POLITICIDE

The attempted murder of the Jewish state

Picture on front cover shows Hamas terrorist bombing of Jerusalem bus in which 21 Israeli civilians perished.

Victor Sharpe

POLITICIDE – Volume Three

The attempted murder of the Jewish state

The Islamist deniers of the Holocaust plot yet another one

POLITICIDE – VOLUME THREE

The relentless attempts by the Arab and Muslim world

to destroy the State of Israel

Written by Victor Sharpe

Copyright © Victor Sharpe 2011

ISBN: 978-1-105-21690-9

Not to be reproduced or distributed in any

manner without written permission of the author.

All rights reserved

Like Volume One and Two of ***Politicide***, this third volume is again dedicated to Vladimir "Ze'ev" Jabotinsky, fighter for his people whom so few chose to follow.

JOSEPH TRUMPELDOR'S MESSAGE:

Born in 1880, Joseph Trumpeldor grew up in the small town of Piatigorsk in the Caucasus region of Russia and spent much of his youth wandering among the foothills of the Caucasian mountain range.

Young Joseph's father was forcibly conscripted into the Czarist army for 25 years. This was the cruel policy implemented by a succession of Czars who hoped that the length of time away from home and family would erase any Jewish identity in the hapless soldiers. But Joseph Trumpeldor's father remained firm in his faith and love of his Jewish ancestry. This proved to be a major influence on young Joseph.

Near the town of Piatigorsk was an experimental agricultural commune created by followers of Leo Tolstoy, the great Russian writer, novelist and social reformer. Tolstoy was an admirer of the Jews and thundered against the anti-Semitism he witnessed in his native Russia.

"Anti-Semitism is a mad passion," he wrote, "akin to the lowest perversities of diseased human nature. It is the will to hate." As for the anti-Jewish persecution he saw in St. Petersburg and the ghettos the Jews were forced to live in, Tolstoy wrote:

"To lock people like wild beasts in a cage, to surround them with disgraceful laws as in an immense circus, for the sole revolting purpose to let loose the murderous mob upon them whenever practicable for St. Petersburg – terrible, terrible!"

The farming community inspired by Leo Tolstoy so impressed young Trumpeldor that he began to dream of helping his fellow Jews escape their misery in Russia and create similar communal farms in the Land of Israel, then ruled by the Ottoman Turkish Empire.

Before long, he was electrified by the Zionist cause–the self-determination of the Jewish people and their national liberation movement. Theodor Herzl had called the first Zionist Congress in 1897 and this began for Joseph Trumpeldor a lifelong belief in Zionism and the resettlement of yeoman Jewish farmers in the ancestral and biblical Jewish homeland.

In 1912, Trumpeldor, now thoroughly disenchanted with the relentless persecution of Russia's and Europe's Jews, arrived in Turkish occupied Palestine that five years later was to be liberated by British forces.

Trumpeldor settled in one of the first agricultural villages to be reconstituted by the Jewish pioneers. It was called Degania. This was what he had dreamed of during his life in Russia, but his stay was to be short lived.

With World War I, when the Turks allied themselves with Germany, Trumpledor was deported to Egypt because of his Russian nationality. It was in Egypt that Trumpeldor joined with arguably the greatest Zionist leader of the 20th century, Vladimir Ze'ev Jabotinsky, and helped form the Zion Mule Corps – a Jewish military unit under the command of Colonel John Henry Patterson.

They were sent to Gallipoli to support the British army and the Anzacs, the Australian and New Zealand troops, under the command of the Australian General Monash, himself a Jewish officer.

This campaign was planned by Winston Churchill, who was blamed for its failure but who had aimed at striking the enemy at the Dardanelles – the soft underbelly – and thus bring the war early to an early conclusion. Though the campaign was fought with immense bravery and high casualties, it ended in a military defeat under the blazing Turkish guns.

We now come to a tragic period: the British government's progressive betrayal of the Balfour Declaration promulgated in November 1917, at the height of the war, by Lord Arthur Balfour, the British Foreign Minister. This promise was later enshrined at the 1920 San Remo conference granting the Mandate for Palestine to Great Britain, with the express purpose of granting within its territory a Jewish National Home. However, when the war ended, British government officials in Palestine began to side with the Arabs.

A mere two years after San Remo, in 1922, Winston Churchill, the Colonial Secretary at the time, was to arbitrarily tear away all the territory of British

Mandatory Palestine that lay east of the River Jordan – 80% of the original geographical area of Palestine.

Britain gave it to the Hashemite Bedouin tribe led by the Emir Abdullah, ostensibly in gratitude for help given to Britain in defeating the Turks.

However T. E. Lawrence, who had led the Arab attacks against the Turkish military, described the contribution of Abdullah and his Hashemite tribe in deprecating terms as, "a sideshow in a sideshow."

Indeed the Zion Mule Corps did far more to assist the British forces in the Middle East Theater. Nevertheless, the proposed Jewish Homeland was now reduced to just western Palestine – a fifth of the original promised area.

Trumpeldor did not live long enough to see the scale of the British government's betrayal, let alone the infamous White Paper of 1939, slamming shut the gates of Mandatory Palestine to the millions of desperate Jewish refugees fleeing the Nazi juggernaut at the onset of World War II.

But he did see the beginning of this process. As early as 1920, there were indications that some British officials had already begun to foment violence by urging local Arabs to attack Jewish farms and villages, even going as far as providing weapons to the hostile Arab bands.

Jewish villages and towns were attacked and the Jews forced, after suffering mounting casualties, to form self-defense units, which were outmanned and outgunned by the Arab irregulars.

In 1920, Trumpeldor, whose military prowess and heroism during the Russo-Japanese War had made him a legendary figure, was sent to a tiny embattled outpost in upper Galilee. The place was called Tel Hai, which translated from the Hebrew means Hill of Life. Tel Hai was a modification of the Arabic name for the site *Talha* meaning an Acacia tree.

Tel Hai had been under severe assault for some time by large numbers of attackers from the nearby Arab settlement of Hulsa. Trumpeldor himself arrived under fire and immediately set about organizing Tel Hai's defense.

Confronted with a relentless barrage of superior firepower and frequent waves of attacks, the defenders fell one by one. And on a Galilean spring day in early March, Trumpeldor himself fell mortally wounded, fighting to the end.

His dying words in Hebrew were: *Ein davar. Tov lamut be'ad artzenu.* Translated into English:

"Never mind: It is good to die for our country."

Joseph Trumpeldor's grave is located near Tel Hai, now a commemorative site adjoining Kfar Giladi. Not long after his heroic death a Jewish village was reborn at the foot of Mount Gilboa where 3,000 years earlier other Jewish military heroes, King Saul and his son, Jonathan, so beloved of his friend David, fell fighting an ancient enemy; the now long extinct Philistines. That village is named in Trumpeldor's honor: Tel Yosef.

So what would Trumpeldor's message be today to the embattled Jewish state? It would probably be this: Fight, fight and fight again. Self-restraint never works in the face of an implacable foe. Build, build and build again throughout the ancestral homeland.

Indulging in self-imposed building freezes to placate enemies and so-called friends alike, while the Arab enemy constructs thousands of illegal buildings with impunity, is insanity.

Defend Israel with all the might that has been given to you, for to lose the precious homeland again and return to the horrors of exile is beyond imagining.

Table of Contents:

Page 4: Joseph Trumpeldor's Message

Page 11: Britain's Mandate & Division of Palestine

Page 12: Foreword by Adrian Morgan

Page 15: Praise by Steven B. Myers

Page 16: Preface

Page 18: Timeline

Page 20: Apartheid is Alive and Well in Araby

Page 25: Abdullah in Wonderland

Page 30: Israeli and Kurdish victims of Turkey

Page 34: Turkish Delight: But not for the Oppressed

Page 38: A Guide to the Perplexed

Page 41: U.N. Insanity: Still a Mad, Mad World

Page 45: The Arab Veil of Deception and the Left

Page 49: The Mosques of War

Page 54: Islam is Islam is Islam

Page 58: The Poisoned Pen

Page 61: How Many More Outrages?

Page 64: Then as Now: Now as Then

Page 67: Israeli Concessions: A Zero Sum Game

Page 72: The Siren Song of Arab Rejection

Page 76: Israel, America and Islam: The Bitter Truth

Page 80: Whose is the Land?

Page 86: Boycotts and Divestments have Consequences

Page 90: The Plague of the un-Jews

Page 95: Forward to the Past

Page 99: Facts Arabs Would Rather Not Admit

Page 104: A People Need Not Annex What is Theirs

Page 108: Go East beyond the River Jordan

Page 113: Lies, Damned Lies, and Erakat

Page 118: Two Nations under Islamic Duress

Page 126: The Security Council: To Veto or not to Veto

Page 131: Obama Knows What Chaos he has Unleashed

Page 136: Take back the Philadelphi Corridor

Page 140: Hillary's War

Page 144: Passover's Gift: Promised and Undivided Land

Page 151: A Bit of History Never Goes Amiss

Page 162: Mahmoud Abbas: A Wolf in Sheep's Clothing

Page 168: Obama's call for Israel to Self-Destruct

Page 173: Trust in the Lord but Keep Your Powder Dry

Page 179: Jews face Jerusalem but Muslims face Mecca

Page 184: Israel's Missed Opportunities

Page 188: The Choice is Ours: What Will it Be?

Page 192: Bodies in the Well

Page 195: Obama and Israel: What if he is Re-Elected?

Page 199: The Ship that Changed the Middle East

Page 205: Tiny Israel: The Ultimate Rape Victim

Page 209: Erdoğan's Not so Sublime Porte

Page 213: Netanyahu's speech and the deafening silence

Page 216: Palestinian Arab Aggression Will Never End

Page 221: Conclusion

Politicide

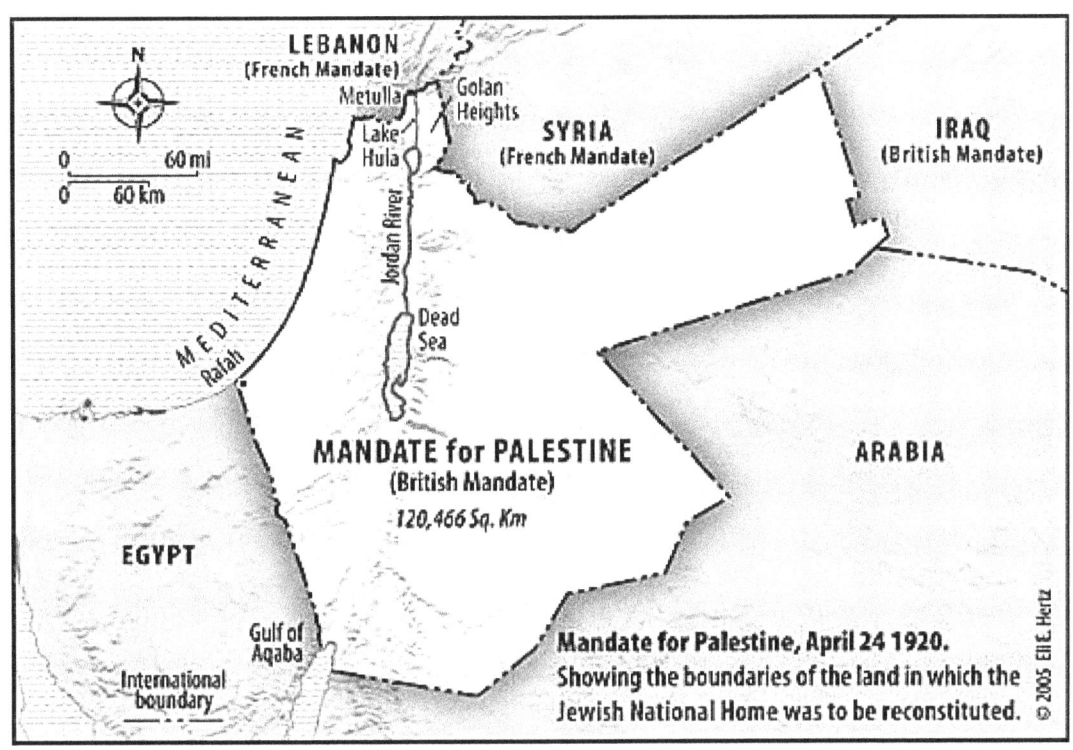

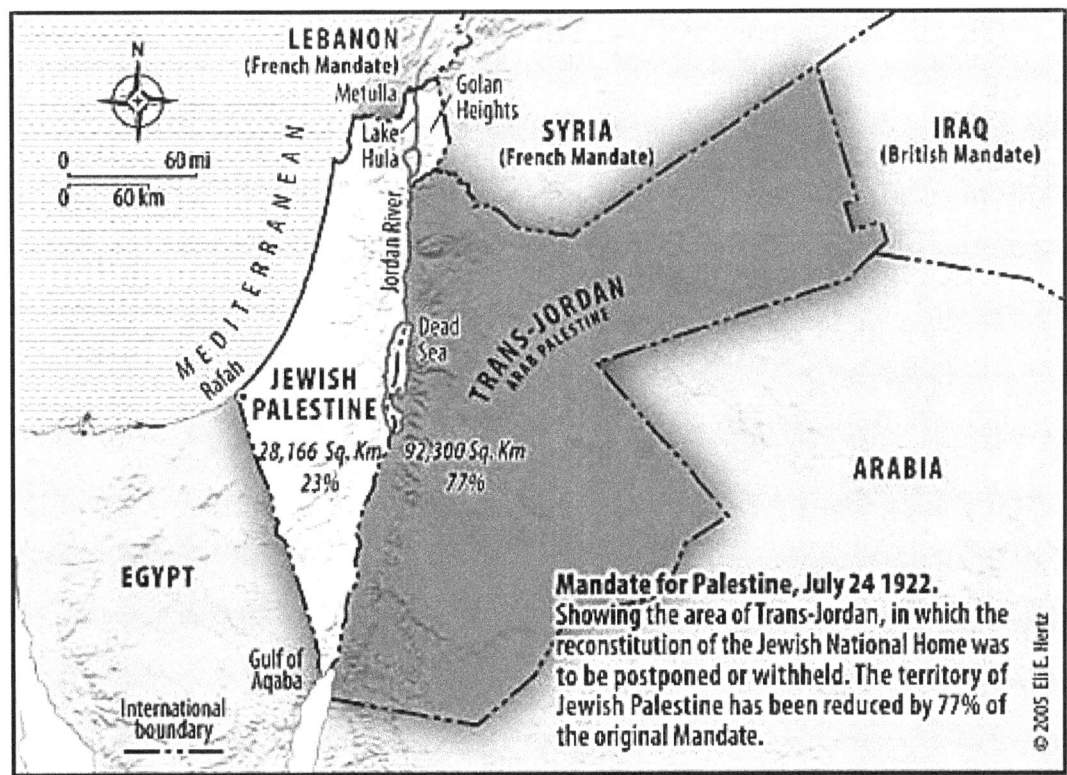

Maps by Myths and Facts

Foreword:

By Adrian Morgan, November 2011 (Cheshvan, 5772)

Editor, Family Security Matters

The third volume of Victor Sharpe's series "*Politicide*" is to be welcomed. At this juncture in time, Israel is at the most vulnerable stage in her history. In 1967, those who were her enemies were easily identifiable. Now, those who casually contribute to the cultural trend of "de-legitimization" come from all walks of life, and many come from the heartlands of Israel's official allies.

There is a need now, more than ever, to address the history of what brought Israel to this point, and to identify how this undermining process takes place. Hamas, among Israel's most virulent enemies, implacably opposed to the existence of the Jewish state, has gained friends in the West. Publicity stunts carried out by Hamas to provoke violence are ignored by the media in the civilized West, and Israel is blamed merely for defending itself.

The passive-aggressive machinations of Hamas and its Islamist and naïf leftist supporters, those who go on convoys or flotillas and constantly claim that Israel deliberately kills Palestinian babies, are reigniting the ancient blood libels that were so damaging to Jews from time immemorial. They do so – they claim – to support the rights of Palestinian people. Yet they stand side by side with those whose outlook is purely medieval. The United Nations gives its ear to Mahmoud Abbas, even though he has said that in a Palestinian state, no Jews should live there. Such bigotry ignores the fact that Israel is the most pluralist and democratic nation in the entire Middle East.

The blood libel continues in the taunts of genocide by those who would exterminate an entire nation and who would deny the very real events of the Holocaust. And yet, so many in the West cannot see how perverse their viewpoint has become. They ally themselves with people in Hamas who religiously believe – as attested in the Hamas Charter, article seven – that at the end of time, that even the rocks and trees will wish to see Jews killed:

> "The Day of Judgment will not come about until Muslims fight the Jews (killing the Jews), when the Jew will hide behind stones and trees. The stones and trees will say O Muslims, O Abdulla, there is a Jew behind me,

come and kill him. Only the Gharkad tree, would not do that because it is one of the trees of the Jews."(Related by al-Bukhari and Muslim)."

Hamas believes the land of Israel is a "waqf" (an endowment from Allah) and the group states in its eleventh article:

"The Islamic Resistance Movement believes that the land of Palestine is an Islamic Waqf consecrated for future Muslim generations until Judgment Day. It, or any part of it, should not be squandered: it, or any part of it, should not be given up. Neither a single Arab country nor all Arab countries, neither any king or president, nor all the kings and presidents, neither any organization nor all of them, be they Palestinian or Arab, possess the right to do that. Palestine is an Islamic Waqf land consecrated for Muslim generations until Judgment Day. This being so, who could claim to have the right to represent Muslim generations till Judgment Day?

"This is the law governing the land of Palestine in the Islamic Sharia (law) and the same goes for any land the Muslims have conquered by force, because during the times of (Islamic) conquests, the Muslims consecrated these lands to Muslim generations till the Day of Judgment."

There is no tolerance, no sense of compromise in this Charter. Yet Western governments, governments that have Muslim advisers who come from the same ranks of the Muslim Brotherhood that also spawned Hamas, urge Israel to make concessions. Israel must remove its "settlements." Israel must give up more and more land. It must negotiate with political movements that have nothing but racist contempt for Jews. Palestinian Authority media, dominated by Fatah, continues the litany of hate, but UNESCO members seek to grant legitimacy to such groups.

There are many players in this drama, and there are many arguments presented to the world at large, which is why it is so important for a voice like Victor Sharpe to be heard. He understands the lay of the land within Israel, and in America and Britain. He understands the complexities of Israeli-Palestinian history and politics and explains these with clarity and accessibility.

Victor Sharpe is a man of great integrity and humanity, and he also knows how to weave the various strands of the political and historical narrative into something that shows the true pattern of events. He is not filled with hate for Israel's neighbours but he understands the guile by which some of their leaders have duped Western politicians and the world at large.

At the time of writing, Hamas is actively seeking another Israeli hostage, to relive the ordeal of Gilad Shalit and ultimately be exchanged for prisoners.

The future looks bleak for Israel right now, and people need to understand what is going on. Too many believe the hype spewed by those who would glamorize the role of groups like Hamas.

If Hamas was so good, why would the sisters of Ismail Haniyeh, the leader of Hamas in Gaza, choose to live as citizens of Israel? They moved to Tel Sheva on the edge of the Negev desert, thirty years ago*.

Kholida, Laila and Sabah know that in the future envisioned by her brother, women would have no rights to walk around unescorted, to have their heads uncovered, and to do business on their own terms. In Israel a woman, Arab or Jew, has always had these rights.

It is important to know the facts, and to let others know. Israel is an oasis of freedom and democracy in a political desert. It is a solitary beacon surrounded by darkness. If its light dies, then so will the light of humanity be forever dimmed.

Adrian Morgan, November 2011. (Cheshvan, 5772)

* *"Hamas leader's three sisters live secretly in Israel as full citizens," Tim Butcher, Daily Telegraph (UK), June 2nd, 2006.*

In praise of Politicide: Volume Three

By Steven B. Myers, November 2011

Editor, Page One Daily and Israel Daily News

Every word of Victor Sharpe's trilogy is well-chosen; even the titles.

He points out that, as Israel finds itself in dire straits, it often forgets God's promises to the Jewish people, and even its own leaders seem willing to compromise, to use the opposition's terminology and to gradually allow Israel to fall either directly into the abyss or into a compromise which will eventually result in the same destiny. If Israel's leaders will not defend its right to its land, who will?

In his latest volume, Victor Sharpe offers timely reminders, encouragement and guidance to Israel's leaders and supporters around the world, reminding them of the biblical, moral, geopolitical and historic realities within which the current debate should be framed.

Samaria, for example, covers much of the ancient Kingdom of Israel. Judea was the other ancient Jewish kingdom, names which date from early biblical times, and reinforce the connection of the Jewish people to the whole land west – and indeed east – of the River Jordan.

Judea was the name of the mountainous southern part of the historic Land of Israel from the 11th century BCE onward. Yet when discussing these ancient Jewish heartlands of Judea and Samaria, why do modern politicians and even Israeli politicians, refer instead to the "West Bank", a minimalist, politically-correct, modern pro-Arab, geographical term of blatant and biased left-wing convenience?

Victor Sharpe sets the record straight. His meticulously researched and written books provide biblical and geographical definitions and historical perspective which every scholar will find helpful in ascertaining often-obscured facts about today's Middle East. He offers constant and much needed shots of discipline and courage to today's leaders and observers.

Preface:

This third volume of *Politicide* continues relating all the main events in Israel and throughout the world since I started compiling my many published articles in book form since that atrocious day when Muslim Arab hijackers flew two planes into the World Trade Center towers in New York City on September 11, 2001.

One plane flew into the Pentagon and another crashed into a field in Pennsylvania after brave passengers succeeded in overcoming their Arab hijackers. Of course, Muslim terror had been a constant plague in the world and, especially, against the tiny Jewish nation that was reborn in the midst of the Arab world in 1948.

Volume Two of *Politicide* ended in December 2009. This third volume follows on from that date and ends towards the end of 2011. At the time of writing this preface, Gilad Shalit, the Israel soldier kidnapped by Hamas terrorists five years ago, has just been released in return for a veritable pact with the Devil. Israel, in order to redeem her soldier, was forced to release over 1,000 Arab terrorists, many of whom committed the most unspeakable atrocities against Israeli men, women and children.

The justified fear is that these sub-human monsters will soon return to kill and maim again. The awful dilemma facing Israel and her embattled population is how to remain a moral nation within the most evil part of the planet, surrounded as she is by millions of Muslim Arabs whose religion teaches them to kill all non-Muslims in the name of Allah.

As in the two previous volumes, I have placed the chapters in the book in the chronological order in which each one appeared as a published article. They were posted in various leading websites and magazines including American Thinker, Family Security Matters, Canada Free Press, Israel National News, The Jerusalem Connection, American Renewal, Page One Daily, Israel Daily News, The Jewish Press, Outpost, and a marvelous little newspaper in the heart of Texas: The Buffalo Gap Roundup.

These chapters mark the triumphs and tragedies of tiny Israel. At this time, Iran and Turkey are increasingly vying for control of the Middle East. Predictably, the brownie points for which each Muslim nation is pre-eminent at any time is how they threaten the Jewish state.

Shia and Sunni Muslims are perennially at each other's throats –Iran is Shia and Turkey is Sunni - but it is Israel, which has the misfortune to bring them together in their unholy alliance of hatred against the Jews.

Turkey has become increasingly Islamized under its Prime Minister, Recip Tayyip Erdoğan, who has threatened Israel's newly discovered oil and natural gas finds in the Eastern Mediterranean. He has also threatened to send Turkish naval forces to accompany and defend any new attempt to send ships to Gaza in order to force Israel to accept vast new arms shipments into the Hamas occupied Gaza Strip.

Meanwhile, Iran, its mullahs, and President Mahmoud Ahmadinejad continue to work feverishly to acquire nuclear weapons, which Ahmadinejad has openly threatened to use against Israel.

Israel thus faces a classic pincer movement against her security. This and the relentless terror war by Hamas, Islamic Jihad, Al Qaida, Fatah, ad nauseum, continues, aided and abetted by a worldwide propaganda wars against the Jewish state, a trade boycott by leftists of Israeli products.

All of these insidious maneuvers are deliberately done with the avowed intention of delegitimizing Israel and creating a diabolical climate wherein her destruction becomes an acceptable fact by a world hellishly seduced into believing that this little and imperiled democracy – situated as it is in the heart of darkness - is the greatest danger to world peace.

This was the demented process the Nazis employed to systematically poison the world towards the hapless Jews who fell under their control. Now the same evil is being used against not individual Jews but against the one and only Jewish state.

Like Volume one and Volume Two, there is much history to read – both biblical and post biblical – in the pages of Volume Three of *Politicide* as well as a clear and concise understanding of what I call the Islamist-Israel conflict.

The conflict is not over territory. It is over the Islamic refusal to accept a non-Muslim state in territory previously conquered in the name of Islam - even though Israel is in its own ancestral and biblical homeland predating Islam by millennia.

As I wrote at the end of the preface for the first volume: "Alas that is what it is, what it always has been, and what it always will be."

Timeline:

*There is a reason we call it Islamic terrorism, and it **isn't** because we falsely attribute motives to the terrorists, but because Islam is the stated purpose and aim of the terrorists.*
Daniel Greenfield

To view all the thousands of individual Muslim and Arab terror attacks throughout the world for previous years, visit
www.thereligionofpeace.com

Islamic Terror Attacks for First Part of 2011

Islamic Terror Attacks for 2010

Islamic Terror Attacks for 2009

Islamic Terror Attacks for 2008

Islamic Terror Attacks for 2007

Islamic Terror Attacks for 2006

Islamic Terror Attacks for 2005

Islamic Terror Attacks for 2004

Islamic Attacks from September 11th, 2001 through 2003

If we are "at war" with Islam it is not because there is something wrong with us, but because there is something wrong with Islam.

Here is the continuation of the timeline of Arab and Islamic terrorist attacks, which I began listing in both Volume One and Two of *Politicide* from that horrific day of September 11, 2001 when America was attacked in New York City.

In Volume Three, I present the ever growing list of almost daily Muslim violence and aggression perpetrated as crimes against humanity.

By clicking on the above mentioned URL, you will view unparalleled numbers of atrocities and massacres committed by Muslims in the name of their religion.

The lists are so long that there is simply not enough room to put them all in this book. But the sheer magnitude of misery and heartbreak that each attack upon peoples of all faiths by followers of the "religion of peace" has, and is, causing is a desolating indictment and a timeline of terror and barbarity that has no end.

Israeli victims of a Muslim Arab atrocity.

Five members of the Fogel family were murdered in March 2011 in their village of Itamar by two Palestinian Arab men who entered their home and knifed them to death, including the two toddlers and baby shown here.

One daughter and her young brother survived. Rabbi Fogel and his wife inspired holiness in all who met them and the rabbi's memory will be enshrined in a new seminary being built in his name in Itamar. Good will prevail over evil.

March 3, 2010

Apartheid is Alive and Well in Araby

We stand in the midst of a new round of Israel-bashing called by the organizers of "Israel Apartheid Week." Those doing the bashing are busy turning logic on its head.

For them, up is down, day is night, and right is wrong. The collected hatemongers of the radical Left allied with the terminally hate-filled Muslim world, their ranks filled with empty-headed and gullible drones, are combining to shriek misplaced support for an Arab people calling themselves Palestinians, who, they allege, are suffering from apartheid. They make this false charge by slandering the Jewish state, equating it with what was once the South African apartheid regime.

According to the upside-down world of the "hate Israel" crowd, Arabs are separated from Jews within Israel just as the black Africans were segregated from the whites within South Africa. This is where facts retreat into the fantasy world one finds within *The Thousand and One Arabian Nights*.

The real apartheid that exists in the Middle East can be found not in Israel, but within the territories currently occupied by the Fatah-controlled Palestinian Authority and the Hamas-occupied Gaza Strip. The Palestinian Arabs ban all Jews from living amongst them. Any Jews found are summarily murdered in cold blood.

This is sanctioned by Fatah and Hamas, who both delight in describing the Arab terrorist thugs as heroes -- even naming streets and town squares in their honor. Any Arabs found to have sold property to Jewish purchasers are summarily executed - often in the public squares and streets of Palestinian Arab settlements.

The geographical territory known as Palestine has, of course, never existed as an independent, sovereign nation in all of human history, and certainly never as an Arab state.

The current territory within the Palestinian Authority and the Gaza Strip formed integral parts of the ancestral and biblical Jewish homeland. Indeed, the Palestinian Authority sits upon the very Jewish heartland of Judea and Samaria, known now by its Jordanian name, the West Bank.

The vast territory east of the River Jordan, now called the Kingdom of Jordan, includes large tracts of land that also formed part of the biblical Jewish and tribal lands.

But now that same vast territory, which extends eastwards to Iraq, north to Syria, and south to Saudi Arabia (dwarfing tiny Israel in size), is also closed by the Jordanian authorities to Jews, who may not live within its borders upon pain of death. In contrast, Arabs, who make up 20% of the overall Israeli population, may live within the reconstituted Jewish state as citizens enjoying equal rights with justice for all.

The Jordanian regime instituted a law in 1954 prohibiting Jews from living in Jordan. They did this by conferring citizenship to all former residents of geographical Palestine - except Jewish ones. Israel's population contains Jews who are white, black, brown, and yellow. It is not an apartheid state based on racial differences or concepts of racial purity and impurity.

Under apartheid South Africa, blacks were not citizens of the country and were not permitted to vote. Yet the loony Left, allied with the hate-filled Islamic world, continues to accuse Israel of a mythical apartheid system while ignoring the Arab and Muslim perpetrators of the actual apartheid that so clearly exists in the Kingdom of Jordan, in the Palestinian Authority, and within the Hamas-controlled Gaza Strip.

The tsunami of anti-Jewish bigotry and malice sweeping the universities in America and Europe is desolating. The boycotts of Israel generated from within academia are built upon a fraudulent ethos of Arab distortions and outright lies, yet they are willingly accepted by gullible students and faculty alike.

It seems that the intellectuals who utter their elitist drivel within the corridors of academe are all too often seduced by novelties. But what it sadly, and so often, reveals is an undeniable truth that intellectualism does not automatically confer intelligence or intelligent behavior. It would be refreshing if the same students, professors, and assorted Israel-bashers could learn how the Arabs who call themselves Palestinians have created for themselves what can be described as anti-history.

So insanely set are they upon a destructive denial of Jewish patrimony that these same Palestinian Arabs have created for themselves a fraudulent narrative denying even the existence of the Jewish Temples on Jerusalem's Temple Mount - despite the overwhelming archaeological evidence of Jewish civilization and history in the land spanning millennia.

This is why Palestinian Prime Minister Fayad called out the Palestinian rent-a-mob to riot in the streets of Hebron and Jerusalem after Israel declared the ancient Jewish holy sites of the Machpela Cave in Hebron and the tomb of the biblical matriarch, Rachel, as national heritage sites.

In Genesis 23:13, we read about the first Jew, Abraham, purchasing land in Hebron from Ephron the Hittite as a burial plot for his wife, Sarah. His son Isaac and grandson Jacob are also buried there along with their wives - the Jewish patriarchs and matriarchs. But this upsets the Palestinian Arabs because the Jewish tombs are within the territory they demand for a state - for them, these Jewish sites are an inconvenient truth.

Another Jewish holy place in what the world likes to call the West Bank is Joseph's tomb in Nablus, or what was once biblical Jewish Shechem. The good Palestinian Arabs recently desecrated the ancient tomb, filling it with rubbish and excrement, to prevent Jewish prayers and pilgrimage at the site. These are manifestations of apartheid - Arab style.

With breathtaking absurdity, the Arabs who call themselves Palestinians make claims of historical and lineal descent from the extinct Canaanites and Philistines. They have bred several generations of children in kindergartens imbued with such frightening nonsense, attended by a love of barbarism and a culture of death.

They have been encouraged in this by the corrupt neighboring Arab leaders, who for some sixty years have stigmatized them as refugees yet at the same time have barred them from living within their own basket-case countries.

From this horrific Palestinian-Arab sectarianism, the culture of death has developed along with an Islamic refusal to ever make a true and lasting peace with the non-Muslim state known as Israel. Indeed, for the Jewish population and for the subsequent State of Israel, there has been relentless Arab terror since the 1920s.

Consider the massacre of Jewish civilians by their Arab neighbors in Judaism's second-holiest city, Hebron - the city that not only houses the Jewish burial place of Abraham, Isaac, and Jacob, but which King David first made his capital.

That Arab atrocity took place in 1929 during the British Mandate occupation. For all those anti-Israel bigots who scream against Israeli occupation, they should know that the so-called West Bank and the Gaza Strip were not occupied at that time.

Indeed, the Jewish state was not reborn until nineteen years later, in 1948 -- yet Arabs were murdering and terrorizing Jews all those years before. They should ask themselves why, after the Israel-Arab war of 1948, when the Egyptians occupied the Gaza Strip and the Jordanians' occupied the so-called West Bank, neither Egypt nor Jordan felt the need to create a new Arab state to be called Palestine. Neither did the Arab residents demand it.

Only after Israel defeated Arab aggression in 1967 and liberated the territories did the Arab world begin to demand the creation of a 23rd Arab state. They should also know that today, some 98% of Arabs calling themselves Palestinians live in both the Arab Hamas-controlled Gaza Strip and the rival Fatah-controlled Palestinian Authority.

There is, in reality, no occupation. So what do they mean when they rant and rave about Israeli occupation, unless it is a call for the very extinction of Israel itself?

There is no such thing as Israeli apartheid against the Arabs. But there most certainly is Arab apartheid imposed upon Jews, who are denied the right to live amongst Arabs even in the ancestral and biblical Jewish heartland, which is occupied and controlled today by the Palestinian Authority and the Islamist Hamas.

It truly is an upside-down world, viewed now through a window so terribly distorted as to bewilder and confuse untold millions. It is much more than an Arab-Israel conflict over territory; it is much deeper than that. It is an Islamic refusal to accept a reconstituted Jewish homeland where once the Muslim foot trod triumphal.

The very fact that the Palestinian Arabs, who are overwhelmingly Muslim, will never accept a tiny Jewish state within the enormous Arab landmass that stretches from Mauritania in the west to Iraq in the east is clear and present evidence of Muslim and Arab apartheid. This empirical fact must be understood.

In that context, I am reminded that it was the Indian leader Mahatma Ghandi who said, "While Hindus, Sikhs, Christians, Parsees, and Jews, along with several million adherents of an animistic religion, all coexisted in relative harmony, one religion that would not accept compromise stood out from the rest: Islam."

It would be an enlightening and seminal moment in these first years of the 21st century if the eyes and ears of the Israel-bashers could be opened with the realization that they have targeted the wrong nation, and that apartheid is alive and well within the Arab world.

April 12, 2010

Abdullah in Wonderland

When Alice fell down the rabbit hole, encountering situations that defied logic and characters who acted in bizarre ways, she was fortunate not to meet Jordan's kinglet, Abdullah II. Kinglet is an apt description for this monarch, first coined by columnist Ruth King.

Jordan's king, a member of the Hashemite tribe, is named after Emir Abdullah, who was assassinated on July 20, 1951 after leaving Friday evening prayers at Jerusalem's Al Aqsa mosque. Abdullah was in favor of making peace with Israel but, like Egypt's Anwar Sadat, he was murdered by Islamic extremists for his moderation.

The assassinated emir was accompanied at the mosque by his grandson, King Hussein, also the present Jordanian monarch's father. In a recent interview in the Wall Street Journal, King Abdullah II announced that at his forthcoming meeting with America's president, Barack Hussein Obama, he will ask the president to pile on yet more pressure upon embattled Israel over Arab territorial demands on Israel's capital, Jerusalem.

The kinglet stated in his WSJ interview that "Jerusalem specifically engages Jordan because we are the custodians of the Muslim and Christian holy places and this is a flashpoint that goes beyond Jordanian-Israel relations."

And here we descend the rabbit hole. Abdullah II chose to hide the unpleasant facts that under his father, King Hussein, not only did Jordan refuse to allow Jews access to their holy sites during Jordan's illegal occupation of East Jerusalem from 1949 to 1967 (including the Old City, the Western Wall, and the Temple Mount), but it desecrated the ancient Jewish graves on the Mount of Olives.

It also ran a road through the cemetery, used many of the gravestones as latrines for the Arab Legion, deliberately destroyed and desecrated scores of ancient synagogues throughout the Old City, and used the Tomb of Simon the Just as a stable. The Jewish inhabitants of the Old City and areas of east Jerusalem, meanwhile, had been driven from their homes and forced to flee to safety in West Jerusalem.

During the nineteen years of illegal Jordanian Arab occupation of the eastern neighborhoods of Jerusalem - an occupation recognized by only Pakistan and Britain - the United Nations not once protested against the rampant and systematic destruction of the ancient Jewish quarter.

Only after the reunification of the city in 1967 and the removal by Israel of the Jordanian pillboxes, barbed wire, and sniper sites was the filth that had piled up over the years along the Via Delarosa (with Christian pilgrims being forced to wade through it) removed and the area cleansed. And only after reunification did the morally challenged United Nations begin its long and hypocritical series of anti-Israel resolutions over Jerusalem.

It is only since Israel was forced by Arab aggression to fight the June 1967 Six Day War and liberate Jerusalem from Jordanian occupation that all religions and faiths are treated with respect and provided free access to their holy places.

On June 4, 1967, former Israeli Prime Minister Levi Eshkol pleaded with the late King Hussein, via the United Nations, not to follow the genocidal boastings of Egypt's President Nasser and attack the Jewish state. Eshkol stated that "we shall not initiate any action whatsoever against Jordan. However, should Jordan open hostilities, we shall react with all our might and he (the King) will have to bear the full responsibility for all the consequences."

The impressionable king, succumbing to Nasser's boast of Egyptian forces already inside Israel, ordered his artillery to open fire along the entire border between west and east Jerusalem. The Egyptians and elements of the Arab Legion had penetrated the southernmost Jewish suburb of Jerusalem, Ramat Rachel, founded in 1926 upon the same site of a Jewish village from biblical times.

It is instructive to note that King Hussein visited East Jerusalem only once during Jordan's occupation and chose to keep Amman the capital of Jordan. Indeed, no Muslim holy place is today the capital city of an Arab and Muslim state. In Iran, the capital is Teheran; it is not Qum or Meshed. In Saudi Arabia, neither Mecca nor Medina is the capital city; it is Riyadh.

Only the Jews regard Jerusalem as both their spiritual and temporal capital city, and they have done so for three thousand years. For Christians, Jerusalem is a spiritual, not a temporal, site. Muslims, even while praying in their mosque on the Temple Mount, face Mecca with their backs to Jerusalem.

My article, titled *"The Two-State-Solution,"* which appeared in volume two, traces the events of some 90 years ago and is an ideal explanation of the historic betrayal by Great Britain toward its obligation to create a Jewish National Home in geographical Palestine and how the entire territory east of the River Jordan (present-day Jordan) was torn away, leaving only the narrow sliver of land west of the Jordan River for the reconstituted Jewish state.

This tiny piece of land, which includes the very biblical and ancestral heartland of the Jews, is now threatened by yet another Two-State-Solution, reducing Israel to only nine miles wide at its most populous region. The present Kingdom of Jordan, over which Abdullah II reigns, is the much larger territory east of the River Jordan stretching east to Iraq, south to Saudi Arabia, and north to Syria.

In 1994, Yasser Arafat's PLO demanded East Jerusalem as the capital city of a new Arab state. All Jews living in such a capital, it declared, will be driven out - or worse. Sound familiar? This demand was first articulated only after the 1967 War and Jerusalem's reunification. Since then, it has become a staple of Palestinian Arab and all other Arab and Muslim rhetoric.

Now Abdullah II impudently claims that the Israeli Prime Minister's actions have brought their two nation's relations to a new low. Again the Alice in Wonderland syndrome is clear for all to see. For Netanyahu has made yet more concessions to bring about peace in the region by agreeing to a freeze on housing for Jews throughout Judea and Samaria (the West Bank).

No concessions have been demanded of the Palestinian Arabs, who continue terrorism against Israeli civilians and indoctrinate their children with vile anti-Jewish hatred - all banned under the Oslo Peace Accords. The Jordanian king even stretches credulity by claiming that Jordanian officials call their relations with Israel a cold peace. He went on to say, "People to people exchanges between our two countries are virtually non-existent and cross border business has largely dried up."

Though Jordan has resisted the Palestinians' attempt to undermine the peace treaty obligations made earlier between Jordan and Israel in 1994, it has nevertheless been Jordan that is the cause of the cold peace with the Jewish state. Animosity toward Israel and the lack of peaceful interchange between the two peoples has been led by Jordan's professional and intellectual organizations. These have included journalists, doctors, dentists, business leaders, artists, and musicians. These groups have opposed all and every form of normalization with Israel.

Any Jordanian Arab who reaches out to Israelis is immediately threatened and blacklisted. It is ironic that Jordan's kinglet allows such a situation to exist while choosing to falsely blame Israel. Could it be that he is afraid of alienating these organizations for fear that the Hashemite control over his kingdom would falter? After all, Jordan's population is three-fourths Palestinian, and the kinglet's greatest fear is a Palestinian Arab coup.

In September 1970, the kinglet's father, King Hussein, fought off a PLO coup d'état led by the arch terrorist, Yasser Arafat, who had created a state within a state inside Jordan. Hussein's Arab Legion killed thousands of PLO terrorists, along with their families, and many fled to Israel for safety - the very same terrorists who had been conducting grisly cross-border raids into Israel.

Since then, Israel has several times warned Jordan of attempts to destroy it from the neighboring Syrian regime in Damascus, which considers Jordan as part of southern Syria. Indeed, Israel even intervened once to forestall an imminent Syrian invasion.

In his meeting with President Barack Hussein Obama, the kinglet will take the predictable anti-Israeli line in order to keep his Arab credentials intact and his Hashemite minority from being overthrown. The kinglet's throne is an uneasy one at best. But what better way to deflect his subjects' growing Islamic radicalization than to heap blame upon Israel for every problem in the Middle East: And this while secretly relying upon Israel to protect his throne.

According to an earlier Pew Global Attitude Project finding, a majority of Jordanians now say suicide bombings and other violent actions are justifiable in defense of Islam. According to the *Jordan Times'* correspondent, Omar Karmi, because of close geopolitical and familial ties, Hamas has a close relationship with Jordan's Islamists, and the Jordanian Islamists' increasing popularity has been given a big boost by Hamas' victory. Jordan's Muslim Brotherhood is and always has been implacably opposed to the 1994 [Jordan-Israel] peace treaty.

Despite the remarkable durability of the Hashemite Kingdom, Jordan's strategic position and its vulnerability remain a given that cannot be ignored in any Israeli security assessment.

Jordan's King Abdullah II dares not buck the growing Arab, Muslim, and worldwide pressure piling on Israel, vastly encouraged as it is by the mendacious and unprincipled anti-Israel bias emanating from the White House and State

Department. He will no doubt echo the tired old mantra that solving the Israel-Palestinian conflict will miraculously solve all world problems and usher in "peace in our time." It is no surprise, therefore, that the kinglet and the American president will have a great time together at their upcoming Mad Hatter's Tea Party.

And no doubt U.S. Secretary of State Hillary Clinton, U.S. Middle East envoy George Mitchell, and American General James Jones will all join together in the "let's bash Israel" festivity while the malevolent Cheshire cat, Ahmadinejad, looks on with an ever-widening grin.

June 6, 2010

Israeli and Kurdish victims of Turkey

Sometime ago, before Turkey chose to lurch further into the deadly embrace of Islamism, I received a plea from a Kurdish friend who remains supportive of Israel's epic struggle to survive among its hostile Arab neighbors. He is also devoted to the Jewish people for he knows of the shared ethnicities believed to exist between Jews and Kurds dating back millennia.

Here is some of my Kurdish friend's impassioned letter from two years ago, which uncannily warned against any alliance with Turkey:

"I wish the Jews in Israel and abroad would know better about the policy of their leaders concerning the Kurds, because it happens in the name of Israel, and that should matter to all Jews. Turkish oppression of the Kurds is unknown to most Israelis. It is hard for me to understand how Israel's cooperation with Turkey does not take into account the misery that it imposes upon the Kurdish people who yearn, as the Jews have for centuries, to be free from terror and persecution?

"Not so long ago, the Jews in Europe endured the Shoah (he used the Hebrew term for the Holocaust - VS) and they know better than anyone else the horrors of that experience. Of course it's not only Israel but the whole world that is pro-Turkish and anti-Kurdish. It is not fair to criticize Israel only, but given the history of the Jewish people, there should be a heightened sensitivity towards Kurdish suffering.

"We Kurds have shared so much culture together and we still remember fondly the Jews who lived with us for centuries. But the Turks waxed and waned in their attitude towards the Jews; sometimes they were tolerant and sometimes hostile. There are many Turks today who share Islamist ideas and proclaim hostility towards the Jewish state. Within Turkey lies the same pestilence of anti-Semitism that exists throughout the Arab and Persian world.

"I remember your moving article in which you categorically made clear that the people who truly deserve an independent sovereign state are the Kurds; not the Arabs who call themselves Palestinians. I also feel deeply that one day there will be an abiding and honorable alliance between the Jewish state and a free and independent Kurdistan.

But arming Turkey, our people's oppressor, is morally and geographically not to Israel's advantage. Israel's cooperation with Turkey is, in reality, a misguided support for political Islam and its oppression of the Kurds. It undermines Israel's credibility with the only true friend it has in the Middle East."

Now in hindsight, it is glaringly obvious how correct my Kurdish friend's warning at the time was.

Turkey is now an enemy of both Israel and the Kurdish people. In a previous letter, as Turkish troops were invading Kurdistan and jet aircraft were bombarding Kurdish villages in northern Iraq, my friend was more pointed in his criticism of the Israeli leadership's shortsightedness. He defended without question what he called, "Israel's cause and the undying truth that Jews are the rightful owners of the historic Jewish lands - now partially occupied by the Arabs.

But he also pointed out that, "the legitimate arguments and rights Israel has are the same rights and truths it denies in its official policy towards the Kurds. For now and for the future, everything looks black. I fear the worst for us. The whole world is against us, and on the Turkish side there is no change...."

Coincidentally, Ruth King, a freelance writer who is a columnist for several magazines, urged those who read, "feel-good stories about Turkey" to remember the ship, *Struma*. In 1941, while carrying 769 Jewish refugees fleeing from the Nazi German killing machine, it was not permitted to land in Turkey and sank with appalling loss of life.

With the reality of Israel's reconstitution as a sovereign nation in its ancestral and biblical homeland has come the equal reality of its uniqueness and isolation within a hostile world.

The rush to bash Israel by hypocritical national leaders and the falsehoods perpetrated by international news agencies such as the Associated Press (AP) despite the video tapes and pictures showing pipe wielding, masked thugs, screaming "kill the Jews," while beating up Israeli soldiers - armed at first only with paint ball guns - is despicable. Thugs, Islamists, and jihadists claiming to be "peace" activists aboard a Turkish ferry boat, with the Turkish Prime Minister's own direct collaboration, should be an indictment of Turkey, not Israel. But this is not a moral world.

The international outpouring of imbecilic hatred towards the embattled Jewish state for merely trying to defend its citizens from a future maritime pipeline delivering lethal weapons and deadly missiles into Gaza to be used to kill Jewish civilians is one of the most depressing indictments of humanity.

In this, Israel shares with the Kurds a familial fate. Both endure relentless aggression from their neighbors. Even though it lives in a terrible neighborhood and desperately seeks friends, Israel must not evade its unique responsibility towards the Kurdish people, who also suffer from the depredations of their hostile neighbors -- especially Iran, Syria, and last but not least, Turkey.

The Jewish state, now undergoing what individual Jews endured for centuries - a bloody and irrational persecution - must now, more than ever, not ignore the Kurds, who remain stateless and shunned by the world and who seek, at last, the historic justice they have craved for centuries but have been denied; an independent state of their own.

According to an article titled "Can Israel make it alone?" written some years ago by James Lewis in the *American Thinker*, Lewis wrote: "Nations have no permanent friends, only permanent interests -- like survival." With the stark reality now of a profoundly less friendly Obama Administration, it is more important than ever to see what he wrote: "If the United States abandons the Jewish State, Jerusalem will have to seek new alliances."

Turkey has now chosen to break its alliance with Israel and instead has sought alliances with rogue states such as Iran and Syria, along with the Hamas occupied and terrorist infested Gaza Strip. It has turned on Israel with a viciousness that is desolating to watch. It is a nation turning its back upon the Ataturk secular revolution of the 1920s. Instead, it is sliding remorsefully back to the 7th century mindset and cesspit that so many of its neighbors wallow in.

The Turkish regime is allowing ant-Semitic films and documentaries to be broadcast relentlessly, thus poisoning the minds of both its secular and Islamist population. One need only hark back to the demonization and vilification spewed against the Jews for years under Hitler in Nazi Germany to see how most Germans behaved and what horrors resulted.

Whether or not President Barack Obama continues to act negatively towards the Jewish state, any new Israeli alliances should include the restoration of a profoundly just, moral and enduring pact with the Kurdish people, and assistance towards creating a future independent State of Kurdistan. That may be the silver lining from the present international flotilla of xenophobic hatred presently sailing towards Israel's shores.

June 18, 2010

Turkish Delight: But not for the Oppressed

In 1974, a flotilla set sail from Turkey. No, it wasn't destined for the Gaza coast carrying thugs and jihadists masquerading as human rights activists - as ill armed Israeli commandos discovered to their cost. No, this was a flotilla of naval ships sailing towards Cyprus as a full-fledged invasion force, illegally employing U.S. arms and equipment.

Later, after Greek Cypriot resistance had been crushed in the north of the island, Turkish forces began to ethnically cleanse almost half of the island from its Greek population, The Turkish military employed hundreds of U.S. tanks and airplanes and 35,000 ground troops, with the result being a land grab by Turkey of 37.3% of Cyprus. Turkey later sent additional flotillas to the island; ships containing 150,000 Turkish settlers who proceeded to colonize the land after some 200,000 Greeks had been driven out and made into refugees.

The capital city of Cyprus, Nicosia, remains today a city divided with barbed wire marking the border like an ugly scar. Though relatively quiet today, pockmarks still cover the walls where bullets struck civilians and snipers held sway. This was how Jerusalem and its Jewish residents also suffered during the illegal Jordanian occupation from 1948 until 1967. This division of the city left its eastern half and the biblical and ancestral Jewish homeland of Judea and Samaria, known by the world as the West Bank, under Arab occupation.

In 1948, the Jewish population of Jerusalem's Old City was expelled by the British officered Jordanian Arab Legion. Only in 1967 were they able to reclaim their homes throughout the eastern half of the Holy City and in the ravaged Jewish Quarter after Israel was forced to fight a defensive war against Jordan, Egypt and Syria. Fifty seven ancient synagogues were desecrated by the Arabs and Jewish gravestones in the Mount of Olives were torn up and used as latrines by the Arab Legion.

Just as now Nicosia is a city divided against itself, so too was Jerusalem before its liberation and reunification. In Cyprus, churches were desecrated and left in ruins. Cyprus and Israel both now endure Turkish aggression. Turkey, with its new found Islamic triumphalism and alliance with the Islamic Republic of Iran, has become a threat to the Jewish state and has become even more obdurate towards any hope of a peaceful settlement with the Greeks in divided Cyprus.

It is interesting to note that just as Britain held and abused the terms of the Palestine Mandate conferred upon it with the express agreement to establish within much of its borders a Jewish National Home, so too did Turkey's occupation of Cyprus. Its use of the terms Greek Cypriot and Turkish Cypriot came to be viewed as a classic "divide and rule" tactic.

Britain and the U.S. helped formulate in the United Nations what became known as the Annan Plan, named for the UN Secretary General, Kofi Annan. But this plan was grossly unfair to the Greek population of the island. Most problematic was the document's inability or unwillingness to address the core issue: Turkey's original and premeditated invasion and aggression.

During their reign, the Ottoman Turks occupied vast areas of the Middle East, Eastern Europe, the Balkans and Greece including Cyprus. They held their empire from 1517 to 1917 and in that time, as Islamic states have always done to their non-Muslim populations, treated them as *dhimmis*; discriminated against, second class citizens.

Throughout the long years of occupation, the *dhimmis* often suffered horrendous crimes committed against them, including in Cyprus. For example, massacres of Cypriot civilians occurred throughout the island and in the city of Famagusta a massacre of the Greek Christian population broke out with the public hanging of Archbishop Kyprianos, three Bishops and Greek Cypriot dignitaries in Nicosia.
Many Christians and Jews were treated as second class citizens with no right to hold office in the Ottoman state.

They were discriminated against and forced to pay the *jizya*, the onerous tax paid by all "infidels" to the Muslim authorities. It was, and remains in some Muslim territories, a veritable protection racket enshrined in Sharia law.

Some Jews who faced expulsion or conversion in Spain and Portugal during the Catholic Inquisition of Ferdinand and Isabella in 1492 and thereafter, converted in mass public events to remain in the Iberian Peninsula. However, most retained in secret their Jewish faith in order to retain their beliefs. Similarly, many Greek Christians in the mainland and in Cyprus converted to Islam but secretly these "*Linovamvakoi*" continued to worship in underground churches and keep Greek culture alive.

In 1978, the Turks sold Cyprus to the British in order to replenish their dwindling financial reserves. Turkey was already fast becoming known as the "sick man of Europe" and would later ally itself with Germany during the First World War, resulting in the destruction of the Ottoman Turkish Empire and the liberation of vast territories - including the liberation in 1917 of Jerusalem.

The 1923 Treaty of Lausanne ended any notion of a legitimate Turkish claim to the overwhelmingly Greek populated island. After World War 2, many British territories began to seek their independence from the Crown. In 1947, the Indian sub-continent was partitioned between the largely Hindu state of India and a smaller bifurcated Islamic state of East and West Pakistan. The result was a bloody conflict between the two religions. East Pakistan later became present day Bangladesh.

In Mandatory Palestine, a territory which had never existed in all of recorded history as an independent, and certainly not an Arab independent state, the Jewish community had supported Britain during the war against Nazi Germany, but had also struggled for its own independence in the tiny territory left to them after Britain's earlier betrayal of the Mandate in 1921/22.

In this, Britain arbitrarily removed from the Mandate all the relatively vast territory east of the River Jordan up to the borders of the newly formed Iraqi state and created yet another artificial Arab state - now known as the Kingdom of Jordan.
The Cypriot people also demanded to be freed of the British yoke following the example of other Crown Colonies and territories. But Turkey reneged on the earlier treaties and a campaign of violence and a land grab was instituted, funded by Turkey.

Cyprus finally gained its independence from Britain on 16th August 1960. In December 1963, Turkey sent commandos into northern Cyprus. Despite UN and international condemnation, Turkey mounted indiscriminate air strikes using chemical weapons and napalm on civilians. And in 1974, we know what took place - a full scale Turkish invasion.

In a moral world it would be eloquent justice for flotillas containing true humanitarians to sail towards Turkey to publicly demand restoration of the national integrity of Cyprus and removal of all Turkish military occupation; of the rights of the Kurdish people for an independent State of Kurdistan; of full admittance of the horrors perpetrated against the Armenian people; and for Turkey to come to its senses regarding the embattled State of Israel by accepting the Jewish state's inalienable right to defend itself against Arab and Islamist aggression emanating from Gaza.

To this day Turkey is ratcheting up its Islamic ambition to restore the old hateful Ottoman Turkish Empire and Caliphate instead of showing any remorse for the atrocities that it and the Ottoman Empire perpetrated against the occupied non-Muslim peoples. It refuses more than ever any recognition or acknowledgment of its crimes against humanity in the past and in the present.

Meanwhile, the Obama Administration, the United Nations, and a deeply immoral world looks on in silence as yet another flotilla of lies and violence prepares to set sail from Turkey and Iran to create a maritime pipeline of advanced and ever lethal missiles for Hamas in Gaza to use against Israeli civilians.

A Guide to the Perplexed

June 20, 2010

I was asked by a friend recently to assist a Christian Zionist lady who had received some anti-Israel propaganda at her church and was perplexed and swayed by the opposing points of view she was reading.

I have taken the liberty of using as my title the same one used in the great work of Moses Maimonides who clarified Jewish law during medieval times.

I have used only the first letter of the lady's name and replied to her as follows:

Dear C,

Israel is the ancestral and biblical homeland of the Jewish people. Not only is it their spiritual homeland but they are the indigenous, native people of the land.

Simply read the Bible. It is not only the word of Almighty God but a remarkable and accurate history book. Though Arab propagandists attempt to accuse Israel of rejecting peace, the facts are that the re-born Jewish state has offered repeatedly to make the enormous sacrifice of sharing its tiny land – no larger than Wales or New Jersey – with its Arab neighbors. But this has been rejected time and time again.

The tragedy is that those Arabs, who call themselves Palestinians, do not want to live in a state side by side with Israel – they want a state instead of Israel.

The ultimate tragedy for the world is that wherever the Muslim foot has trod triumphal – as in the 7th century Arab invasion of the Jewish homeland – the land is forever considered in Islam as part of the *Umma*, the Muslim community.

If it is subsequently liberated from Muslim occupation, it must be recovered through endless war. Thus, it is considered in the *Dar al-Harb*, the House of War.

This means that Islam will not permit any non-Muslim state to exist in land the Muslims consider was once theirs. The same applies to Spain and Portugal, which once were conquered by Muslim armies, along with vast areas of France, Italy, Sicily, the Balkans, Southern Russia, Greece – even up to the very gates of Vienna in Austria. All these territories were once invaded and conquered by Muslim armies and must be returned to Islam according to Islamic teaching.

I merely write the above so that you will see that whatever Israel offers the Arab and Muslim world in a heartfelt plea for peace it will always be rebuffed and rejected.

The terrible proof of this is the breathtaking concession that Israel made in 2005. It took the immense risk for peace and left the Gaza Strip for the Arabs to begin creating a nascent and peaceful nation, which would hopefully build schools, libraries and hospitals and all the trappings of a civilized and democratic state.

Israel's government at the time even forcibly removed the 10,000 Jewish villagers from their productive farms throughout the Gaza Strip and left the greenhouses and agricultural infrastructure behind for the Arabs to use. Instead, the farms were trashed and the remaining synagogues desecrated.

Meanwhile the exiled Jews still live as refugees inside Israel. Shortly after, the Islamist Hamas organization, which calls in its charter for the slaughter of the Jews in Israel and the destruction of the re-born Jewish homeland, launched a bloody civil war against the Fatah organization and occupied the Gaza territory.

Immediately, Hamas began to fire missiles into Israeli schools, kindergartens and civilian homes. To date, Hamas has launched some 12,000 rockets into Israeli villages and towns and continues to smuggle in ever lethal and advanced weapons to kill and maim Israeli civilians.

Israel's amazingly risky decision to leave Gaza and help the Arabs to create the beginnings of a viable and peaceful state were torn to shreds by the Hamas and

Islamic jihad terror machine, which now has given the world empirical proof that the Arabs who call themselves Palestinians want NO peace with Israel, ever.

One vital matter you must also understand is that there has never, in all of recorded history, been an independent – let alone Arab independent – state of Palestine.

That word was created and employed by the Roman Emperor Hadrian, who destroyed the Jewish homeland in 135 AD, and who renamed it Philistia, which morphed into Palestina and Palestine.

Hadrian knew that the ancient and hated enemies of the Jewish people were the Philistines and he chose to insult the surviving Jews by changing the name of their homeland.

The land remained merely a geographical territory in name only, just as Siberia and Patagonia, for example, are not independent nations but merely geographical regions.

Despite an endless succession of alien occupiers, Jews always remained in the land in whatever numbers they could sustain. Wherever Jews lived throughout the long years of dispersion, Israel was and is always a focal point in the synagogue service. The very agricultural cycles of Israel are celebrated in various Jewish harvest festivals.

No other people has such an inextricable religious and national relationship with the Promised Land; a special place that the first Jew, Abraham, was led to by God and through Isaac and Jacob – not Ishmael – became a special people unto the Lord. In time, Moses, the Lawgiver, led the Jews from Egyptian bondage back to the Promised Land and the biblical narrative thus proceeds from there.

C, please do not be swayed by emotional claims from the Arab world, and from those in your church who would deceive you as they have themselves been deceived, unless you can find the truth and the proof to back up their statements.

Feel free to run them by me at any time if it helps. I will certainly be willing to answer your questions.

July 1, 2010

United Nations Insanity: Still a Mad, Mad World

"Our faith was born there, as was our language, our nationhood, our pride. It is incumbent upon us to defend - even if we all die."

If you read those words, you would be forgiven for believing they were uttered as a declaration of eternal Jewish love and support for Jerusalem and Zion. You would be wrong. Fill in the blank and you will discover that they were uttered by Serbian Deputy Prime Minister, Draskovitch, some twelve years ago while referring to Kosovo. The Serbs lost their ancestral heartland of Kosovo to the Muslim Turks a little over 600 years ago at the Battle of the Field of Blackbirds.

Serbs never stop dreaming of lost Kosovo; it is now part of their national yearning for its eventual return, though the present occupation of Kosovo by the Albanian Muslims casts a giant shadow over any hope for its redemption.

Still it is the hoped for return that unites most Serbs, just as Jerusalem's reunification and restoration to the Jewish people unites most Jews.

Six hundred years is a long time for a people to weep over its still lost heartland. Jews themselves wept over the loss of their Jerusalem for a far, far longer period –

almost 1,800 years during the long exile before Jerusalem's liberation from alien occupation in that momentous and miraculous summer of 1967.

Draskovitch was reflecting upon the unbearable pressure the U.S. Clinton Administration, through NATO, exerted upon the Serbian people even to the extent of a high level bombing campaign, which destroyed all the bridges in Belgrade and took the lives of hundreds of Serbian civilians.

According to an article written by Elyakim Haetzni for Arutz Sheva Israel National Radio, a reporter asked Draskovitch if he "did not want his country to become a part of the West and to share in its wealth?" The Deputy Prime Minister replied: "Not if the price is Kosovo."

Like Israel today, the Serbs were the target of a hostile media. Muslim atrocities against the Christian Serbs were played down almost to exclusion while Serbian massacres of Muslims were banner headlines. As far as the media was concerned, the Serbs were: "Guilty until proven guilty."

That is how Israeli Prime Minister, Binyamin Netanyahu recently described much of the international media's present day attitude towards Israel's attempt at self-defense in the face of a premeditated campaign of anti-Israel demonization and de-legitimization.

John Cleese, the wonderfully funny British comedian who was part of the earlier Monty Python Flying Circus and who played the part of the memorable manic proprietor of the British seaside hotel, Fawlty Towers, said on a recent You Tube video that, "now that I am sixty six years old, I can see that the world is completely mad."

The current occupant of the White House, Barack Hussein Obama, acting as the chief appeaser during this century's first decade, speaks loudly about foreign tyrants but pounds his desk with a feather when it comes to reining in the aggressive ambitions of Iran and North Korea.

In that Temple to Hypocrisy, the United Nations, the U.N. Human Rights Council, whose members include all the most barbaric and repressive rogue regimes one can imagine, spend their time ignoring their own human rights abuses and target only one tiny nation: Israel. Dozens of breathtakingly biased resolutions have been cast against the Jewish state without once ever referring to the appalling history of Palestinian Arab terror that Israel has, and is, forced to endure.

The mad world denies human rights to the Tibetans whose land has been swallowed up by the Communist Chinese. It denies human rights and self-determination to the Kurdish people who endure great hardship at the hands of Turkey, Iran, Syria and Iraq. It denies justice to the Greek Cypriots whose island is 33% occupied in the north by Turkey.

And where is the meaningful UN intervention in the Sudan in which the Arab Muslim north has already slaughtered millions of black Christians, Muslims and animists? Yet all the time, a massive flow of US and European Union tax payer money is poured down a veritable black hole in the deluded hope that it will bring freedom and democracy into Arab-Muslim lands.

Billions of dollars have already been syphoned off into hidden tax havens, be they by despotic and corrupt leaders in the Palestinian Territories, in Iraq, Afghanistan, or throughout the Middle East and south Asia.

According to Matthew Rosenberg, writing in the June 28, 2010 edition of the Wall Street Journal, "more than $3 billion in cash has openly been flown out of Kabul International Airport in the past three years. Most of the funds are being moved by often secretive outfits called '*hawalas*' money transfers with roots in the Muslim world stretching back centuries."

But in this mad world, western politicians and leaders are seemingly devoid of understanding the simple fact that Islam will not ever truly embrace democracy for Islam means submission to the will of Allah, not as democracy teaches; submission to the will of the people.

Seeing the West in its present day descent towards a new dark gulf, I am reminded of Winston Churchill's lament of Britain's similar descent in the 1930s.

Replace his mention of the British nation six months before Munich with that of America today and his words ring uncannily true for all of us as we endure the trillions of dollars of debt piled on by President Obama and the Democrat party while witnessing the rising peril of Islamic triumphalism.

He said: "I have watched this famous island descending incontinently, fecklessly, down the path which leads to a dark gulf. It is a fine broad stairway at the beginning, but after a bit the carpet ends.

"A little farther on there are only flagstones, and a little farther on still these break beneath your feet … if mortal catastrophe should overtake the British nation, historians a thousand years hence will still be baffled by the mystery of our affairs.

"They will never understand how it was that a victorious nation, with everything in hand, suffered itself to be brought low, and to cast away all that had been gained by measureless sacrifice and absolute victory – gone with the wind!"

July 7, 2010

The Arab Veil of Deception and the Left

Though they will not expose it in the media, Arab-Muslim anti-Israel activists feel a profound and debilitating sense of humiliation at the inherent failings of their own societies. So what better way to deflect their dissatisfaction within Araby than to employ the language of the Left - in particular, such phrases as "national liberation" and "anti-apartheid" - with which to level false charges against the embattled Jewish state?

It doesn't matter to these Arab-Muslims, to their few Christian-Arab apologists, or to their leftist and progressive amen chorus that Israel is dwarfed by an enormous Arab landmass, which is 570 times greater than that of Israel - a state no larger than Wales or New Jersey. Indeed, the leftists, while ironically turning on the one state in the Middle East that provides its people with freedoms no Arab or Muslim country will ever provide, choose to embrace the Arab falsehoods. Why is this? It is because the Left is terrified of being perceived as racist. Yet by their very own actions and words, they are just that.

The Left buys the Arab and Muslim lies against Israel because they believe that the Arabs can never change for the better. That is pure racism of the worst kind. The corollary to this put-down of an entire Arab ethnicity is that the Left refuses to admit that it is the Arab-Muslim culture that actively engages in the very evil practices that they falsely hurl at Israel. And where do you find apartheid, racism, repression and torture? Why, in the very Arab-Muslim world the Left supports and embraces.

Leftists will always invoke liberal values, but if they truly cared about them, they would first address the Arab-Muslim political culture that by its very nature is inimical to liberalism. And when such leftist hypocrisy is exposed, the Left always retreats to the tawdry defense of hurling charges of Islamophobia and racism at all who attempt to correct it.

Indeed, left-wing attempts at silencing critics who question the Left's manic obsession of only attacking Israel merely continue to hurt the millions of Arab-Muslims who suffer within societies still rooted in a 7th century mindset. The leftist and progressive so-called human rights activists and college-age drones, while obsessed with attacking the Jewish state, remained astonishingly silent on the massive human rights abuses endemic in the Arab and Muslim world.

Gaza's shops are full of every commodity; their people are well-fed, despite what the mainstream media tells you. Gaza's Hamas occupier (the same Islamic terror machine that calls in its charter for the slaughter of Jews and the violent destruction of Israel) continues to be the recipient of billions of dollars from the European Union, the United Nations, and even from American taxpayer money, courtesy of Barack Obama.

But it is Gaza that remains the object de jour of the loony Left while the suffering Kurds, the disinherited Tibetans, and the black victims of Arab tyranny and genocide in Darfur are conveniently ignored. The Left fails to appreciate that it is empirically racist to have lower expectations for non-Westerners.

If the radical Left and progressives (today's communists by another name) are so concerned about "justice and peace" - words which have now become terminally tarnished by their utterances in the mouths of so many hypocrites and charlatans - they should be challenged about how their persistent and obsessive attacks on Israel wound terribly the Jewish survivors of Palestinian Arab terror, or the Jewish refugees from the Arab and Muslim world. Or is Jewish blood of no consequence to the radical Left?

If the Left, radical and otherwise, is for justice, why then do its members ignore the Jews who were persecuted, uprooted, and forced from their homes in Araby into exile simply because they were Jews? The question every leftist should be asked is why does the Left not demand justice for these victims instead of obsessively attacking the ancestral and biblical homeland these Jewish refugees now live in?

One wonders if leftists truly understand geographical, historical and political realities in the Middle East and North Africa from which some 800,000 Jews were brutally expelled - a number greater than those Arabs who needlessly followed the commands of their corrupt leaders and left their homes during the 1948 Arab-Israel War.

One wonders if leftists know that in 1922, Britain tore away almost 80% of Mandatory Palestine that lay east of the Jordan River and arbitrarily created a new Arab state today called Jordan? Or that, in reality, Jordan is Palestine? Do the leftists and progressives know, or even care, that Jews were immediately and ethnically cleansed from four fifths of Arab occupied areas - parts of the very land they had been promised by the British government in 1917 as a future national Jewish home?

Do the masses of college students in the U.S., who flock to the siren call of the mendacious Arab anti-Israel disinformation machine, realize that the Arab-Muslim nation has spread over nearly 12 million square kilometers in the Mid-East and North Africa?

Do these same college-age students ever ask themselves why so many educated, intelligent young Arabs and Muslims become suicide killers and massacre thousands - mostly fellow Muslims - and why so many millions of Muslims applaud their atrocities? Why does the Left remain so strangely indifferent in the face of the indoctrination of so many young, susceptible Arab and Muslim minds by hate-filled imams?

These facts should repel Western college and university students who would fiercely reject the notion that they too are being indoctrinated. But it seems that by their willing acceptance and espousal of the disinformation they receive from the Left, and from the highly sophisticated and well-financed Arab propaganda machine, they are themselves being indoctrinated.

Perhaps the narrative will finally change within Western campuses. The pendulum will swing back. Perhaps the students, the potential leaders of the future, will come to understand that Israeli Jews try to survive on a tiny sliver of land between the Mediterranean Sea and the River Jordan - a mere forty-plus miles at its widest - and all that is left to them from the original Palestine Mandate.

And even the very ancestral and biblical Jewish heartland of Judea and Samaria (the so-called West Bank) is required by the world to be torn away from that narrow strip and given to the Arabs to create yet another Arab state. But such a mini-state will be composed of hate-filled Muslim-Arabs who have undergone decades of anti-Jewish indoctrination and who desire one thing only: the violent destruction of what is left of Israel. This is no peace process. This is future genocide.

Perhaps the Western students will come to realize that despite the torrent of Arab-Muslim lies against Israel, the Left's eager embrace of such lies aided and abetted by the willing connivance of so many extreme leftist tenured professors, Israel's Muslim neighbors will never accept a non-Muslim state on land upon which the Muslim foot once trod triumphal - even though the Jewish inhabitants preceded Islam by millennia.

Perhaps, perhaps, they may even come to realize, before it is too late, that their own Western societies are threatened by Islamic triumphalism and the covert introduction of Islamic sharia law. Or will they and the Left continue to exist under a horrifying veil of deception?

On the day Israel was reconstituted in its ancient homeland, the Muslim-Arabs tried to exterminate it. They have been trying ever since, be it by all-out wars, by relentless terror, or by the current stratagem of de-legitimization and demonization of the Jewish homeland using thugs and jihadists on "peace flotillas" posing as human rights activists.

July 13, 2010

The Mosques of War

Of the three monotheistic religions, Judaism is considered the mother faith and the other two, Christianity and Islam, her daughters.

The first daughter, Christianity, under the influence of the early church fathers, rejected the mother and distanced herself from Judaism, even to the extent of changing the Sabbath from the seventh day, Saturday, to Sunday and renaming it the Lord's Day. Seventh-Day Adventists retain Saturday as their Sabbath.

The younger daughter, Islam, under Muhammad, turned on both the Jewish and Christian tribes of Arabia, who declined to accept that Muhammad was the Messenger of God and the "Seal of all the Prophets." Both Jews and Christians rejected the claim of the new faith that it alone ushered in "God's final revelation."

After Rome embraced Christianity under Constantine, the Church fathers increasingly used temporal powers to discriminate against the Jews and proscribe and mock the practice of their faith. In time, this led to the horrors of the Crusades, the Catholic inquisition, forced conversions, pogroms, and ultimately, to the Holocaust.

Islam's followers tolerated those they called the "people of the Book," the Jews and Christians, whose faith was based upon the Bible. But Islam, too, practiced forced conversions, pogroms, massacres, and the discrimination of Jews and Christians through the practice of *dhimmitude*, whereby the "infidels" were forced into second-class status and forced to pay a tax, the *jizzya*, as a penalty for remaining outside the Islamic faith while under Muslim control.

Like Christendom, Islam often forced the Jews to live in ghettos, called *mellahs*. Islamic authorities were the first to coerce Jews into wearing distinctive and often humiliating clothing, preceding the German Nazis by centuries. The Nazis and their European allies forced the Jews into wearing a yellow Star of David, thus marking them for death.

But history is replete with accounts of both daughter religions fighting each other for centuries over territory. When not slaughtering each other, they both often turned upon the hapless and stateless Jews, who, for the most part, had no allies and were unable to defend themselves.

The mother has ample reason to weep at the ferocious degradation and scorn her daughters have heaped upon her with such violence and ingratitude. But many Christians - not all - have come to the realization that biblical Jewish roots are inextricable from their own and that their faith is fatefully incomplete without an acknowledgment of those roots.

Islam, too, is immensely indebted to Judaism. According to Abraham I. Katsh, author of *Judaism and the Koran*, "... like the Jew, the Moslem affirms the unity of God, that He is one, eternal, merciful, compassionate, beneficent, almighty, all-knowing, just, loving and forgiving.

"Like Judaism, Islam does not recognize saints serving as mediators between the individual and his Creator and both faiths believe that each individual is to follow a righteous path and secure atonement by improving his or her conduct and by practicing sincere repentance. But there is another essential and integral part of Islam not shared with Judaism: *Jihad*."

As Katsh points out in his book, originally written as far back as 1954, the duty of Jihad, the waging of Holy War, has been raised to the dignity of a sixth canonical obligation, especially by the descendants of the Kharijites. [...]

To the Moslem, the world is divided into regions under Islamic control, the *dar al-Islam*, and regions not subjected as yet, the *dar al-harb*.

Between this 'area of warfare' and the Muslim dominated part of the world there can be no peace. Practical considerations may induce the Muslim leaders to conclude an armistice, but the obligation to conquer and, if possible, convert never lapses. Nor can territory once under Muslim rule be lawfully yielded to the unbeliever. Legal theory has gone so far as to define as *dar al-Islam* any area where at least one Muslim custom is still observed.

Thanks to this concept, the Moslem is required to subdue the infidel, and he who dies in the path of Allah is considered a martyr and assured of Paradise and of unique privileges there.

Here one can understand clearly that peace - true and lasting peace - between Islam and nations that adhere still to Judeo-Christian civilization, or to Hinduism, Buddhism, or all other faiths, is a forlorn and baseless hope.

The "peace process" between Israel and the Palestinians, for example, is thus a grand illusion, endlessly fostered by Western politicians and diplomats, along with self-deluded Israeli leaders, who all refuse to see a reality that has existed since Islam's creation in the 7th century.

And it is in one abiding respect that this endless spiritual and temporal conflict is seen in its most practical and historical context - the conversion of places of worship into mosques.

The result has been that since the time of Muhammad, synagogues, churches, Hindu temples, Zoroastrian temples, and pagan shrines have been all too often violently converted into mosques.

After the conquest of Mecca in the year 630, Muhammad transformed the Black Stone in the Ka'aba, which ancient pagan Arabs had worshiped, into the paramount Islamic holy place. It became known as the Masjid al-Haram, or Sacred Mosque.

During the Arab invasions of neighboring lands in the Middle East, North Africa, and beyond, under the new banner of Islam, numerous synagogues and churches were converted into mosques. In Damascus, Syria, the church of St. John is now known as the Umayyad Mosque. Also in Syria, the mosque of Job was originally a church.

The Islamic tide swept into Egypt, and many Christian Coptic churches were converted into mosques. From North Africa, the conquests continued into Spain and Portugal, where again churches were converted into mosques. Interestingly, many churches had been built upon the sites of earlier Roman temples. But during the re-conquest of the Iberian Peninsula by Christian armies - the Reconquista - these same mosques were reconverted into churches.

In Gaza, the Great Mosque of Gaza was originally a Christian church. In Turkey, the Hagia Sophia Church was converted in 1453 into a mosque and remained so until 1935, when it became a museum. Indeed, the Ottoman Turks converted into mosques practically all churches and monasteries in the territories they conquered.

The most well-known mosques, built upon previous non-Muslim holy sites, are the Al-Aqsa mosque on Jerusalem's Temple Mount and the Dome of the Rock, also built upon the site of the two biblical Jewish Temples.

There are four holy cities of Judaism: Jerusalem, Hebron, Safed, and Tiberias. Hebron is the second-holiest city, and in it is the burial place of the Jewish Patriarchs and Matriarchs, known as the Cave of Machpela, where Abraham and Sarah, Isaac and Rebekah, and Jacob and Leah are buried.

Herod the Great constructed an enclosure for the burial site. During the later Christian Byzantine period, a church was built upon the site, but this was destroyed in 614 by the Persians. Later, the Arab-Muslim invaders built a mosque in its place.

Jews were not permitted to worship at their nearly-four-thousand-year-old holy place by the Muslim Arabs. They could only ascend to the seventh step leading to the tombs. Indeed, they were refused this right as a place of worship from the 7th century until 1967, when Israel liberated the territory from the Jordanian occupiers.

Even before the Israeli liberation, a horrifying massacre of Jewish residents in Hebron, by their Arab Moslem neighbors, took place in 1929 while under the British Mandate of the geographical territory known as Palestine.

Prior to the present-day Palestinian Authority assuming control of the city of Nablus, which was the ancient biblical Jewish city of Shechem, the Tomb of Joseph, the biblical figure, was a place of Jewish pilgrimage.

When it was handed over to the PA, as one of seemingly endless Israeli concessions, the tomb was desecrated by a Moslem mob, which proceeded to convert it into a mosque.

On the Indian subcontinent, Hindu temples were similarly converted into mosques. Lately, Hindu nationalists have reconverted some mosques into temples, and, as in so many other parts of the world, considerable bitterness exists between Moslems and members of other faiths or those of no faith.

Mosques now occupy vast numbers of places of worship for other faiths. In Algeria, the Great Synagogue of Oran is now a mosque after the Jewish population was driven from Algeria. Many other synagogues throughout the Arab world are now mosques after the Jewish inhabitants were expelled.

In the 1974 invasion of Cyprus by Turkey, many Greek Orthodox churches in northern Cyprus were converted into mosques. And the process continues.

Saudi Arabia invests endless billions of dollars to build mosques throughout the world. The international blanketing of cities with mosques is just another expression of jihad. In Western Europe, most famously renamed *Eurabia* by the writer, Bat Yeor, there may soon come a time when there will be more minarets than steeples.

Perhaps the most egregious and blatant example of Islamic triumphalism is the planned construction of a giant mosque in New York, almost upon the site of the horrific destruction of the Twin Towers by Moslem terrorists acting in the name of Allah.

The proposed mosque is to be opened in 2011 on the very anniversary of the September 11, 2001 atrocity - a flagrant insult to the memory of the thousands of innocents who died at the hands of Moslem fanatics and believers, most of them Saudis.

But this, after all, is what jihad is all about. Subdue the "infidel" at all costs. The Islamic obligation to conquer and convert the unbeliever must never lapse. Its tangible manifestation can also be characterized as the mosques of war.

Islam is Islam is Islam

August 4, 2010

To quote the old proverb: "If it walks like a duck, quacks like a duck, looks like a duck, it must be a duck." So it is with Islam. There is no radical Islam, no hijacked Islam, no corrupted Islam, no extreme Islam and no moderate Islam: There is simply Islam.

Listening to White House spokesman, Robert Gibbs, answering questions from reporters about the planned 15 story high mosque mere yards from ground zero was revealing. He said: "I think you've heard this administration and the last administration talk about the fact that we are not at war with a religion but with an idea that has corrupted a religion."

There again is that oft repeated phrase that the religion of Islam has been corrupted. But do Gibbs and his boss, Barack Hussein Obama, truly believe that Islam is a peaceful religion and not without a major pillar called jihad with its dire implications for all non-Moslems or, as the Muslim world likes to describe them: infidels.

One still hears the phrase by well-meaning but misguided individuals that Islam means peace. No. Islam means submission; not submission to the will of the people as in a democracy, but solely to the will of Allah. And Moslems may not ever question the teachings of the prophet Mohammed.

Islam also teaches that it is superior to all other religions. It is Islam über alles. The Moslem is taught that Judaism and Christianity perverted the will of Allah and Islam received the superior revelation requiring, therefore, that Jews and Christians ultimately submit to Islam.

Islam bases its ideology on five pillars – Witness to Allah and his prophet Mohammed; Prayer five times daily facing Mecca and the Ka'ba; Almsgiving to the poor and to the mosque; Fasting during the month of Ramadan; and Pilgrimage to Mecca.

But there is a sixth pillar called jihad. This is now the greatest of all threats to Judeo-Christian civilization. Indeed one can say that much of the world faces an existential threat to its survival, not from the manufactured and erroneous science of global warming but from global jihad.

According to Abraham Katsh, who wrote the following as far back as 1954 in his book on the Koran:

"The duty of Jihad, the waging of Holy War, has been raised to the dignity of a sixth canonical obligation … To the Moslem, the world is divided into regions under Islamic control, the Dar al-Islam, and regions not subjected as yet, the Dar al-Harb.

"Between this area of warfare and the Muslim dominated part of the world there can be no peace. Practical considerations may induce the Muslim leaders to conclude an armistice, but the obligation to conquer and, if possible, convert never lapses. Nor can territory once under Muslim rule be lawfully yielded to the unbeliever. Legal theory has gone so far as to define as Dar al-Islam any area where at least one Muslim custom is observed.

"Thanks to this concept, the Moslem is required to subdue the infidel, and he who dies in the path of Allah is considered a martyr and assured of Paradise and of unique privileges there."

Now we can see how there will never be a true and lasting peace by the Muslim Arabs – who call themselves Palestinians, or by the Arab and Muslim states – with Israel. Islam will not allow it. So it is pointless, therefore, and against God's Covenant with His people, to give away one single centimeter of biblical and ancestral Jewish land to the so-called Palestinian Arabs or to anyone else.

Nor can there ever be peace between Muslim Kosovo and the Orthodox Christian Serbs or between Muslim Pakistan and Hindu India, to name a few of the endless Muslim engendered wars raging in the world today. The simple reason is that Islam will never countenance or accept peace with any non-Muslim neighbor: Never.

Jihad requires the Moslem believers to spread what they consider "Islamic truth" by all means, especially by the sword. Now in our modern world, the sword gives way to the most lethal and devastating weaponry in man's military arsenal. That is why the leader of Iran, Mahmoud Ahmadinejad, seeks the ultimate nuclear weapon to destroy Israel and usher in what he believes to be the Islamic messiah, the 12th Imam.

As I've written previously, Islam, through jihad, is to spread what is called in Arabic, Dar al-Islam, the "House of Submission" meaning those lands occupied and controlled by Islamic states and under Sharia law. Those nations not yet conquered by Muslim forces are in what is called the "Dar al-Harb: the House of War, and must be eventually overcome by endless war.

Islam seeks to impose Sharia law wherever it gains control. It is based upon the Koran and the Sunna and has not been reformed or modified since the 7th century. It can never be changed.

That is why we see on the front page of the Times magazine the horrific photograph of the 18 year old Afghani girl whose nose and ears were cut off by her husband, acting according to Islamic Sharia law. Her offense was that she had fled from her cruel family and in-laws and, as a mere woman under Taliban Islamic rule, she had little or no rights.

Saudi Arabia invests endless billions of dollars to build mosques throughout the world. The international blanketing of cities with mosques is just another expression of jihad. In Western Europe, most famously renamed Eurabia by the writer, Bat Ye'or, there may soon come a time when there will be more minarets than steeples.

Perhaps the most egregious and blatant example of Islamic triumphalism is the planned construction of a giant mosque in New York, almost upon the site of the horrific destruction of the Twin Towers by Moslem terrorists acting in the name of Allah.

The proposed Cordoba Mosque (named after the Islamic defeat of Christians in Spain during the 8th century) is to be opened in 2011 on the very anniversary of the September 11, 2001 atrocity – a flagrant insult to the memory of the thousands of innocents who died at the hands of Moslem fanatics and believers, most of them Saudis.

It is depressing to see and hear liberals such as White House spokesman, Robert Gibbs, and New York Mayor, Michael Bloomberg, denigrating principled opponents of the giant mosque, accusing them of being against religious freedom.

This is a canard and as baseless as the claim by proponents of the building of a mosque at ground zero as being merely Muslim outreach and interfaith understanding.

What liberals and "progressives" fail to understand by the very location of the mosque is what jihad is all about. Subdue the "infidel" at all costs. For Moslems, the Islamic obligation to conquer and convert the unbeliever and impose Sharia law must never lapse.

The Poisoned Pen

August 11, 2010

Then said Satan: "This besieged one, how shall I overcome him?
He has courage and ability, he has weapons and imagination.
So he said: I shall not take his strength, nor muzzle nor bridle him.
Nor soften nor weaken his hands, only one thing I shall do;
I shall dull his brain and he will forget that he is in the right."

So wrote the Israeli poet, Natan Alterman, in his poem, *Gone like a Dream*.

He was expressing his deep anxiety over the weakening resolve and steadfastness of the Jews of Israel and of the Diaspora in their support for the reconstituted Jewish state.

For long decades, in the face of unrelenting Arab Muslim hostility and aggression, the Jews were imbued with a deep conviction of the rightness of their cause.

Many still do and fight against an unremitting and hostile world that would consign Israel to the abyss, but far too many today have fallen away and been seduced by an overwhelming onslaught – not of military might – but by a war of ideas, however false and twisted those ideas are. The success of those lies has sapped the will of many and confused many more.

We have all heard of the Big Lie theory that was so successfully enunciated and practiced by Adolf Hitler's propaganda minister, Josef Goebbels.

The theory essentially posits that people will believe in a lie if it is big enough and repeated enough times.

Goebbels knew that most people had a scant understanding of a situation but when they heard the same lie repeated again and again they would begin to accept unquestionably what was being told to them.

Goebbels put it this way: "The rank and file is usually much more primitive than we imagine. Propaganda must therefore always be essentially simple and repetitious. The most brilliant propagandist technique will yield no success unless one fundamental principle is borne in mind constantly … it must confine itself to a few points and repeat them over and over."

The Muslim Arabs have learned this lesson all too well for they have succeeded in doing what years of Arab and Islamist warfare and terror have failed to do. They have isolated the Jewish state as never before and won millions around the globe to their cause by demonizing Israel with the Goebbelian technique of the Big Lie theory.

Arab Muslim spokespersons have become adept at smoothly repeating a few enormous lies, often wrapped in pseudo-emotion, that coerce so many uninformed but well- intentioned listeners who then fall for them – hook, line and sinker.

A typical technique by such Arab Muslim propagandists is to create a lie and deliver it with conviction. As soon as the lie is exposed for what it is, the Arab or pro-Arab propagandists merely moves on to the next big howler. And so it goes – an endless and unashamed armory of pernicious falsehoods masquerading as facts.

And in the court of public opinion, the victim of those manufactured myths, Israel, now becomes the victimizer and oppressor to so many people and thus further marginalized and demonized.

Leftists and Marxists rush to embrace the cause of the Arabs, who call themselves Palestinians, seeing through a dark mirror a warped comparison of the successful and creative Jewish state with Lenin's attack on capitalism – and if the Jewish state is surrounded by self-oppressed and failed Arab societies, so much the better. Add to this Ionesco like 'Theater of the Absurd' a mainstream international media, which eagerly loves to be manipulated by Arab and Muslim regimes, and you have a perfect storm.

This then is the metaphysical challenge to Israel as it resists both the violence of overt Muslim Arab physical aggression and the equally diabolical violence of the poisoned pen and the mendacity of the misspoken word.

The old aphorism goes: 'Sticks and stones may break my bones but words will never harm them.' Oh! But they do.

And the Arab Muslim world has learned, just as Josef Goebbels knew, that if you lie about a people and bear false witness against them, you prepare them with your hateful words for an extermination that millions around the globe will willingly accept and excuse.

Satan is busy. He hates the light of Israel. He hates the creativity, the progress and the freedoms that Israel, like America, spreads throughout the world.

He enjoys the ultimate absurdity that spews from the Islamic Republic of Iran as the new 'Haman,' Mahmoud Ahmadinejad, calls the United States the 'Great Satan' and Israel, the 'Little Satan.' Oh, how delicious that irony is to the real Satan.

But the dark forces of Arab and Islamic hate know that they will not prevail if they fail to extinguish the flickering candle of light in the world. Israel is that illuminating candle and will surely endure despite Satan's eternal quest to snuff it out.

It says in the Apocrypha's Book of Esdras 2: "I shall light a candle of understanding in thy heart, which shall not be put out."

It should also be understood by the forces of hate and darkness, those who worship death, not life, that the flame of a single candle can light untold millions more.

August 16, 2010

How many more Outrages?

The question has to be asked yet again: How many more outrages will President Barak Hussein Obama commit before America finally wakes up?

Speaking at a White House dinner to celebrate the Muslim month of Ramadan, Obama took the opportunity of the festive meal, the Iftar, eaten after the day's fasting, to announce his unswerving support for the building of a fifteen story mosque mere yards from the hallowed site of Ground Zero in New York City.

By making this proclamation, surrounded by members of the Muslim community, which sadly included some – perhaps many – who overtly or covertly support Hamas and other Islamic jihadist organizations, President Obama turned his back on America and, like his earlier speech in Cairo to the Muslim world, callously again embraced Islamic triumphalism.

Make no mistake, the construction of this particular mosque, so near to the scene of America's worst attack upon its soil, will send a clear message to the Islamic world that the jihadists have triumphed against what they call the "Great Satan."

The mosque's very existence, so terribly close to where Jihadists from Saudi Arabia deliberately flew two airliners full of innocent passengers into the twin towers and murdered nearly three thousand civilians, will send a rallying cry to untold millions more Moslem men and women throughout the dysfunctional Arab world to become willing martyrs for Allah.

Plans for the mosque's alleged opening on September 11th, 2011 - the tenth anniversary date of the massacre of the innocents - exposes the degree of mendacity and cynical exploitation practiced by so many in the Muslim world.

The completed mosque, rising high over the scene where the remains of some victims still remain eviscerated somewhere in the rubble as the towers fell because of that harrowing and dastardly atrocity, may well mark the beginning of the end of the United States of America as we have known and loved it.

Sharia law is already poised to begin stealthily replacing the Constitution unless we choose as a people to say no to this mosque at this time and in this place. Build your mosques elsewhere. Not here! Not here!

There is freedom of religion still in America but Muslim symbols are immensely strong in the world of Islam and this mosque, to be known as the Cordoba mosque, will be saturated with Islamic symbolism - replete with memories of Christian victories over Islam in Spain.

The soaring mosque at Ground Zero will thus be sweet revenge to many Moslems and a powerful vindication for their belief of Islam's superiority over Christianity, Judaism and every other religion on Earth.

That Obama chose to support what he surely knows is a Koranic injunction to all Moslems to win the world for Allah through the building of a mosque at the site of an 'Islamic victory' says much about this 44th president of the United States of America.

Thomas Wolfe once wrote: "It makes the world safe for hypocrisy."

But there will be those who will still make the untenable claim that this particular mosque is merely to be an interfaith center, a place for Moslems in America to reach out to non-Moslems. Therein is our eventual oblivion. It will be an epochal defeat for America and the Constitution we hold dear.

Winston Churchill, describing the fearful implications of Munich in the House of Commons on October 1938 said: "We have sustained a defeat without a war."

The construction of this particular mosque at Ground Zero will be a tangible reminder of America's own Munich and fearsome events will follow.

Through our espousal of those twin idiocies, Political Correctness and Multiculturalism, we will bow our heads to an implacable ideology that scorns and mocks our 'brotherly love' and has nothing but contempt for what it perceives as American weakness.

August 25, 2010

Then as Now: Now as Then

When you enter an Arab bazaar you are expected to bargain. Not to do so is almost considered an insult to the Arab trader: More than that it marks you as almost worthless and beneath contempt.

The same attitude exists towards the non-Arab and non-Moslem that enters into negotiations with an Arab interlocutor. If you come seeking genuine negotiations with an open heart and a willingness to make concessions as a tangible expression of your desire to reach an honorable agreement, you are considered a fool and, again, worthy only of contempt.

Thus Binyamin Netanyahu comes to Washington, DC in order to sit with Mahmoud Abbas, Chairman of the Palestinian Authority along with the Jordanian Kinglet Abdullah, the Egyptian President Hosni Mubarak and the U.S. President Barack Hussein Obama on September 2, 2010. It will likely be a fatal trap for the Israeli leader.

Predictably, the Arab side will call for pre-conditions even though Netanyahu has been assured by the Obama regime that there will be no such demands permitted. But Abbas, coached by the Arab League, has already demanded that the freeze on Israeli building within parts of Jerusalem be extended throughout all of Jerusalem and within Judea and Samaria (otherwise known as the West Bank by its Jordanian name) and that it must continue indefinitely – by which Abbas means permanently. The crafty bazaar traders know only too well how to bamboozle the innocent non-Arab. Obama will, of course, find an equally duplicitous formula to accept the Arab demand and Israel will be brutally pressured accordingly as it has been time and time again.

And true to type, PA Chief Mahmoud Abbas (Abu Mazen), has sent a letter to the Quartet (US, EU, Russia, UN) saying he will abruptly terminate the direct talks with Israel if Israel resumes construction.

Here again are shades of the arch-terrorist, Yasser Arafat, walking out of peace agreements as he did before with the degrading image of Secretary of State, Madeline Albright, shamefully running behind and begging him to return.

The Americans, mediating the process, did not agree to the PA's demand to make the talks conditional on an extension of the freeze. Chief PA negotiator and veteran dissembler, Saeb Erekat, acknowledged this recently. However, he added that the Americans "allowed us to understand that if the direct talks are renewed, it would be far, far easier to yet again persuade Israel to extend the freeze indefinitely."

Israel had announced a ten-month freeze on all new Jewish construction in Judea and Samaria nine months ago. It was done in the hope and belief that this would bring the Palestinian Authority to the negotiating table. But 9 months of stagnation passed with the PA refusing to agree to direct talks.

It is only now, as the freeze is about to expire, that the PA has agreed to the talks, while threatening to end them if the building freeze ends. Prime Minister Binyamin Netanyahu has repeatedly stated that the freeze will end on Sept. 26.

Israel, for its part, wants any new Arab state that is carved out of Judea and Samaria to be demilitarized and for recognition by the Palestinian Arabs of Israel as the 'national state of the Jewish people." It is a remote possibility that either of those demands will be met from the Arabs who call themselves Palestinians.

It had been expected that Abbas would pressure Israel regarding the freeze shortly before it expired. Danny Dayan, Secretary-General of the Council of Jewish Communities in Judea and Samaria, said: "I suspect that right before the construction freeze ends six weeks from now, Abu Mazen will agree to direct talks on condition that the freeze be extended. That will put Netanyahu in a very tight spot."

There is ample precedent for such Arab double dealing and mendacity. A few weeks after the Oslo agreement was signed between Israeli Prime Minister Rabin and Yasser Arafat on the White House lawn, Arafat, who was the unelected leader of the Palestinian Arabs, went to Johannesburg and in a mosque there made a speech in which he apologized to his fellow Moslems.

He said, "Do you think I signed something with the Jews which are contrary to the rules of Islam? That's not so. I'm doing exactly what the prophet Mohammed did."

Arafat was reminding his Moslem audience about the deception of Hudabiya. The prophet Mohammad had made an agreement there with the Kuraish tribe of Mecca during which he and his followers would honor a peace treaty for 10 years.

But during the period, Mohammad created a veritable army numbering thousands and after a mere two years into the treaty, feeling himself strong enough, he arbitrarily broke it, marched on Mecca, and destroyed the Kuraish tribe, slaughtering the men and enslaving the women.

He did this by manufacturing a flimsy excuse in order to make a surprise attack and thus it has become an article of Muslim faith to break any peace treaty signed with non-Moslems or, as they are called, 'infidels.' Hudabiya is thus the Muslim template for all dealings with non-Moslems and Arafat, following Mohammed's example, broke his agreement with Israel by turning the Oslo Peace into the Oslo War in which thousands of Israeli civilians were slaughtered and maimed.

Norwegian diplomat and United Nations envoy Terje Röd-Larsen, a key player during the Oslo Peace Process in the 1990s, later admitted that "Arafat lied all the time." Lying to infidels is also a device sanctioned and encouraged in the Koran and the Hadith. Nothing changes in the Middle East bazaar. It has always been the same, then as now and now as then.

Israel may well enter into another trap with dire implications for its future. Lies will swirl around during the meeting like cigarette smoke and it is not at all sure that Netanyahu will be able to see clearly what he is agreeing to through the thick and deadly haze.

September 1, 2010

Israeli Concessions: A Zero Sum Game

With Israeli Prime Minister, Binyamin Netanyahu, about to sit with Arab leaders and President Barack Hussein Obama in the White House, some have likened Netanyahu to a minnow surrounded by circling sharks.

Present will be Egyptian President Hosni Mubarak, Jordan's kinglet, Abdullah, the Chairman of the Palestinian Authority, Mahmoud Abbas, and the joker in the pack, President Obama, at the 'peace' talks – peace being an oxymoron with the news that four Israelis, including a pregnant woman, were slaughtered Tuesday evening by Arabs near Hebron.

Never before has an Israeli leader been coerced into a White House meeting where the American president has displayed such extreme partiality to the Muslim and Arab world and barely disguised hostility to the Jewish state.

The talks are already stacked against Prime Minister Netanyahu who had been promised both by Obama and his Secretary of State, Hillary Clinton, that there would be no Arab preconditions imposed upon him. But there most certainly are and they will be at the top of the anti-Israel agenda. Most prominent will be that demanded by Mahmoud Abbas who has already threatened to bolt the talks if Israel does not make the six month self-imposed Israeli building freeze in Judea and Samaria, as well as within Jerusalem itself, permanent.

It was a trap of his own making when Netanyahu, with the best of intentions, announced the voluntary freeze. It was obvious that the Arabs and Obama would lean heavily upon Israel to extend it beyond its September 26 expiration date; in other words to make it a permanent fact.

The irony is that Netanyahu ordered the six month building freeze as another in the long line of Israeli concessions in order to encourage Abbas to attend peace talks. But the wily Abbas made his demands just prior to the talks, which goes to prove yet again that the road to Hell is paved with good intentions.

The entire purpose of the talks is to give Obama a photo-op and an opportunity to force Israel into accepting a two-state solution. President Obama has already made the creation of a Palestinian state his primary foreign policy goal and he is determined to turn the screw on the Jewish state even as the U.S. economy sinks further and further into the abyss.

But what are the frightful dangers to Israel's survival should a new Arab state - one hostile in the extreme to Israel - be carved out of what is biblical Judea and Samaria (the West Bank), leaving Israel a mere nine miles wide at its most populous and vulnerable region? The views of non-Israelis immediately after the June 1967 Six Day War are as pertinent today as they were then.

A secret memorandum was issued by the United States Joint Chiefs of Staff (JCS) shortly after Israel liberated the West Bank from Jordanian occupation. The Golan Heights had also been taken from the Syrian army, which had used the dominant heights solely to rain artillery barrages down upon Israeli farmers in the Hula Valley and fishermen on the Sea of Galilee.

The Sinai had been wrested from Egyptian control after Egypt's Nasser had moved his armies into the peninsula to threaten Israel. Subsequently the Gaza Strip was liberated from Egyptian occupation.

The conclusions of the JCS were that any peace settlement between Israel and the Arab belligerents would only succeed if Israel retained certain territories vital for its continued existence and survival.

The areas the Joint Chiefs declared as the minimum defensible borders for the Jewish state included the Golan Heights, the western half of Samaria (the northwestern part of the West Bank), all of Judea (the southern part of the West Bank), the Gaza Strip and several portions of the eastern Sinai Peninsula.

This, of course, occurred before the world became obsessed with the creation of an Arab terror state within the narrow 44 mile wide territory between the Mediterranean and the River Jordan.

Since that report in 1967, the Begin government gave away all of the Sinai. Under Prime Minister Ariel Sharon and his deputy, Ehud Olmert, Israel gave away the entire Gaza Strip in 2005, with catastrophic consequences for the Jewish state.

Ehud Barak, Israel's present Defense Minister, had years earlier withdrawn from the southern Lebanon security strip, thus allowing the Islamist Hezbollah to fill the vacuum with dire consequences for Israel. After Israel endured over 10,000 incoming missiles from Hamas-occupied Gaza, a war was finally launched by Israel to remove or nullify the threat.

To date it has not succeeded and missiles and mortars continue to target Israeli civilians though not at the levels that existed before Israel's Operation Cast Lead. Hamas occupied Gaza remains a lethal dagger pointing into the heart of Israel. And behind Hamas and Hezbollah is the nexus of all Islamic terror: Iran.

Israel is under the greatest pressure in years from an American administration to give away the ancestral Jewish heartland of Judea and Samaria. President Barack Obama is perceived by many to be a clear and present danger to the very survival of the reconstituted Jewish state.

In the aftermath of the Six Day War, the US Joint Chiefs were not interested in Jewish patrimony or Biblical history. They were solely concerned with the strategic necessities for Israel's survival in a very bad neighborhood. That is why they set out what the bare minimum retention of territory for Israel should be.

Col. Irving Kett (USA, ret.) also prepared in 1974 an Army War College study on Israel's security needs. His study was called, "A Proposed Solution to the Arab-Israel Conflict."

In it, he strongly suggested that, from a military point of view, Israel's borders should be constituted to make it a compact state with natural boundaries on all sides - the Jordan River to the east, Golan Heights to the northeast, the Litani River in the north, the Mediterranean Sea to the west and the historic boundary with the Sinai Peninsula to the south. As a direct result and consequence of Arab aggression, most of those borders had been attained by Israel at one time or another.

Now Sinai, the Gaza Strip and the security zone in Southern Lebanon have all been given away to an implacable Arab enemy as Israeli concessions and gestures of peace.

Irving Kett had not been aware that another memorandum had been produced earlier, on June 29, 1967, for Secretary of Defense Robert McNamara by General Earle Wheeler, chairman of the JCS, at the direction of President Lyndon Johnson. That study was declassified in 1983 and recommended that Israel keep all of Judea, the western half of Samaria, the Golan Heights, the Gaza Strip and two significant parts of east and south Sinai. The similarity between the memorandums is quite remarkable.

Colonel Kett pointed out what the IDF has always known, but what too many Israeli politicians preferred to ignore; namely, that there is vital strategic value in the mountain range which forms the spine running through Judea and Samaria. The highlands run some 54 miles from Jenin in the north to Hebron in the south and dominate Israel's coastline.

The Jordan valley, which is part of the Great Rift Valley that extends down into East Africa, lies deep below sea level. The mountains rise up to form a massive defense barrier against any Arab and Muslim invasion attempt from the east. The mountain spine is 12 miles wide and Israel simply cannot afford to vacate it.

It was assumed for years by both the Israeli military and politicians that if a Palestinian Arab state came into existence it would have to permit an Israeli defense line on the Jordan River (the Allon Plan), and that such a state would have to be demilitarized.

The answer, of course, would be to have made permanent the suggested boundaries proposed in both Kett's memorandum and the earlier JCS report of some 40 years ago. Events have moved on since then. The Palestinian Authority in the West Bank would never agree to this and Hamas in Gaza would scornfully dismiss it out of hand. The Arabs have become even more vicious in their anti-Jewish rhetoric and behavior, and a jihadist Iran has all but encircled the Jewish state through its Islamist proxies in Gaza and Lebanon.

The Arab-Israel conflict is not, and never has been, merely a war over territory. It is, and always has been, a religious war. Islam will never accept a non-Muslim state, whatever size or shape it may be, within lands previously conquered by Muslims in the name of Allah.

The "Two-State -Solution", so beloved of President Obama and President George Bush before him, requires Judea and Samaria to be given away to the Palestinian Arabs. But the Arabs have no intention of making peace, which should be enough for an Israeli government and Prime Minister with intestinal fortitude to defy the world's pressure for the Jewish state to slowly and surely disappear.

After all, Prime Ministers David Ben-Gurion, Menachem Begin and Yitzchak Shamir all said "no" to American presidents in the past and prevailed.

Interestingly, Colonel Kett had also suggested that the Palestinian Arabs be resettled in a state in the Sinai. The other famous suggestion has been that Jordan is Palestine, which is based upon the historical fact of the first "two-state solution" enacted in infamy by Great Britain some 88 years ago.

Even President George W. Bush, when visiting Israel as Governor of Texas, was moved to utter, "The whole of Israel is only about six times the size of the King Ranch near Corpus Christie." Yet even he, after becoming president, called for a "two-state solution" west of the Jordan River.

Pushing Israel back to the "Auschwitz borders", as Abba Eban called them, where the Jewish state is only nine miles wide at its most populous region, is what the "two-state solution" is all about. The dread euphemism "Final Solution" comes to mind.

Hopefully Binyamin Netanyahu will stress the territorial insanity of that fact over and over to President Obama in the White House. But it will avail him nothing. Accordingly, I am not holding my breath.

September 3, 2010

The Siren Song of Arab Rejection

Another round of peace talks between Israel and the Palestinians began yesterday at the White House. Present were the two Arab leaders and autocrats who are putatively at peace with Israel, Egypt's Hosni Mubarak and Jordan's kinglet, Abdullah.

But, as we shall no doubt see, they will exert their Arab bona fides within the Arab-Muslim world by displaying how hard they can lean on the Israeli Prime Minister, Binyamin Netanyahu. Not to do so invites threats from the hostile Arab and Muslim street.

Despite promises by both President Obama and Secretary of State Hillary Clinton that there will be no preconditions imposed at the talks, Palestinian Chairman Mahmoud Abbas has already made it abundantly clear that he will most certainly demand preconditions and bolt from the peace conference if they are not met: Blackmail?

What he insists on is a permanent freeze on building homes within Jewish communities in Judea and Samaria (aka the West Bank). On September 26, 2010, the self-imposed Israeli building freeze expires.

It was rigorously enforced by Israel, with all the hardships it imposed upon Israeli families, as a goodwill gesture to Abbas to encourage him to attend peace negotiations. Abbas refused up until the very last moment to agree to attend, which underlines the familiar and dreary reluctance by the Palestinian leadership to truly enter into genuine peace talks with the Jewish state.

So, finally, he will attend, but true to type, he could not resist saying that: "if upcoming direct talks between Israel and the PA will fail, Israel would be to blame if it continues to build in Judea and Samaria."

In a televised speech, Abbas said, "Israel alone will bear the responsibility of threatening these negotiations with collapse and failure if it continues settlement expansion in all its forms."

And recently, Saeb Erakat, the wily and disingenuous chief Palestinian negotiator, was reported as stating that Israel must choose "settlements or peace."

The Arab strategy is to make the so-called settlements -- within the territory liberated in 1967 by Israel from Jordanian occupation -- the acid test for peace. But it is a red herring, or perhaps in this case, a red shish-kebab.

If there were no Jewish communities within Judea and Samaria (the biblical ancestral Jewish heartland), it would make no difference to the conflict. The Muslim Arabs would still not accept a Jewish state in any territory previously conquered by Muslim force of arms in the name of Allah.

Before the 1967 Six-Day War, Arab regimes never permitted a single Jew to live in the Jordanian-occupied West Bank or Egyptian-occupied Gaza Strip, and not once was there any intention by Jordan, Egypt, Syria, or Lebanon (the Arab states having borders with Israel) to make peace with the Jewish state.

Listen today to sermons in mosques within the Arab world; the desire to destroy Israel has not abated one iota. It is the relentless Arab rejection of Israel that is at the very heart of the conflict, not the so-called settlements.

In one of his clearer-thinking moments, Thomas Friedman of the New York Times wrote, "To think that the Palestinians are only enraged about settlements is also fatuous. Talk to the 15 year olds. Their grievance is not just with Israeli settlements, but with Israel."

In other words, like their elders, they follow the Muslim line that no non-Muslim state must be permitted to exist and must be warred against perpetually until it is no more.

But Arab rejection predates the modern 1948 reconstitution of Israel within its ancient homeland. In 1937, the British occupiers of Mandatory Palestine appointed the Peel Commission, which proposed a partition plan to separate Jews and Arabs.

The Jews were offered a sliver of land, mostly along the coast, representing a mere 10% of historic geographical Palestine. Remember that in 1921-22, Britain had already torn away all of the Palestinian land east of the River Jordan (amounting to nearly 80% of the mandatory territory and three times the size of present-day Israel) and had given it to the Arab Bedouin Hashemite tribe. Jordan subsequently announced its independence in 1946.

The Jewish leadership reluctantly accepted the 1937 partition. The Arabs -- no surprise -- rejected the plan outright. Instead, again no surprise, the Arab leadership fomented and organized violence and terror against the Jewish inhabitants.

The same occurred with the 1947 U.N. partition of geographical Palestine. The Jews accepted; the Arabs rejected. In 1967, the Arab leaders again rejected any agreement to Jewish sovereignty. Just nine days before the June 5, 1967 outbreak of the Six-Day War, Gamal Abdul Nasser, President of Egypt, clearly enunciated what he had in store for the Jewish state. He said, "Our basic objective is the destruction of Israel. The Arab people want to fight."

And the Iraqi president, Abd-al-Rahman, was equally belligerent. He said, "Our goal is clear: to wipe Israel off the map."

But after the resounding and crushing 1967 Israeli victory over a constellation of Arab armies, Israel's Foreign Minister, Abba Eban, offered to give away territories in exchange for peace.

A victor rarely comes to the defeated party and offers to give away the fruits of victory, but Israel, now as then, sought peace above all else. Sadly but predictably, the Arab world meeting in Khartoum responded with the infamous "Three No's" to Israel's unheard of offer: "No peace with Israel, no recognition of Israel, no negotiations with Israel."

At the peace talks in President Obama's White House, the Egyptian and Jordanian leaders now abide by a peace treaty with Israel, but one upon which both have imposed an Arctic frigidity whereby the normal intercourse between friendly neighboring states is not permitted by them to exist.

Netanyahu will face the same implacable rejection of Israel as always exists, which forms the fundamental reason for the dreary Arab and Muslim strategy of using one excuse after another to render true peace negotiations an exercise in futility.

They will never embrace the Jewish state in the Middle East, but merely use their immense powers of dissimilitude to blame Israel for the absence of peace with one red herring after another. Today it is the so-called settlements. If that fails, there are countless other excuses in their deceptive armory.

To prove the point, even if Israel were foolish enough to commit national suicide by giving to the Arabs the strategic high ground that stretches north and south in Samaria and Judea and which overlooks the Israeli coastal plain, the words of a Fatah Central Committee member, Rafik Natche, are startlingly ominous. He said:

"Hamas says all of the territory belongs to us from the sea to the river and we want to take it in one fell swoop. But the Fatah, which is the armed wing of the PLO, thinks it is more efficient to proceed according to the Step by Step plan. The two organizations are in agreement on the final goal. Our discord is only on the method to adopt in order to achieve the goal."

In other words, the Arabs know that to obtain a state - not living side-by-side with Israel, but in place of Israel - the first step must be to gain disputed territories.

They already have Gaza, which the Israelis gave to them in 2005 in the hope of a true and lasting peace, even forcing out ten thousand Israeli villagers from their homes and farms. Instead, Israel received for its pains a relentless barrage of thousands of lethal missiles targeting its civilian population.

With Israel's unpleasant experience of concession after concession to the Arabs, including the disastrous Gaza experience and the creation of the Palestinian Authority, the vain hope is that the Arab leadership finally recognizes that peace is a two-way street.

It is tragically apparent, however, that barring a miracle, it will be Israel yet again that is leaned upon to make more concessions imperiling its own security. If Netanyahu remains steadfast that the building freeze ends as agreed, then the ever-present threat of Palestinian aggression will once again erupt.

But if he extends the freeze, it will gain Israel nothing and merely embolden the Arab side to demand ever more. Netanyahu will be told by Presidents Obama and Mubarak, as well as by the Jordanian kinglet Abdullah, that Israel must take "risks for peace," which is code for national suicide.

Then there is the joker in the pack, President Barak Hussein Obama, who is the most extreme, radical left-wing president in America's history, who sympathizes with the Muslim world and is no true friend of Israel. Meanwhile, the Arab attendees of the peace talks, as always, will give nothing in return.

Israel, America and Islam: The Bitter Truth

September 13, 2010

Islam will never accept Israel or any non-Muslim land including the United States of America. It cannot do so and still be called Islam. That said there is no future, in particular, for the Jewish state if it believes that the Muslim world will ever accept it in true and lasting peace.

Israel, which is on the front line against resurgent and triumphal Islam, has to accept the dismal fact that it cannot ever have peaceful neighbors who will not at every opportunity wish to destroy it. Israel must continue, therefore, to prosper and thrive as a state in the knowledge that it can never let down its guard.

Even with a Muslim Arab sword of Damocles hanging over it, Israel can survive and grow. Though the Jewish state yearns for peace, more so than most other civilized societies do, the very external threat can be turned to great advantage militarily, politically, socially and economically.

Even in the fractious politics of Israel, nothing keeps internal divisions at bay more than when the barbarians are at the gates. Since the great Zionist leaders of the likes of Theodor Herzl, Vladimir Ze'ev Jabotinsky, David Ben-Gurion, Menachem Begin and Yitzchak Shamir have passed from the scene, there has been a long and depressing parade of weak and incompetent Israeli leaders and politicians who have brought unnecessary disaster down upon the state.

Prime Ministers Yitzchak Rabin, Shimon Peres, Ariel Sharon, Ehud Barak and Ehud Olmert, were all resistant to accepting the bitter truth that even if Israel shrunk to one downtown city block in Tel Aviv, the Arab and Muslim world would still not recognize a Jewish state or agree to live with it in peace and harmony. Why would it not? The answer to that question is Islam itself.

True peace can never be achieved between Muslim and non-Muslim nations. Islam mandates the faithful to spread Sharia and jihad through territorial conquest or, as in the case of Israel, by reclaiming what Muslims believe they have lost.

Even though the native and indigenous peoples of Israel are the Jews, and even though the Land of Israel was given to the Jewish people in an eternal covenant with God, it does not matter to Islam's adherents, for wherever the Muslim foot has once trod triumphal, that territory is forever regarded as Islamic.

If such territory is lost to Muslims, then Allah has been diminished and the land must be retaken. Peace, then, is merely a mirage in the desert sands.

Too many world leaders fail to understand the Muslim mindset. Israeli leaders, who of all people should know better, still fall into the fatal trap of believing that the Western model of lasting peace between nation-states can equally apply in the Middle East between Muslim and non-Muslim nations. It is a fatal fallacy.

The conflict between Israel and the Arabs in general, and between Israel and those who call themselves Palestinians in particular, is not territorial. It is theological.

It is part of the existential conflict that has existed between Islam and the rest of the non-Muslim world since the 7th century.

Much of the Islamic world now feels empowered, as perhaps never before, and seeks global domination with renewed vigor. Global jihad is the tangible and growing threat to the world; not global warming.

The policies of the Jewish state must be ordered within the recognition of that reality; somber and depressing as it may be. But only when world leaders understand the nature of Islam's theological rejection of a genuine and irrevocable peace with Israel, and Israeli leaders realize the uselessness of trading tangible and ancestral land for a delusional "peace," will a long and overdue realism finally enter the conflict.

What we witness today is Israeli Prime Minister, Binyamin Netanyahu, under enormous pressure from the most hostile American president in Israel's history, demanding that Israel make suicidal concession to the deceitful leader of the Palestinian Authority. Abbas is a miserable Holocaust denier, which should place him beyond the pale of every Israeli leader.

But America is under the same Islamic onslaught as Israel, though the threat is not as immediate. Nevertheless, the mosque planned for construction, a mere 600 yards from hallowed ground zero, where body parts from the nearly 3,000 people murdered by Muslim hijackers still remain under the twisted steel and concrete tomb, would be a tangible and symbolic manifestation of Islam's triumph over America. It must not be allowed to be built for if it is, America will begin its fateful descent into becoming the United States of Dhimmitude.

As for Israel, Abbas has predictably imposed the pre-condition that he will bolt the ongoing "peace" talks unless Israel makes its self-imposed building freeze in Judea, Samaria and parts of Jerusalem permanent. This Arab leader is interested only in taking whatever he can from the Israelis while giving nothing, absolutely nothing, in return.

The not so secret reason is that as a Muslim he is not permitted to make peace with a non-Muslim. Yet so many liberal and left-wing Jews inside and outside of Israel, remain infuriatingly blind to these simple facts just as in America so many liberals of all non-Muslim religions and denominations live under a veil of deception.

Great fears justifiably exist about the Obama regime and its abiding hostility towards Israel compared to the obsequious 'bending of the knee' by this American president towards the Islamic world and his deliberate inaction over Iran's nuclear threats.

Even with the strongest backbone in the world, Prime Minister Netanyahu must be wondering just how strong he can be in resisting US pressure to make yet more Israeli concessions to the PA, especially if there has been some implicit or explicit linkage on action against Iran. It is increasingly apparent that Divine intervention is desperately needed to withstand the growing constellation of existential dangers Israel is facing from friends and foes alike.

Israeli leaders must look to their own people's Biblical history. They must see again the nature of their enemies as spelled out in crystal clear clarity by the Almighty through the words of the Jewish prophet Jeremiah:

"They dress the wound of my people as though it were not serious, saying, 'Peace, peace,' but there is no peace. We looked for peace, but no good came." Think of the disasters that Israeli leaders like Yitzhak Rabin, Shimon Peres and Yossi Beilin have brought upon the Jewish state. They were the architects of the Oslo Accords, which we now more accurately call the Oslo War.

The premise of those failed accords, which inflicted terrible suffering on so many Israelis, was for Israel to accept that its ancestral and Biblical lands can be given away to implacable enemies in order to make them peaceful and accept what was left of the Jewish state.

Only the great Shepherd (God Almighty) can protect Israel from her enemies. The world hardly shrugged at the barbaric slaughter of four Jewish civilians near Kiryat Arba by Palestinian Arabs, including the murder of a young woman, nine month's pregnant. It is almost axiomatic that when Israel is invited to yet another round of "peace talks" by a U.S. president and the State Department, Jewish civilians perish in one Arab atrocity after another.

It seems that no recent Israeli government has been able to face the task of fully protecting the residents of Israel. Therefore, in this time of growing worldwide anti-Jewish hatred and fearsome threats to the reconstituted Jewish state God alone, the true guardian of Israel, is there to protect it.

It was the prophet Joel who reminded his fellow Jews in his time that the Covenanted land must never be given away, for as he said:

"In those days and at that time, when I restore the fortunes of Judah and Jerusalem, I will gather all nations and bring them down to the Valley of Jehoshaphat. There I will enter into judgment against them concerning my inheritance, my people Israel, for they scattered my people among the nations and divided up my land." Joel, speaking G-d's words, then proclaimed: "The Lord will roar from Zion and thunder from Jerusalem; the earth and the sky will tremble. But the Lord God will be a refuge for His people, a stronghold for the people of Israel."

Islam's followers in overwhelming numbers consider America the "Great Satan" and Israel the "Little Satan." An old saying among Muslims, who relish ultimate victory over Jews and Christians is: "First the Saturday people; Next the Sunday people." Allahu al-Akbar, meaning Allah is greater, is the 1,400 year old war cry against all non-Muslim peoples. Only by both Israel and America upholding the Divine underpinnings and foundations of their respective nations can they withstand and defeat the onslaught of triumphalist Islam.

September 20, 2010

Whose Is The Land?

Yet again an American administration, this one with decidedly pro-Muslim attitudes, is attempting to create a new Arab state called Palestine within the heartland of ancestral Jewish territory known by the biblical names: Judea and Samaria. But most of the world chooses to know the area by the Arab name of West Bank, a name first applied by its Jordanian occupiers between 1948 and 1967.

Sadly, too many Israeli leaders, politicians and journalists have repeatedly used the Arab name instead of insisting upon using the biblical and ancestral Jewish names, which in Hebrew are *Yehuda* and *Shomron*. In doing so, they have foolishly ceded much of their patrimony.

In fact, Arabs don't like the name *Yehuda* because it is the Hebrew name meaning Judea and for them it is the inconvenient truth that Jews, *Yehudim*, originate from Judea - *Yehuda* - the southern region of the very territory they now demand for their Arab state. Twenty two Arab states already exist in a land mass greater than that of the Unites States of America. Israel itself is no larger than Wales or New Jersey.

Israelis and even pro-Israelis have fallen into the trap of using what has become in English the pejorative term "settlements" instead of villages for the Jewish communities established in Judea and Samaria.

This has been a self- inflicted wound, which carries with it the premise that these communities are imposed upon another peoples' land. That could not be further from the truth.

Many of the Jewish communities within Judea and Samaria are built upon ancient Jewish villages and towns that existed in biblical and post-biblical times. They are merely the rebuilt and re-constituted habitations where Jewish ancestors lived. But the Arabs who call themselves Palestinians want the land and the expulsion of all Jews living in it. Apartheid: Arab style.

Apart from the patriotic souls who have returned to the biblical heartland and whom the world, especially the Left, vilifies as "settlers," many Israelis still make the mistake of using terms such as "West Bank" or beyond the "Green Line," meaning beyond the old 1967 Israeli border, which at its most populous region was only nine miles wide.

George Bush, when Governor of Texas, visited Israel and reportedly remarked about the tiny width then of Israel by saying: 'Why, in Texas, we have driveways longer than that."

There are only two occasions when the geographical territory known as Palestine had a political association. The first was after Rome defeated the second Jewish uprising against Rome. The Emperor Hadrian renamed Judea in Latin, *Palaestina*, eventually becoming Palestine, as an insult to the Jews by using the name of their ancient biblical enemy, the Philistines. This term lasted from 135 AD until the Arab invasion in the 7th century.

The next time the territory was called Palestine in a political context was during the British Mandate in the first decades of the 20th century. But throughout history, no independent, sovereign nation called Palestine ever existed. Certainly there was never an Arab state with such a name. In fact, from the time of the Arab conquest until the British occupation and Mandate, it was never a name on the world's political map.

The territory was always a portion of some greater empire, be it Arab, Mamluk or Turkish. The few inhabitants who wandered across its empty landscape never considered themselves a national entity. It was merely a territory primarily warred over by conflicting Islamic dynasties ruling from Baghdad, Cairo, Istanbul or Damascus. A Kingdom of Jerusalem existed during the Crusader period, created by Christian knights with no historic claim to the land.

The first Jew, Abraham, entered Canaan, modern day Israel, some 4,000 years ago and purchased land in Hebron – one of Judaism's four holy cities; the others being Tiberias, Safed, and the jewel in the crown: Jerusalem. Abraham, his son Isaac, and grandchild, Jacob, along with all but one of their wives, are buried in Hebron. You can read the biblical passage in Genesis 12: verses1 to 3 and 12.

The Jewish faith is unique in that it enshrines a people, a national group, in an inseparable bond with a special land: the Land of Israel. Its geographical position along the eastern shore of the Mediterranean Sea lies between Asia and Africa, and between the river valleys of the Nile and Euphrates. This meant that it was fated to be a bridge between warring empires: Egypt to the southwest and, in turn, Assyria, Babylonia and Persia to the East.

When Rome became the controlling empire of the lands adjoining the Mediterranean basin and beyond, it controlled both the Nile Valley and the approaches to the eastern territories. This reduced the importance of Judea to a minor province.

Theologically, and historically, the Land of Israel is the birthplace of first Judaism and secondly, Christianity. The followers of Islam, realizing the attachment of Jews and Christians to their respective historic holy sites in the land, chose to create within the Koran and Hadith the claim that Mohammad ascended to heaven on a winged horse from Al-Aksa, meaning the farthest place, but in later years - for political and triumphalist reasons - they predictably chose it to be Jerusalem.

Thus a political claim on the Holy City was artificially established, which was made tangible by the Muslim mosques of Al-Aksa and the Dome of the Rock built upon the very site of the two ancient Jewish temples. Mosques are built throughout the world on top of holy places or hallowed sites of non-Muslim faiths.

This is Islamic practice and should be a dire warning to all as we witness the present day Islamic attempt to build a victory mosque a mere 600 feet from hallowed Ground Zero where Muslim terrorists destroyed the Twin Towers.

After Hadrian's defeat of Judea and the slaughter of hundreds of thousands of Jews, with many more taken as slaves, the land was almost denuded of its inhabitants. However, Jews remained in whatever numbers they could sustain and there is ample archaeological evidence of Jewish villages and synagogues existing throughout the Byzantine period from the Golan in the north to southern Israel, including in Gaza.

It is false to believe that Jews only returned in the late 19th century. On the contrary throughout the nearly two thousand years of exile, Jews never stopped returning to join existing communities in the land.

Despite often brutal alien conquests of the land - from the Babylonians in 586 BC, Muslim Arabs in 637 AD, Crusaders in 1099 - up until the British capture of the land from Ottoman Turkey in 1917 - there has been a continuous Jewish presence. In the Diaspora, Jews found refuge wherever they could and retained a spiritual bond with their ancestral homeland. In synagogues around the globe, Jews face towards Jerusalem, which is synonymous with Zion, and utter prayers for a return to Zion and Jerusalem.

The vast majority of Arabs living in Mandatory Palestine in 1947 were not the descendants of Arabs who had lived in the land for thousands of years as Arab and pro-Arab propagandists would have you believe.

Rather, the Arabs were immigrants, or children of immigrants, mostly illegal, who came in the late 19th century and early 20the century from Egypt, Syria, and even as far as Sudan, to take advantage of the opportunities in agriculture and industry the Jewish pioneers were creating.

These Arabs immigrated to a new land from their stagnant countries of origin; the Jews, on the other hand, were returning to their ancestral homeland.

The eternal Jewish capital, Jerusalem, is now demanded by the Arabs who call themselves Palestinians. In the current "peace talks" Judea and Samaria are in grave danger of being turned into an Islamist terrorist bridgehead, which will threaten what is left of Israel just as Gaza, which Israel relinquished to the Arabs in 2005, has become a nightmare for the Jewish state.

The Arabs demand that Jerusalem be re-divided as it was during the Jordanian occupation from 1948 to 1967. And the world applauds these demands, even desiring to celebrate the re-division of Jerusalem as it celebrates the reunification of Berlin.

How strange, but we live in strange times. Jerusalem has never been the capital of any people other than the Jews and never, in all recorded history, has it ever been the capital of an Arab state.

It is only a matter of time before Israel is blamed by the Obama regime for any failure of the peace talks. It is long overdue, therefore, for the Jewish state to do what I and many others have been urging for so long and which Mr. Goodenough, a Christian writer, so tellingly implores in this portion of his article:

"As the second round of Israeli-Palestinian peace talks wrapped up in Sharm e-Sheikh on Tuesday, US Mideast envoy George Mitchell offered no evidence of progress on the issue of West Bank "settlements."

Calling them, "West Bank settlements," instead of Jewish villages and towns in Samaria and Judea! Why, it's as if almost all Israelis have resigned themselves to calling their land 'not our land.'

"This course has been followed for so long now. And truly, in the world of 21st century international politics, it is hard, some would say impossible, to reverse.

"Whose is the land? This is the battle: You have to announce, declare, proclaim, and assert: "Samaria and Judea is our land. It is Jewish land. It is the cradle of our nationhood, the home and the burial place of our founding fathers, the geographical furnace in which our nation was formed and forged. Our roots are irremovably planted here and they will not be severed.

"And you have to vow: We will build on this land; we will develop it; we will live in it, we will grow in it, and we will die in it. We will never give one inch of it away."

This then is the stark but long overdue choice Prime Minister Binyamin Netanyahu has before him. And not only him but all Israelis who have been seduced into using the nomenclature of a world, which exults in delegitimizing the Jewish presence in its tiny homeland.

Israelis did this because they yearned for peace. But from the Muslim Arabs, peace will never come. And even now, according to the Debka Security Report,

Netanyahu is proposing to give away most of the Golan – biblical Bashan – to Syria in return for yet another worthless piece of paper.

Finally, remember these words written by Ruth Wisse in her book: *If I am not for myself*: "Arabs, having conquered more civilizations than any other people in history, are in the weakest position of all to deny the rights of a single, tiny Jewish state.

Indeed, Jews have more concurrent rights to their land than any other people on this earth can claim: aboriginal rights, divine rights, legal rights, internationally granted rights and pioneering rights."

Ms. Wisse has also stated that, "Jews have set themselves up as a comfortable punching bag for the rest of the world."

She is correct. The time is now long overdue for Israel to be the lion; to finally end once and for all the nonsense that peace talks with the Arab and Islamic world represent, and to no longer be the international sacrificial lamb.

October 1, 2010

Boycotts and Divestments have Consequences

The latest weapon employed by Israel bashers is the boycott. It is a device being considered by a host of groups and organizations to selectively end all investments in companies doing business with Israel and to boycott stores and retail outlets selling Israeli products.

It is known as the Boycott, Divestment, and Sanctions campaign (BDS). Their inspiration comes from the decade's old failed boycott of Israel by the Arab League.

Within the last week, I was asked to prepare a one page flyer to be used in Port Townsend, Washington State, to combat an anti-Israel boycott resolution initiated by two leftist and radical members of a Food Co-Operative. The flyer was derived from an earlier article I had published defending Israel against the usual false charges and libels heaped upon the embattled Jewish state.

Several hundred copies of the flyer were distributed among the four hundred or so members who attended the board meeting. Fortunately the message in the flyer succeeded in beating back the anti-Israel resolution: A small victory in an ongoing war, yet the same miscreants who proposed the boycott in Port Townsend threaten to attempt the same boycott in the Spokane, Washington, Co-Op.

Several years earlier, a resolution to divest investments in Israeli companies was submitted by the leadership of the Presbyterian Church at its 216th General Assembly. Among the reasons the Presbyterian leadership gave for boycotting the Jewish State at that time was Israel's security fence, which it compared to the Berlin Wall.

Of course, the Communist regime in East Germany erected their wall to trap its citizens and suppress their freedom of movement. Sadly what those who formed a relatively small but influential committee within the Church omitted to explain to the general membership was that the purpose of Israel's security fence was, and is, to protect its citizens from attacks by Palestinian Muslim terrorists. Nor did they choose to echo Israel's stated aim, which is that the security fence would go once Palestinian terror permanently ended: Sadly, a vain hope.

The Church's divestment campaign, aimed solely against Israel (not against states that routinely persecute Christians and disseminate crude anti-Jewish propaganda, such as Sudan, Saudi Arabia, Iran, or the Palestinian Authority itself) had consequences damaging to Jewish-Christian relations, to the integrity of the Presbyterian Church, and upon the influence it had.

It emboldened the Episcopal Church and the World Council of Churches to also plan divestment from Israel. Fortunately wiser heads prevailed and the clique within the Presbyterian Church was eventually voted down. Yet the danger still remains.

If members of the liberal churches decide to fall in line with the boycott against Israel - joining the leftist constellation of so-called "peace" and "justice" groups that proliferate among the universities and colleges - they should at least have the courage of their convictions and begin by throwing away their computers. Why?

Well most of Window's operating systems were developed by Microsoft-Israel. The Pentium NMX Chip technology was designed at Intel in Israel. The Pentium 4 microprocessor, the Centrium, and Core processors were entirely or in part designed and developed in Israel.

Those boycotting Israeli products had better take note that Microsoft and Cisco built their only R & D facilities outside of the U.S. in Israel. Voice mail technology was developed in Israel; so was the technology for the AOL Instant Messenger (ICQ). And horror upon horror, the cell phone was an Israeli invention.

But these are only technologies. Perhaps divestment and boycott supporters should check their personal medications. They should refuse any products made by Teva or Abic. They will have to suffer from colds and flu this coming winter and purchase more expensive cholesterol lowering drugs; but that's a small price to pay for their campaign against Israel.

Trouble is, those wretched Israelis have also developed a simple blood test that distinguishes between mild and more severe cases of Multiple Sclerosis and Parkinson's disease.

So if all who embrace divestment from Israel and boycott Israeli products in the stores know of any family or friends suffering from MS or Parkinson's, tell them to ignore the Israeli patents that may more accurately diagnose their symptoms and bring relief.

If they have, or know of, young children with breathing problems, tell them that the anti-Israel boycott will not allow them to accept another medical breakthrough - the Child Hood. Although it replaces the inhalation mask with an improved drug delivery system that provides relief for child and parent, it must remain unacceptable because the Israelis invented it.

If a boycotter has a family member who is a stroke victim and who is severely disabled and unable to move their bodies or communicate, do not tell the patient that an Israeli device provides the ability to write an e-mail, to communicate and steer a wheelchair by sniffing.

The revolutionary device identifies changes in air pressure inside the nostrils and translates these into electrical signals, which can then be used either to write messages or to move a wheelchair. But dear boycotter, please don't tell a soul, especially a suffering soul.

Oh, and if the divestment freak knows someone who has paralyzed hands, he or she better not mention yet another Israeli made device, which electronically stimulates hand muscles and provides hope to millions of stroke sufferers and victims of spinal injuries.

Those wicked Israelis have also tried to help women who undergo hysterectomies each year for the treatment of uterine fibroids. Israel's ExAblate 2000 System is a welcome breakthrough, but keep it quite – better to divest and boycott, isn't it?

In fact, Parkinson's disease patients can also benefit from deep brain stimulation techniques, developed through the Movement Disorder Surgery program at Israel's Hadassah Medical Center, which eliminates the physical manifestations of the disease.

But, again, keep that quite too as it would be hypocritical for liberal church members and loony leftists to benefit at the same time they are divesting from Israel or boycotting its products.

So due to their divestment campaign and boycotts, they will have poor health, no computers or cell phones. After all, those technologies were developed in Israel of all places.

Of course, the boycotters could suggest to retailers, hospitals, and pharmacies that they replace on their shelves the nasty Israeli products with those manufactured in Gaza and the Palestinian Authority. A few such Arab products come to mind: Kassam missiles, exploding suicide belts, and racist, anti-Semitic 'literature' that will bring joy to the hearts and minds of every neo-Nazi.

Now reflect on the massive contribution Israel is making to all the peoples of the world – including the Palestinian Arabs – in medicine, science, agriculture, security and communications.

Not bad for an embattled people living in a tiny country no larger than Wales or New Jersey.

October 3, 2010

The Plague of the un-Jews

Some years ago, posing as a supporter of the PLO, I infiltrated an Arab anti-Israel meeting held in a room above a London pub. There were mostly Arabs present with a sprinkling of non-Arabs, mostly local Brits.

Among the Brits was a man who told the audience that he was also a Jew and hated Israel. His self-loathing was limited to his Jewish ancestry, for he displayed no lack of modesty as he stood up and spewed hate against his own people and hostility towards the increasingly embattled Jewish state.

But in all the bile that fell from his lips, he revealed a total lack of knowledge about Judaism and Jewish history - certainly he exhibited no understanding of the rebirth of Israel in its ancestral and biblical homeland or of the immense odds of its survival in the face of enormous Arab and Muslim aggression. His trope was merely to echo the fashionable Arab and pro-Arab propaganda of "the poor Arabs and the nasty Israelis."

All he seemed to want to do was ingratiate himself with those Arabs in the misguided belief that they would award him with what he personally lacked in his own sad life: fame and name recognition. If he could achieve that by denigrating and abusing the people from whom he sprung, then so be it.

For him, the means justified the ends. What he did not realize was that the Arabs looked upon him with no respect; rather, they treated him with contempt, using him as a useful idiot.

I thought of him when I considered the U.K. pro-Palestinian group of Jews - overwhelmingly leftists - who attempted to sail to Gaza from the Turkish-occupied north of Cyprus in order to bring aid and comfort to the Hamas occupiers of the Gaza Strip.

Among the left-wing British Jews was one Yonatan Shapira, who defaced a wall near the Warsaw Ghetto monument with a slogan describing the Arabs in Gaza as suffering like the Polish Jews in the ghetto. However, unlike the Arabs in Gaza, the Jews were slaughtered, and the few survivors gassed, during the Holocaust.

Before boarding the yacht, the Israeli Navy transmitted two warnings to the boat, which refused to turn back and sailed farther into the blockade area. According to the Jerusalem Post, Israeli Foreign Ministry spokesman Andy David called the left-wing Jews' claim to be bringing aid to Gaza "ridiculous" and labeled the voyage "a politically motivated provocation."

Emanuele Ottolenghi, in a commentary, said: "There is a certain irony in the fact that a boat full of "Jews for Justice for Palestinians" set sail for Gaza from Northern Cyprus.

Northern Cyprus is an illegally occupied territory that belongs to EU-member Cyprus, seized by force in 1974 by the Turkish army. Its legal status as a fictionally independent state is only recognized by Turkey. The Turkish military forcibly removed hundreds of thousands of ethnic Greeks from that territory and settled its own population to permanently alter the ethnic balance of the area.

And this arrival of "The Ship of Fools" occurred even as Hamas thugs shot yet another nine-month pregnant Jewish woman in Judea and continue firing lethal missiles from Gaza into Israeli villages and towns. Thankfully, unlike the poor pregnant woman and four other Jewish civilians who were slaughtered two weeks earlier in Judea by Hamas gunmen, she survived and gave birth to a healthy baby after a C-section.

I also thought of the man in the room above the London pub when I recently read that an Israeli self-hater, Professor Illan Pappe, was visiting India in order to demonize Israel and encourage a boycott by Indians of the Jewish state.

Professor Pappe, well-known as an extreme leftist and one of a handful of Israeli professors who support an academic boycott of Israel, criticized the Arab world for "not doing anything" against Israel.

In view of the decade's long history of barbaric terrorism perpetrated by Arabs against Israeli civilians; this was an oxymoronic statement if ever there was one.

Another speaker at the event in India was Richard Falk, formerly the United Nations Human Rights Council envoy to Gaza and to Judea and Samaria, or what most of the world calls by its Jordanian Arab name: the West Bank.

During his term with the grotesquely misnamed U.N. Human Rights Council, Falk was the envoy for this despicable organization, one made up of the most egregious rogue states on earth and worst human rights abusers. This committee spends all its time ignoring the horrors perpetrated by its own members and concentrates solely and obsessively on heaping slanders and falsehoods upon Israel.

Falk, yet another Jewish self-hater, had no conscience in condemning Israel for such actions as dismantling illegally built Arab structures in Jerusalem and deporting four senior Hamas terrorists from the city.

Indeed, Israeli officials criticized Falk as "redundant at best and malicious at worst" and accused him of lacking any objectivity. Predictably, this same Falk had no condemnation for the Muslim terrorist attack in Mumbai in 2008, during which the terrorists deliberately attacked Chabad House and cruelly murdered eight Jews, including a rabbi and his young wife.

I mention this only because it reveals the depths of the pathological sickness the Jewish self-haters are consumed by. But we have to understand that this is not something new that has existed only since Israel was reconstituted in 1948 in its ancient homeland.

For centuries, since the destruction of Jewish Judea in 70 AD and the second uprising against the Roman Empire, which lasted from 132 to 135AD, the Jews were stateless, seeking refuge wherever they could find it within Christendom and the Islamic world.

The relentless persecution of the stateless Jews during the following nineteen hundred years or so led to some individuals wishing to shake off the crushing burden. Unlike the vast majority of Jews who endured endless torment, often through martyrdom, a few sought to evade it by converting or, in many instances, aiding and abetting the very persecutors of their fellow Jews.

Like the man in the room above the London pub, they sought to ingratiate themselves, but, again like him, they were considered "useful idiots."

In this last year of the first decade of the 21st century, it seems that there is an endless procession of such secular, left-wing men and women who spring from the Jewish people but who know very little if anything about their faith and history. I call them the un-Jews.

These people are from mostly the higher strata of society: academics, writers, musicians, the intelligentsia, etc. But the glue that binds them is their total ignorance and arrogance. They are drawn overwhelmingly from the Left - a spurious and problematic home from which venomous attacks upon Israel routinely emanate.

Again these un-Jews feel compelled to find acceptance in this Theater of the Absurd that is known as the Left. The un-Jews thus, yet again and again, seek to ingratiate themselves with their non-Jewish cronies by railing against only the Jewish state - ignoring all the horrors of the Sudan, of Iran, and of the despotic Arab and Muslim world. They care not for the disinherited Tibetan people who live under Chinese occupation. They care not for the Serbian people who see their own ancestral heartland of Kosovo snatched from them by Muslims.

Only the struggle by Israel, the one and only beleaguered Jewish state, attempting against great odds to survive and seek its own self-determination in a hostile world, inspires within the un-Jew such demented loathing.

It is the vile behavior of the un-Jews towards Israel that allows the non-Jewish anti-Semites to be open about their own deep-seated pathology and bigotry. After all, they can say with equanimity, Jews themselves are criticizing Israel, so that gives us a free pass to libel the Jewish state and support the Muslims and Arabs in their genocide against the Jews. You can find a list of these miscreants, these un-Jews, in an article by David Solway in Front Page Magazine.

Writer Ruth Wisse describes how the liberals and leftists are undermining the Jewish people's own liberation and self-determination movement, Zionism - the return to Zion and Jerusalem, words which are synonymous with each other. Her extraordinary book, a must-read, is titled *The Liberal Betrayal of the Jews*.

Michael Savage, the conservative talk show host, aptly describes liberalism as a "mental disorder." The un-Jews who endlessly spew their venom against their own people are at the forefront of creating organizations that are patently one-sided shills for the Arab and Muslim terror and genocide machine.

Such organizations are readily transparent by their names, which always include words such as "justice" and "peace." These once-precious words have been bastardized by the leftist and peacenik organizations - home to so many of the un-Jews. Now those two words, epitomizing the higher ideals of humanity, have become bitter ashes in the mouth.

What is most egregiously and lamentably insulting is how the un-Jews claim to espouse authentic Jewish ethics and morality. They do not. They exhibit a devastating ignorance and profound shallowness of what Judaism teaches. Their breathtaking ignorance misrepresents the divinely inspired Jewish ideals and love of life, which is in such stark contrast to the Muslim worship of death.

October 17, 2010

Forward to the Past

Edmund Burke, British statesman and philosopher, known for his famous aphorism "all that is necessary for the triumph of evil is for good men to do nothing," also uttered other words of wisdom.

Reflecting on the parlous condition of the stateless Jews in his time, Burke was moved to observe the following:

Having no fixed settlement in any part of the world, no kingdom nor country in which they have a government, a community and a system of laws, they are thrown on the benevolence of nations ... If Dutchmen are injured and attacked, the Dutch have a nation, a government and armies to redress or revenge their cause. If Britons be injured, Britons have armies and laws, the law of nations ... to fly to for protection and justice. But the Jews have no such power and no such friend to depend on. Humanity, then, must become their protector and ally.

But of course, humanity, except for a few exceptional and honorable individuals, did not protect the hapless Jews. They were alone in a bleak and ever-dangerous world.

Speaking after the Second World War and the Holocaust, which reduced the world Jewish population in the space of nearly seven dread years from eighteen million to barely twelve million, Andrei Gromyko, the Soviet Union delegate to the United Nations, said,

The fact that no Western European State has been able to ensure the defense of the elementary rights of the Jewish people and to safeguard it against the violence of the fascist executioners explains the aspirations of the Jews to establish their own state. It would be unjust not to take this into consideration and to deny the right of the Jewish people to realize this aspiration.

Gromyko was addressing the U.N. during the passage of Resolution 181, which granted the re-born State of Israel Jewish sovereignty at last in its ancestral and biblical homeland. The territory was then the geographical territory known as Palestine, under the occupation of the British Mandate.

However, despite Gromyko's fine and humanitarian words, the Soviet Union went on to support Arab dictators in several wars against Israel, aiding and abetting Egypt, Syria, and the PLO in relentless acts of anti-Israel aggression.

But it was not only because of the Holocaust that Jewish aspirations for a return to Zion existed. That yearning had existed for millennia, and Jews continued to return to the now-stagnant and barren land of their fathers in whatever numbers and whenever they could.

In 1894, a young Austrian Jewish journalist named Theodore Herzl traveled to Paris, France to witness a trial against a Jewish military officer, Alfred Dreyfus. This officer was falsely accused of treason by the French High Command. The trial led to outrage among many writers and artists as they witnessed the specter of growing anti-Jewish excesses within civilized France. Emil Zola's *J'Accuse* was a searing indictment of the French military and society.

Herzl, who believed that Jews could freely assimilate into the wider European populations and who thought that at long last, they had found equality throughout Western Europe, was devastated. The outpouring of such hate towards an innocent man in civilized France, primarily because of his Jewish faith, irrevocably altered Herzl's earlier assumptions.

He began to believe that for the Jews, the only salvation was a return to the ancient physical and spiritual homeland. Herzl went on to found modern Zionism, the movement supporting the Jewish people's own right of self-determination and their national liberation.

Even before Herzl began to work tirelessly for the dream to become a reality, a great thinker and leading exponent of the European Enlightenment, Jean Jacques Rousseau, wrote of the Jews' plight:

These unfortunates feel themselves to be at our mercy ... What will they dare say without laying themselves open to our accusing them of blasphemy? ... I shall never believe I have seriously heard the arguments of the Jews until they have a free state, schools and universities, where they can speak and dispute without risk. Only then will we be able to know what they have to say.

And it came to pass. The long and seemingly endless statelessness and trail of tears, stretching over nearly two thousand years from the Roman defeat of ancient

Judea, came to an end on November 29, 1947. The U.N. voted in favor of the creation of a Jewish and an Arab state. Even before that date, Jewish universities and schools had indeed sprung up as Rousseau had hoped.

Though the Jewish remnant had, like some wondrous Phoenix, risen again from the charnel house of Europe and accepted the tiny and perilously truncated state in the hope that they could realize their own destiny in peace, the Arab League rejected outright the existence of any Jewish state. Tragically, in May 1948 -- immediately upon Israel's declaration of independence -- the Arab armies invaded.

Miraculously, the Jewish State, outnumbered and with few arms to defend the nascent nation, beat back the Arab forces. But Arab and Muslim hostility remains to this day and is becoming ever more dangerous to the continued existence and survival of the Jewish state.

The European nations who treated the once-stateless Jews so harshly now heap calumny upon the reconstituted democratic Jewish state. Indeed, to their shame, many European governments are complicit with some of their own radicalized citizens in accusing Israel of violating basic human rights -- this while totally ignoring the horrors routinely inflicted upon women and non-Muslims throughout the undemocratic Arab world. As for the Tibetans, Kurds, Serbians, and all others who deserve justice, the Israel-bashers have little or no time for their suffering.

Baseless charges of "apartheid" are routinely hurled at Israel by an orchestrated and heavily funded constellation of leftists, progressives (aka communists), and those who for whatever murky reasons choose to demonize one state alone: Israel.

The supreme irony in the apartheid slander is that, alone in the world, only Israel saved black populations (the ancient black Jews of Ethiopia) and brought them to a country, not as the Europeans and Muslim Arab slave traders did as slaves, but as free men and women.

To quote William Safire: "For the first time in history, thousands of black people are being brought to a country not in chains but in dignity, not as slaves but as citizens."

Now, if you need proof of real apartheid, simply look at the demands of the Palestinian Authority, Israel's so-called "peace partner," that all Jews living in territory the Arabs want for a state must be ethnically cleansed.

And look at Jordan, which sits on four-fifths of the original geographical territory of Palestine, and in which no Jews are allowed to live. Now that's apartheid by any other name.

As the world nears the end of the first decade of the 21st century, democracy is under increasing assault from Islam. It is not beyond reality that we may see both Europe and America subsumed under growing Muslim populations and Judeo-Christian civilization giving way to ascendant Islamic rule.

Whether Israel, so perilously placed as it is on the front line against resurgent and aggressive Islamic power, will be supported by the Europeans and Americans is for the near future to witness.

Europe, or Eurabia as it is likely to become unless it urgently wakes up, is almost lost under its self-inflicted political correctness, multiculturalism, and growing subservience to creeping Sharia law. But if the unthinkable occurs and the United States Constitution is replaced by Sharia Law, then a new Dark Age will lie ahead, and democratic civilization and religious freedom as we have known it will crumble away: And all this while the Amen chorus of fools hurl their unfounded slanders and invective against the embattled Jewish state.

It would be horribly ironic if Burke's aphorism was forgotten and the triumph of evil, which he warned against, comes to be. But this time, not only will Jews return to a stateless existence owing to the unbearable loss of their restored homeland, but vast numbers of non-Jews, by resisting forced conversion to Islam, will join them in shared statelessness and a veritable vale of tears.

Dhimmitude, the terror under which Jews and Christians were forced to endure Islamic tyranny for centuries, will return with a vengeance, and much of the world as we have known it will needlessly stumble forward into the past.

November 23, 2010

Facts Arabs Would Rather Not Admit

Statue of Maimonides at Cordoba, Spain.

I was complimented the other day by a reader of one of my recent articles, titled, *Lies, Myths and Obama*, which dealt – as many of them do – with the history of Israel: biblical and post-biblical.

I had included in the article the following sentence: "Only one people has ever made Jerusalem its capital and only one people ever established their ancestral and biblical homeland between the River Jordan and the Mediterranean Sea: the Jews."

I had also added that: "the Jews were the aboriginal inhabitants of the Land for millennia before the Muslim religion was created."

The reader, nevertheless, had correctly pointed out that most people, because they have been exposed for so long to anti-Israel Arab propaganda, believe that there has not been a continuous Jewish presence in the Land for the last 2,000 years.

They are thus unaware that the territory was never *Judenrein* (that is empty of a Jewish presence). And Arabs would rather you forget also that Jews lived for millennia in Mesopotamia and in what became later known as British created Iraq.

Indeed Jews had resided for 3,000 years in that territory from the Babylonian Captivity onwards. It was when Israel was reborn in 1948 that the Iraqi Arabs drove the Jews from their ancient homes, turning them into refugees who found sanctuary in Israel; an impoverished country barely able to support them at the time.

More Jewish refugees were created than Arab refugees as one Arab state after another in the Middle East and North Africa drove out their Jewish populations: A crime, which hardly is ever recognized.

Arabs and their anti-Israel supporters try to convince the world that the Jews just appeared in the early 20th century after being dispersed for two thousand years from their biblical homeland. That is a flat out lie and flies in the face of recorded history. But facts never seem to matter to Arabs and pro-Arabs. So this brief history lesson will be for them an inconvenient truth.

Let me start by quoting from an article written in The Weekly Standard, May 11, 1998 by Charles Krauthammer:

"Israel is the very embodiment of Jewish continuity: It is the only nation on earth that inhabits the same land, bears the same name, speaks the same language, and worships the same God that it did 3,000 years ago. You dig the soil and you find pottery from Davidic times, coins from Bar Kochba, and 2,000-year-old scrolls written in a script remarkably like the one today advertising ice cream at the corner candy store."

The Jewish People trace their origin to Abraham, he who is called the Holy Convert, the first Jew, who established the belief in only one God, the creator of the universe. Abraham, his son Yitzhak (Isaac), and grandson Jacob (Israel), are referred to as the patriarchs of the Israelites who lived in what was then the Land of Canaan; later to become known as the Land of Israel. They and their wives are buried in the Ma'arat HaMachpela, the Tomb of the Patriarchs, in Hebron, Judaism's second holiest city. (Genesis, Chapter 23).

The name, Israel, derives from the name given to Jacob (Genesis 32:29). His 12 sons were the ancestors of the 12 tribes that later developed into the Jewish nation. The name Jew derives from Yehuda (Judah) one of the 12 sons of Jacob. You will find the names of the tribes listed in Exodus 1:1. Yehuda (Judea) is also the biblical name of the southern region of what the world calls by its Arab name – the West Bank. Shomron (Samaria) is the northern half.

Modern Israel shares the same language, culture, and Jewish faith passed through generations starting with the founding father Abraham and the Jews have had a continuous presence in the land of Israel for the past 3,300 years.

Menorah plundered from the Temple, depicted on Arch of Titus, Rome

In 70 AD, Rome destroyed the Holy Temple and conquered the Jewish nation, yet only part of the population was sent into exile. Even after the Second Jewish Revolt against the continuing cruel Roman occupation, Jews, though banned from Jerusalem, survived for centuries in other Jewish towns including Rafah, Gaza, Yavne, Ashkelon, Jaffa and Caesarea as well as throughout Galilee and the Golan.

Ruins of synagogues built in post-biblical Byzantine times are found scattered throughout the Golan and an epic act of Jewish resistance to the Roman legions took place at Gamla, high upon the Golan Heights. Here again, the Jewish presence predates the modern Syrian claims to the Heights by millennia.

Interestingly, early seventh century battles raged between the Persians and the Byzantines over the Land of Israel. The Byzantines were oppressing the Jews and a Jewish general, Benjamin of Tiberius, was able to raise an army of twenty thousand Jewish men from villages and towns in northern Israel to support the Persian cause against the oppressors.

This again points to extensive Jewish life in the land well after the erroneous Arab claim that Jews had not lived in the land during the last 2,000 years.

The height of Jewish prominence was again achieved in the tenth century. In Tiberius, by the shores of Lake Kinneret, the Sea of Galilee, a symbol system for Hebrew vowels was created which eventually gained universal acceptance.

But with the advent of the Crusades in Israel during the 12th century, and the massacres of thousands of Jews in Jerusalem and throughout the land, the Jewish population reached its lowest point. But Jewish populations again revived, strengthened by new Jewish immigrants arriving constantly from the Diaspora.

Many such returnees settled in Safed, Tiberius, Hebron and Jerusalem.
These are the four Holy Jewish cities of the Land with Jerusalem, north, south, east and west, the eternal 3,000 year old Jewish capital and veritable jewel in the crown.

Jews traveling from Europe, such as the remarkable medieval explorer, Benjamin of Tudela, had to overcome immense perils while crossing lands at war with one another. They had to avoid death or capture by bandits, or at sea from North African pirates and Crusaders based in Cyprus or Malta.

That they came at all, however, remains a tribute to the earliest efforts to keep Israel populated with its aboriginal and ancestral folk and abide by the religious commandments to go up to the land of Israel.

A brief list of Jews returning to the ancestral land reveals a constant arrival of people joining existing Jewish villages and communities, themselves always at the mercy of alien occupiers. According to the Center for Online Judaic Studies, here are just a few of the names of early Jewish returnees:

1075:1141 Yehuda Halevi, poet.
1135: 1204 Moses Maimonides, philosopher.
1210: Settlement in Israel of three hundred French and English rabbis.
1267: Nachmanides arrives in Israel.
1313: Estory Haparchi arrives: The first geographer of Israel.
1538: Renewal of rabbinic ordination in Safed.
1561: Joseph Nasi leases Tiberius from Turkish sultan.
1700: Yehuda HeChasid and his followers arrive in Jerusalem.
1777: Large Hassidic group settles in Galilee.
1797: Rabbi Nachman of Bratzlav's trip to Israel.
1808: Disciples of Elijah, Gaon of Vilna, settle in Jerusalem.

This very partial list of Jewish immigrants, who arrived well before the 20th century, is an inconvenient truth to the Arab and pro-Arab propagandists who would have you believe their myth that the Jews only arrived much, much later.

The national coins, the pottery, the cities and villages, the ancient Hebrew texts…all support the empirical fact that Jews always had a continuous presence in that land for over 3,000 years.

The fact that Jewish villages and towns were to be found in all parts of the ancient homeland and throughout all the preceding years, up until the present time, dwarf any claims that other people in the region may have; especially the Arabs who today call themselves Palestinians.

A People Need Not Annex What Is Theirs

November 24, 2010

The very fact that the Israeli Knesset passed a bill that would require a referendum before any land officially under Israeli sovereignty is surrendered, specifically the Golan Heights and Jerusalem, is in itself a tacit admission by the present Israeli government that at some future time the very thought of giving away these parts of the ancestral and biblical Jewish homeland may be entertained.

That is treachery most base; treachery to the living Torah; treachery to Jewish history; treachery to Zion; and last but not least treachery to the eternal Holy Covenant made between God and the Jewish people. Liberals, leftists and secular folks may not like being told this, but it is a truth that cannot shrivel away.

Prime Minister Binyamin Netanyahu's office rejected the idea that the referendum law would hurt the chances for peace negotiations between Israel and its neighbors. But when did it become an accepted truism that a so-called peace between Israel and the Arabs, those who call themselves Palestinians, requires that Israel gives to them it's very biblical birthright for a mess of potage?

Have the Oslo Accords, the Wye Agreement, the Roadmap, ad nauseum, all now superseded the eternal possession of the Jewish people to their God given homeland? It would seem so, and that is a monstrous tragedy so enormous as to spit in the face of the Almighty and make the very angels in heaven weep.

Netanyahu said: "A referendum prevents an irresponsible agreement and on the other hand makes it possible to achieve a strong public backing for an agreement that will respond to Israel's national interests."

There again. The word "agreement" and the implicit suggestion that the Golan Heights, ancient biblical Bashan, the homeland of the Tribe of Manasseh, may be given away in an, oh, so base agreement with the Syrian Arabs.

The referendum bill also covers United Jerusalem, but then if the Knesset votes more than two thirds to give away parts of Jerusalem to the hateful Arabs, known as Palestinians, in order for them to create a new Arab capital that has never existed in all of recorded history, it will be a sin so abhorrent that I fear God's wrath.

And all this political foolishness is to appease the present occupant of the White House who is a clear and present danger to the very existence of Eretz Yisrael, the Land of Israel. All this erodes the millennial and inalienable rights of one people alone – the Jewish people – to the land between the River Jordan and the Mediterranean Sea. Indeed, there should be demands made upon the artificial entity known as the Kingdom of Jordan for the return of biblical Gilead – the ancestral homeland of the Jewish tribes of Gad and Manasseh.

Prime Minister Netanyahu's government and previous governments stretching back to that of Yitzhak Rabin, all betrayed Jewish patrimony in the Land of Israel. They have accepted the Arab and pro-Arab lie that Israel "occupies" Arab territory – specifically territory belonging to a fraudulent Arab people who have come to call themselves Palestinians. This stupidity has torn a grievous, self-inflicted wound into the very psyche of Jews within Israel and the Diaspora.

Notice that the referendum refers only to Jerusalem and the Golan because they were "annexed." Does that fact make them special? These are Jewish lands and there is no need to annex what already belongs to the Jewish people. Notice too, that Judea and Samaria are not included in this foolish attempt to bargain over an illusory "land for peace" deal with the Arab world. The reason given is that Judea and Samaria have not been annexed.

Again! So what? These lands are the very warp and woof, the very fabric and fiber of Jewish history during and after biblical times. Whether they were or were not annexed is mere sophistry.

I was looking back at what Professor Talia Einhorn wrote in 2003 about Judea, Samaria and Gaza, or as it is known by its Hebrew acronym, Yesha: meaning Yehuda, Shomron and Azza.

She was commenting on the 'slip of the tongue" by then Prime Minister Sharon who used the word "occupation" in reference to Israel's presence in Yesha. In 2003, Yesha still included Gaza. It was abandoned in 2005 for the sake of peace! She stated clearly then that Israel, the Jewish state, is not an "occupying force" in Yesha:

"Up until 1948, Judea, Samaria and Gaza were a part of the British Mandate. In the 1948 War of Independence, Egypt illegally grabbed the Gaza Strip and Jordan took Judea and Samaria, the 'West Bank.'

"Egypt did not claim sovereignty in Gaza but Jordan deigned, in 1950, to annex Judea and Samaria. This annexation was not recognized by international law. The Arab nations objected to it, and only Britain and Pakistan recognized it – and Britain did not recognize the annexation of eastern Jerusalem.

"In 1967, after the Six Day War, these territories – which were originally meant for the Jewish Nation's National Home according to the Mandate Charter – returned to Israeli control."

Professor Einhorn added that: "…according to international law, Israel has full right to try to populate the entire Land of Israel with dense settlement and thus actualize the principles set by the League of Nations in the original Mandate Charter of San Remo in 1920.

"At that time, the mandate to the Land of Israel was granted to the British and an introduction to the mandate charter states clearly that it is based on the international recognition of the historic ties between the Jewish People and the Land of Israel.

"Clause II of that mandate charges Britain with 'ensuring the existence of political, administrative, and economic conditions that will guarantee the establishment of the Jewish national home in the Land of Israel."

We, of course, know how that turned out. Britain reneged on its promises and undertakings. Britain tore away 80% all of the mandate territory east of the Jordan River in 1922 and gave it away to the Emir Abdullah.

There is nothing, therefore, in international law that requires the creation of a Palestinian state between the Jordan River and the Mediterranean. Professor Einhorn pointed out that the UN Partition Resolution of November 29, 1947 merely recommended that a Jewish and Arab state in what was the geographical territory known as Palestine "shall come into existence."

Though the Jewish leadership accepted the partition plan, it was, as we all know, rejected utterly by the Arab states, which thus voided the UN's recommendation of any legal basis.

So the fact that what is left of Yesha – Judea and Samaria – has not previously been the subject of an Israeli annexation is neither here nor there. It is empirically the Land of Israel by all that is holy. And if that's a dirty word to some, so be it.

Simply put: The Jewish people do not annex land that already belongs to them. And the Jewish people cannot be called settlers in their very own ancestral and aboriginal homeland.

Now if those facts are understood and hammered home again and again by every Israeli and every Jew in the Diaspora, think of the power and the glory that will illuminate the world as the veil of deception is finally torn from the world's eyes.

Go East beyond the River Jordan

December 9, 2010

The phrase "Two State Solution" has been embraced by politicians and journalists alike, repeated endlessly, and touted as the panacea for a "just and equitable" solution to the Israel-Palestinian conflict.

It has assumed the repetitious role of a muezzin's call to Islamic prayer. But it is based on erroneous geography and history; on a mixture of wishful thinking, naiveté and a brilliant Arab propaganda campaign of disinformation and falsehood. To understand why, it is necessary to learn a small but vital chapter of Middle Eastern history.

Shortly after the conclusion of the First World War and the total defeat of the Turkish Ottoman Empire, which had ruled most of the Middle East for 400 years, Britain was made trustee by the League of Nations for the whole of the geographical area known as Mandatory Palestine.

Incorporated within the Mandate was the 1917 Balfour Declaration, which specifically referred to the historical connections of the Jewish people with Palestine and to the moral validity of reconstituting within it the Jewish National Home.

The British Mandatory power, however, arbitrarily tore away 80% of the Palestine Mandate in 1921/22 giving it to the Hashemites, a Bedouin tribe with links to Mecca. Only the land west of the River Jordan remained from the original territory promised to the Jewish people as a National Home.

Jewish residency was immediately forbidden in all the lands east of the River Jordan, which in time became known as Trans-Jordan and then as the Kingdom of Jordan.

The U.N. Partition Plan of 1947 created two states, Jewish and Arab, which were roughly equal in size. But these two states were to occupy only the remaining western geographic area of Mandatory Palestine – from the Mediterranean Sea to the River Jordan – barely 40 miles wide and a mere 20% of what now remained of Mandatory Palestine.

This plan was accepted by the Jewish leadership with deep reservations but as a pragmatic solution to the plight of the 850,000 plus Jewish refugees who were being driven from Arab lands at the time of Israel's rebirth and as a refuge for the remnant of European Jewry who survived the Holocaust.

The State of Israel, thus reconstituted in part of its ancient and biblical homeland in May, 1948, was immediately invaded by seven Arab armies whose aim was to completely destroy it and drive the surviving Jews into the sea.

The Jordanian Arab Legion, led by British officers, invaded and occupied the eastern half of Jerusalem along with Judea and Samaria (the so-called West Bank), driving the Jews out of their towns and villages. In the south, the Egyptians invaded and occupied the Gaza Strip, similarly driving the Jews from their homes.

The Jewish state astonished the world by surviving the Arab aggression. The Arab states, however, totally rejected the existence of a Jewish state in the Middle East and an uneasy armistice remained in force routinely broken by acts of Arab terror and war.

Interestingly in April, 2009, the Holocaust denying leader of the Palestinian Authority, Mahmoud Abbas, Israel's supposed peace partner, rejected any willingness to accept Israel as a Jewish state; a sure indication of the falsity of any Arab claim to live in full and lasting peace with Israel. He has repeatedly rejected accepting Israel as a Jewish state; repeating his rejection this last month.

True, a peace exists today between Israel and Jordan and between Israel and Egypt but it is a frigid, cold and precarious peace with neither Jordan nor Egypt truly interested in full and mutually beneficial relations.

The creation of a Palestinian Arab state within the mere 40 miles separating the Mediterranean and the Jordan River is a recipe for war and for the piecemeal destruction of the Jewish state.

Such an Arab state will more than likely soon fall under the control of the Islamist Hamas movement, itself a branch of the Muslim Brotherhood, which seeks a worldwide Islamic Caliphate. Gaza, and what it has become, is living proof of Palestinian Arab genocidal intentions towards Israel.

The Iranian mullahs, perhaps soon armed with nuclear weapons, will have a command and control base within the territory already given away to the Arabs. They will be ensconced in Gaza on the eastern shore of the Mediterranean Sea, interested in launching ever more lethal terror against what is left of Israel and threatening Europe. If Israel foolishly gives away parts of Judea and Samaria, there will be no part of Israel or Jerusalem safe from Palestinian Arab missile attacks.

Israel will again be reduced to a nation a mere nine miles wide at its most populous region. When President Bush was still Governor of Texas he flew over Israel's tiny width and remarked, "…why, in my state we have driveways longer than that."

That is the most likely outcome of the current proposed Two-State Solution west of the Jordan River, which the Obama Administration is pushing with the flawed zeal of a misguided zealot. But to truly create a just and equitable solution to the Israeli-Palestinian conflict, there must be a Two-State Solution on both sides of the River Jordan.

To repeat: The present day Kingdom of Jordan occupies four-fifths of geographical Palestine. This territory consists of the land east of the River Jordan, extending north to Syria, east to Iraq and south to Saudi-Arabia.

Compared to Israel, it dwarfs the Jewish state yet it originated in an act of unprincipled perfidiousness by the British government of the day and remains an Arab state that has from its inception forbidden Jewish habitation within its borders. This is ethnic cleansing and Apartheid, Arab and Muslim style.

Even though the so-called Kingdom of Jordan includes territory promised in Britain's 1917 Balfour Declaration and by the League of Nations as a Jewish National Home, the territory is currently made up of 75% Arabs who call themselves Palestinians with the remainder being Hashemite Bedouins.

As it exists on land originally forming four fifths of Mandatory Palestine, and as the population is three fourths Palestinian Arab, it follows that the "just and equitable" solution to the creation of a Palestinian Arab state should be within the present day Kingdom of Jordan and, therefore, east of the River Jordan.

The Arabs who call themselves Palestinians, and who choose to remain in Judea and Samaria, should be required to end all terrorism against Israel – hardly an onerous demand – and by finally living in peace could flourish within an Israel whose territory would now formally extend east from the Mediterranean Sea to the Jordan River. That would still only be a distance of barely 40 miles at its widest. The United States in comparison is some 3,000 miles wide.

Israel would now formally give up 80% of the originally mandated territory but would now possess all of her biblical and ancestral Jewish lands – with the exception of biblical Gilead east of the Jordan River, which is in present day north-western Jordan.

If there is a desire within the international community to truly arrive at a "just and equitable" solution, then this would be it. Of course, if this was a perfect world, it would satisfy historical, geographical, religious and ethnic considerations. But, alas, it is anything but a perfect world and the fanatical desire among so many Arab and Muslim nations to wipe out all vestiges of a Jewish state is, perhaps, insurmountable.

Nevertheless, it can do no harm to raise it in the corridors of power and promote and articulate it far more forcefully as a truly "just and equitable" solution.

The accepted wisdom now exercising the minds of Obama, his problematic advisors, the State Department, and the legions of people around the world who have succumbed to the churning mills of the Arab propaganda machine, is that there exist a people called Palestinians with a distinct history who lived in an independent Arab state called Palestine.

It is a lie, perhaps the greatest scam in history, swallowed by so many in direct proportions to the amount of times it has been repeated. It is a fraudulent history of a fraudulent people in a fraudulent land. Indeed, there has never in all of recorded history existed an independent, sovereign Arab nation called Palestine. Just look at what the Arabs themselves have said about a mythical Palestinian history.

Here are the words of a local Arab leader, Auni Bey Abdul-Hadi, speaking in 1937 before the Peel Commission, which was considering partition of the Palestine Mandate, west of the River Jordan:

"…There is no such country as Palestine! …That is a term the Zionists invented! …There is no Palestine in the Bible."

Professor Philip Hitti, the Arab-American history professor at Princeton, said in unambiguous words before the 1946 Anglo-American Committee:

"…There is no such thing as 'Palestine' in history, absolutely not."

And here is the PLO executive committee member, Zahir Muhsein, March 31, 1977, in an interview with the Dutch newspaper, Trouw:

"The Palestinian people do not exist. The creation of a Palestinian state is only a means for continuing our struggle against the state of Israel for our Arab unity. In reality today there is no difference between Jordanians, Palestinians, Syrians and Lebanese. Only for political and tactical reasons do we speak today about the existence of a Palestinian people, since Arab national interests demand that we posit the existence of a distinct 'Palestinian people' to oppose Zionism.

"For tactical reasons, Jordan, which is a sovereign state with defined borders, cannot raise claims to Haifa and Jaffa. While as a Palestinian, I can undoubtedly demand Haifa, Jaffa, Beer-Sheva and Jerusalem. However, the moment we claim our right to all of Palestine, we will not wait even a minute to unite Palestine and Jordan."

President Obama showers the Arab and Muslim world with favors. No favor could be more eagerly snatched at than that of Israel abandoned by this American President to the tender mercies of the ever circling mullahs, imams, kings and dictators.

Israel in its own historic territory, extending east to the Jordan River and living next to a much larger Jordan/Palestine state, itself extending east of the Jordan River to the borders of Iraq, Syria and Saudi-Arabia, is the moral, just and equitable solution to the conflict. But it will never happen so long as Islam remains un-reformed and Muslims continue to believe that no non-Muslim state can be permitted to exist in land previously invaded and conquered in the name of Allah.

The corollary to this is that the Jewish state must not ever give away any more of its aboriginal, ancestral, biblical, spiritual and physical homeland to a people whose Islamic faith demands of them no recognition or acceptance ever of Israel.

December 17, 2010

Lies, Damned Lies, and Erakat

I wrote an article once titled: *Lies, Damned lies, and Palestinian Propaganda in Descending Order.* That title paraphrased British Prime Minister, Benjamin Disraeli's 19th century aphorism: *Lies, damned lies, and statistics in descending order.*

Few have mastered the art of dissimilitude more than long time Palestinian Arab spokesman, Saeb Erakat, who continues to be taken seriously by the ever gullible western media.

Now in his late middle age, Erakat continues to spew howlers as he has been doing for several decades, yet he still retains the confidence of mainstream western journalists and reporters – especially those of the Left. So, true to form, Erakat chose The Guardian newspaper, one of Britain's most left leaning and anti-Israel dailies to let fly another howler.

According to Erakat's recent Op-Ed in The Guardian, there are now seven million Palestinian Arab refugees. This is seven times the number of Arabs who foolishly left their homes in 1948 when ordered to do so by the corrupt Arab League, while at the same time seven Arab armies were invading the fledgling and re-born Jewish state with the intention of committing genocide against its Jewish citizens.

Incidentally, 850,000 Jewish refugees were systematically driven from their homes throughout the Arab world. Most found refuge in Israel. And the 200,000 Arabs (including some 100,000 who were later allowed by Israel to return) who ignored their leaders and remained in Israel now number 1.2 million; some 20% of the Jewish state's population. But Erakat would never mention those facts.

The Arab leaders who call themselves Palestinians often accuse Israel of committing a "holocaust" against the Palestinian Arabs. At the same time, they inflate the numbers of these same Arabs in an almost precipitous and distorted bell curve.

If only the Jewish victims of the real Holocaust would have suffered in such a fashion, there would not have been six million dead but - using Erakat's bizarre mathematics - forty million additional Jewish souls alive today.

That is the extent of the lies, damned lies, and statistics that people like Erakat routinely spew. The tragedy is that so many in the West are ever willing to swallow such garbage. But let's look at Erakat's career as a propagandist.

This is the man who bamboozled the world on CNN in April 2002 by baldly stating that Israel had, "massacred at least 500 people in Jenin and that women and children were missing."

This outrageous lie was effectively dismissed by Colin Powell himself and its falsehood subsequently confirmed by the UN, which went on to report that 56 Arabs were killed (34 of them armed combatants) in fighting by the IDF against Palestinian Arab terror squads infesting the Arab city. This is the city from which some 28 suicide bombers had infiltrated the Jewish state, perpetrating atrocities against hundreds of Israeli civilians during the previous 18 months. Erakat knew his words were false, but he also knew the effectiveness of the "big lie."

No Arab civilians were missing. However, many of the 22 civilians killed were used as human shields by the Arab terrorists – in itself an Arab war crime that remains unpunished.

Erakat's outright lie was hardly challenged, nor his credibility dented. After all, he has made a perverse career of half-truths, mistruths and spectacular falsehoods over several decades while acting as a Palestinian spokesman and negotiator in what is called the, "peace process."

In the latest round of indirect talks between the Israelis and the Palestinian Arabs, brokered by George Mitchell at the behest of his master in the White House, Barack Hussein Obama, Erakat is again, front and center, obfuscating and manipulating the clueless media in the way he knows best.

In an article by Bret Stephens titled *Liar, liar* in December 2002, published in the Jerusalem Post, it was pointed out that up to that date, "Erakat has had no less than 11,382 citations in the English language press since 1988" – a veritable Niagara Falls of falsehoods that have done so much to poison the minds of countless readers against Israel. Since then the torrent of Erakat whoppers has washed away any sense of historical accuracy.

Here are a few of the many deliberate lies Mr. Erakat has uttered:

In the International Herald Tribune (11/26/05), Saeb Erekat wrote, "Israel is a nuclear power boasting the fifth-largest military in the world." Correction (1/3/06): "While there are various ways to measure military strength, in terms of manpower alone and counting both active service members and reservists, Israel's military ranks 18th globally, according to data in the latest edition of *The Military Balance*," a reference by the International Institute for Strategic Studies."

Erakat has often claimed to the Western world and through its media that, "Palestinians are committed to two equal states for two peoples." Sounds nice to western ears, but facts tell a very different story.

Well over 60% of Arabs calling themselves Palestinians reject outright such an Erakat claim. And Mahmoud Abbas himself, the Chairman of the Palestinian Authority, rejects utterly any willingness to accept Israel as a Jewish state. Erakat can provide no evidence that he or his cronies seek peace, while Israel can show three peace offers in the past decade.

But, according to the current Palestinian narrative and effectively conveyed by Erakat, the fault for the absence of negotiations or peace lies with Israel.

Erakat claims repeatedly that, Israeli villages in Judea and Samaria, which Erakat describes in the anti-Israel nomenclature as "settlements in the West Bank," cover 42% of the disputed territory when in fact they control barely 5% of the ancestral and biblical Jewish heartland.

Bret Stephens pointed out in his December, 2002 article that, "Erakat says 'settlers' are stealing Palestinian water resources. Yet almost all 'settlers' are linked to the central Israeli water grid and do not use local wells." What is fact is that the Arabs pollute the scant water resources and aquifer within Judea and Samaria and the very term, Palestinian water resources, is to implicitly pre-judge whose land it truly is.

He also mentioned that, "Erakat says Israel plans to deprive Palestinians of everything but 'an insignificant presence in Jerusalem.' Yet at Camp David, much of east Jerusalem was theirs for the taking. They refused it."

Hitler's propaganda minister, Josef Goebbels, proved that telling a big lie over and over again ensured that most people would come to believe it. However, Saeb Erakat also proves that if you tell a multitude of small lies over and over again, a multitude of people will believe them without question.

Erakat's career has been just such a monument to dissimilitude. Sadly, there are many people anxious and willing to accept any nonsense uttered by such a master of deceits.

According to Israel National News, Saeb Erakat has criticized Prime Minister Binyamin Netanyahu for mentioning the Jewish people's historic ties to Jerusalem as described in the Bible.

He accused the prime minister of, "using religion to incite hatred and fear." Biblical references it seems are now considered hate mongering by the Islamic world. The Holy Jewish Bible refers to Jerusalem and Zion, which are synonymous, 850 times.

The Holy Christian Bible refers to them some 154 times. The Holy Koran does not refer to Jerusalem at all. Instead the Koran commands Muslims to: "… fight and kill the disbelievers wherever you find them, take them captive, harass them, lie in wait and ambush them using every stratagem of war." Koran 9:5. Propaganda is a stratagem of war and Mr. Erakat knows all too well how to wage it.

Erakat has often sought to dismiss the inextricable 3,000 year old Jewish ties to Jerusalem and has claimed that Jewish heritage on the Temple Mount, the site of the two ancient Jewish Temples, are a threat to Islam.

The neighborhoods illegally occupied by the Jordanian regime from 1948 to 1967 are now claimed by the Palestinian Authority as the future capital of a PA state. They include the Old City, the City of David and the Temple Mount. But Jewish residents of these very neighborhoods were expelled from them by the British officered Jordanian Arab Legion in 1948.

Erakat has states several times that, "East Jerusalem cannot continue to be occupied if there is to be peace." This too will be believed by many in the international corridors of power and the media, even as they know in their heart of hearts that if Jerusalem was again divided – like Berlin once was – there still will never be peace from the Arabs.

Saeb Erakat will continue to obfuscate and dissemble in his inimitable fashion, ever hiding the empirical fact that the Muslim world will never accept a Jewish state however much of its biblical and ancestral patrimony it gives away in pursuit of peace. Erakat well knows that even if Israel shrank to one downtown city block in Tel Aviv its existence would still be a provocation to the Arabs who call themselves Palestinians.

The one truth that Erakat will always hide is that the Palestinian Arab leadership will never accept a "two state solution." They want no Jewish state side by side with their Arab and Muslim state.

Indeed, they ultimately want one state stretching from the Mediterranean Sea to the borders of Iraq – that is an Islamic state, including the present day Kingdom of Jordan, in which neither Jews nor Hashemites will be permitted to remain.

This entity will inevitably become a Hamas controlled state willingly tied to the baleful influence of the Islamic Republic of Iran – an extension of Islamist and jihadist influence on the very doorstep of Europe and a bridgehead for the dreamed of worldwide Islamic Caliphate.

Two Nations under Islamic Duress

December 29, 2010

In the 14th century, the Byzantine Empire began to crumble, finally falling to the Ottoman Turks in 1453. But in 1389, the Ottoman Turkish sultan, Murad, 1, began to lead his forces against the armies of the Serbian prince Lazar.

The Serbian prince had already been active in resisting increasing Muslim raids against Christian lands in the Balkans and had called his barons, knights and warriors together to ask them if they should fight or become slaves, dhimmis, to the Muslims. The decision was made to fight although their forces would number some 35,000 against a Turkish Muslim host of 100,000. But better to fight than to be enslaved.

The place chosen to make a stand against the Muslim Turks was at Kosovo Polje (the Field of Blackbirds) in Kosovo - the heartland of the Serbian nation. It was in June, 1389, on St. Vitus Day (Vidovdan), that the rival forces met.

Prince Lazar reviewed the serried ranks of his foot soldiers and the mass of his cavalry, but he saw facing him a Muslim horde with a sea of waving flags upon which were emblazoned the Islamic crescent. He called upon all Serbs on that day saying: "Whoever is of Serbian descent and fails to come and fight in Kosovo, may his name be cursed for as long as his lineage should last."

The battle began at first with Serbian successes and the great Serbian hero, Milos Obilic, killed the Turkish Muslim sultan, Murad. For a while the Turks were in disarray but they managed to recover and by their sheer weight of numbers ground down and defeated the Serbian army.

It was not a mere military defeat, but the end of Serbian independence and the beginning of 500 years of Christian suffering under the Muslim yoke. But worse still, the Serbian heartland of Kosovo was lost. For the Serbian people, the blood shed at the Battle of Kosovo in the Field of Blackbirds marks Kosovo as eternally Serbian.

Another year in history that haunts the memory of a different people, who also suffered the loss of their heartland, is the year 70 AD. It was in that terrible year that the Roman general, Titus, finally came with overwhelming force against the Jewish capital city, Jerusalem.

Suffering for decades from appalling persecution by Roman procurators such as Rufus, Gratus and Pilate, and their legions, the Jews finally rose up against the occupation of their ancient land and at first won great victories. But the superpower of its day, the Roman Empire, sent legion after legion to relentlessly grind down Jewish resistance.

Jerusalem was surrounded by Titus and his forces. Every tree within 20 miles of the city was cut down to make a wooden siege palisade around the city walls. Both fruit and olive trees as well as immense stands of cedars - some over 1,000 years old - were cut down; trees which the Jews had planted and nursed for centuries. In this, there is an eerie similarity from the past to the present. Today, the forests in Israel planted as long ago as 100 years by Jewish pioneers are often targeted by Arab Muslim arsonists, Palestinians, who gleefully burn down the trees.

Jerusalem was finally destroyed after a frightful siege in which hundreds of thousands died of disease and hunger. Eliezer, one of the leaders of the resistance managed to escape with his followers and their families to the immense rock of Masada that overlooks the Dead Sea.

There, high upon the mountain that had been a winter palace of King Herod, the 960 Jewish men, women and children held out for three years. But in the end, Eliezer called them together and asked if they should surrender. Rather than be enslaved or crucified they took their lives.

Before that they had witnessed some one hundred thousand Jewish resistors crucified by the Romans in an immense and ghastly forest of crosses surrounding Jerusalem. In this, yet more trees from Judea and Galilee had been cut down turning the once fertile land into a howling desert.

It was later in 133 AD that the Second Jewish Revolt under the legendary Jewish warrior, Bar Kochba, broke out against continuing Roman depredations and occupation, which also was successful in the first years of the uprising. But finally, the Emperor Hadrian and his legions destroyed what was left of the Jewish state in 135 AD and - in a frightful insult to the Jewish survivors - renamed the Jewish homeland, Palestina, after the hated and long extinct biblical enemies of the Jews; the Philistines.

Centuries pass but history has an almost supernatural way of repeating itself. Fast forward to the twentieth and twenty first centuries and both Serbia and the Jewish homeland are linked by eerie circumstances. Both are falsely demonized in the mainstream press as aggressors when, in fact, they are the victims, and both are under relentless aggression from Islam.

But let us consider the new gold of our times and how it shapes politics and war: Oil, which greases the machinery of geo-politics and lubricates the revenge and envy that nation states harbor towards each other.

The need for oil makes and destroys states and peoples and too often befouls humanity. It is still a necessary evil, but much of this black gold happens by fate to lie under the sands of the Arab Middle East and the Islamic Republic of Iran and thus morphs into a terrible weapon wielded by Arab despots and Islamo-fascist fanatics.

The late 20th century's insane rush to create Kosovo as yet another Muslim autonomous region in the heart of the Balkans, was a testament to the curse of oil.

Ever ready to enrich their economies, the Europeans and, sadly, the Clinton Administration combined to appease and placate the Arab and Muslim kings, emirs, imams and assorted dictators.

The price demanded by the Saudis and the Gulf States for example was, as always, a steep one; namely to pave the way for more and more Muslim influence throughout the world.

The Saudis constantly pour billions of their petrodollars into Europe and North and South America in order to build lavish mosques where Wahhabi imams propagate extremist forms of Islam. European and American universities hold out their begging bowls to receive Arab money and in return help facilitate the spread of anti-Israel and anti-Western falsehoods masquerading as Middle East studies.

The phenomena of the so-called sovereign funds are instruments through which European and American financial institutions receive desperately needed infusions of Arab money to bail themselves out of their own greed and monetary shortcomings. And the financial help bestowed upon them always comes with strings; thus adding yet another layer of Arab and Muslim pressure.

Islamist influence grows with every passing day. Facts are being created on the ground, which are changing the demographics and national characteristics of one European state after another.

And it was in Europe that Arab oil drove the creation of a Muslim statelet, Kosovo, which is rapidly becoming a radical Islamist Balkan beachhead, filled with jihadists from around the Islamic world, ready to threaten what is left of Christian Europe. In time it will inevitably become a springboard for terror into both the United States and Russia.

The U.S. State Department's Nicholas Burns some years ago had congratulated the Kosovars in obtaining their independence from Serbia. This was a betrayal of the Serbian people and has left a disfiguring scar on the United States. For the Serbian people, the province of Kosovo is their very ancestral heartland.

The long suffering Serbs were forced to witness the witless and perfidious Western powers rip away Serbia's heart while their hated ethnic Albanian and Muslim historical enemies took possession of it. The Serbs, in fact, call Kosovo their "Jerusalem." That is how holy they consider their lost homeland.

And we must realize that Israel, too, is threatened by the same evil created by Arab oil. The Arabs who call themselves Palestinians demand Judaism's eternal holy city of Jerusalem and the Jewish heartland of Judea and Samaria (known by the erroneous Arab name, the West Bank). In this, the baleful influence of President Barack Hussein Obama looms, just as the Serbian people's heartland of Kosovo was stolen from them with the connivance and brute force of President Clinton and his diplomats, Richard Holbrooke and Madeleine Albright.

Under relentless U.S State Department pressure, the Israeli government of Prime Minister Netanyahu is enduring the same attempt at the dismemberment of its biblical, ancestral, aboriginal, spiritual and physical Jewish heartland as the brave and ill served Serbian people suffered with the loss of their beloved Kosovo.

Although Serbs living in enclaves within Kosovo are still holding on from being completely driven from their homes, the price of creating a Muslim Palestinian state is the expulsion - the ethnic cleansing - of all Jews from its proposed territory. In other words, it is even worse for the Jews as a new Arab state called Palestine will be judenrein - the forcible removal of Jewish villages and their inhabitants. And this unthinkable outrage of ethnic cleansing will be sanctioned by President Obama and the immoral United Nations under cover of the misnamed peace process.

Jordan is historically in possession of nearly 80% of Mandatory Palestine and its population is over 75% Palestinian. There already thus exists a de facto Palestine. Israel is a mere 40 miles wide from the Mediterranean Sea to the River Jordan and it is within this narrow strip of land that a new Arab and Islamic state would be carved from the biblical Jewish heartland. The world demands that Israel return to the highly vulnerable armistice lines that existed before June 5, 1967 when it was only nine miles wide at its most populous region.

These are the striking similarities between the Serbs and the Jews. Serbia originally lost its province of Kosovo after being defeated in battle by the Muslim Turks. Like the Jews, who in their 2,000 years of exile dreamed of restoring their ancient homeland and their holy city of Jerusalem from alien conquerors, so too the Serbs dreamed of Kosovo and wove their folk music and national identity around the lost Serbian heartland.

Kosovo was partially restored to Serbia but it was not to be for long. Judea and Samaria was liberated by Israel in its defensive 1967 Six Day War. But the world is coming against Israel and in 2011 will bring terrible pressure upon the Jewish state to again abandon its very biblical and ancestral heartland and give it to a terrorist and Islamic state called Palestine.

During the late 1990s when President Clinton and his Secretary of State, Madeline Albright, launched a disgraceful war against the Serbs, the Serbian Deputy Prime Minister, Draskovitch said of Kosovo: "Our faith was born there, as was our language, our nationhood, our pride. It is incumbent upon us to defend Kosovo, even if we all die."

His words were uttered as American bombers, repainted in NATO colors, bombed Serbia for several months inflicting some 3,000 civilian deaths and destroying all the bridges over the Danube River in Belgrade. This was not America's finest hour but it is now largely dead and buried by the mainstream media and by the leftist professors proliferating throughout universities and colleges: Institutions of lower learning as the remarkable Talk Show host, Michael Savage, justifiably calls them

The same mainstream media rarely, if ever, tells us about Serbia's passion during the many centuries leading up to the present and latest shameful act of the West. When Serbia was part of Yugoslavia, it was the Serbs who fought alone and unaided against the German divisions during World War 2; fighting them to a standstill. No other people alone in occupied Europe achieved that remarkable and heroic feat.

Croatia allied itself with Hitler and established a Nazi state. The Croatians exterminated hundreds of thousands of Serbs and tens of thousands of Jews. If you visit the Yasenovatz death camp in Croatia, you will find Jews and Serbs buried there together in mass graves.

The anti-Jewish Arab Mufti of Jerusalem during the British Mandate, Haj Amin el-Husseini, who spent many days with Hitler in his Berlin bunker plotting the destruction of Mandatory Palestine's Jewish population, encouraged the Bosnian Muslims to form several SS divisions, which subsequently carried out mass murders and deportations of Jews to the German death camps.

Serbia emerged from the Second World War with the distinction of defeating the German invasion and inflicting severe losses on the German army. But the Serbs paid a terrible price, losing nearly 2,000,000 dead or some 12% of their population. The Serbian partisans, who included many Jewish fighters, were able to save thousands of Jews from death at the hands of the Croatian, German and Bosnian murderers.

During the Balkan Wars of the 1990s, the Croatians expelled some 250,000 Serbs from their homes in the Krajina district. As soon as the Muslims in Kosovo received autonomy in 1974, they drove out 400,000 Serbs. At the same time a vast influx of ethnic Albanians fleeing Communist rule, flooded across the border to take the place of the disinherited Serbs. Albanian Muslim birth rate was so high that within 60 years the population within Kosovo grew from 70,000 in 1947 to 2,000,000 by 2004. Similarly, the Arab Muslim population within Israel has grown from some 200,000 in 1950 to 1.2 million in 2010.

The Serbian people have been reduced to only 10% of their original population in Kosovo. Ethnic cleansing against the Serbs began long before the Western press ran their lurid stories of Serbian ethnic cleansing against the Bosnian Muslims. Predictably, the mainstream press ignored the earlier attacks by the Muslims against the Serbs, which first led to the war.

The lesson for Israel is that foreign powers have conspired to strip the expendable Serbs of their ancestral heartland and give it to the Muslims. In doing so, these same western powers believe that by placating and ingratiating themselves with the oil rich Arab and Muslim world they enrich their own economies. After all, Serbia does not possess any known oil reserves.

Israel, too, has been until quite recently bereft of meaningful reserves of oil. It too is thus expendable. The pressure upon Israel to give away its own ancestral, historic, spiritual and biblical heartland in Judea and Samaria (the West Bank) grows relentlessly and insidiously.

Sadly and tragically, there has not existed since the time of Prime Minister Shamir an Israeli government or leader with the intestinal fortitude and spiritual certitude to adamantly and resolutely resist the cynical and perfidious machinations of western leaders. Israel desperately needs a leader who can talk to the world as Draskovitch once spoke for the Serbian people. Perhaps Prime Minister Binyamin Netanyahu may yet be that leader, though he has not fully removed the fears of many Israelis.

Carloline Glick, writing in the Feb 23, 2008 edition of the Jerusalem Post summed up the Israeli government's confusion at that time: "What the Serbs made NATO fight its way in to achieve, Israel is offering NATO on a silver platter." She added, "… the lessons of Kosovo are clear. Not only should Israel join Russia, Canada, China, Spain, Romania and many others in refusing to recognize Kosovo.

It should also state that as a consequence of Kosovo's independence, Israel rejects the deployment of any international forces to Gaza or Judea and Samaria, and refuses to cede its legal right to sovereignty in Judea, Samaria, Gaza and Jerusalem to international arbitration." Israel gave Gaza to the Arabs in 2005 in the hope the Arabs would create a peaceful Palestinian state. They did not. Hamas occupies Gaza and has bombarded Israel with over 12,000 missiles since 2005 and vows the extermination of the Jewish state.

Serbia and Israel must be supported by all who still cherish morality over expediency. Historical correctness must in all such cases trump so-called political correctness. As goes Serbia, so goes Israel.

Neither nation deserves to become victim to the international greed for black gold and the attendant groveling acceptance by oil-importing states to the demands of the oil producing dictatorships and Islamic theocracies. The failure to withstand Islamic triumphalism is dhimmitude or death.

The Security Council: To Veto or not to Veto?

January 24, 2011

"America is the greatest, freest and most decent society in existence. It is an oasis of goodness in a desert of cynicism and barbarism. This country, once an experiment unique in the world, is now the best hope for the world."

The above words were written by Dinesh D'Souza, but they are not the words you will ever hear from America's present president, Barack Hussein Obama. In Dinesh D'Souza's intriguing new book, *Understanding Obama's Rage*, the author opines that President Obama is an anti-Colonialist and that he acquired his rage from his biological and Kenyan father: Barack Obama, Senior.

This rage against the ex-colonial European powers and America's own history explains why Obama is cool also towards Britain, which colonized much of Africa, including the East African territory which eventually became known as Kenya.

Obama senior came from a family that had converted to Islam. He hated the British occupation and he espoused strong socialist views. At the same time, his personal life was devastated by alcohol and he finally died after leaving a tavern drunk and driving his car into a tree. All this, according to Mr. D'Souza, is in the president's own book, Dreams from my Father.

Barack Obama's very book title is revealing. The dreams are from his father not of his father. In this we see how the president has taken his father's rage into himself. The president for example was, according to D'Souza, strangely apathetic and disinterested when General McChristal came to him with a new plan to win the war in Afghanistan.

The reason for his lack of interest was because Obama then as now does not want to win the war but, instead, seeks any way in which to quit Afghanistan.

The father's influence beyond the grave has made President Obama believe that America is, as Da Souza, points out, the bear that must be tamed. In other words, Obama believes the United States is a colonial power exploiting other countries, such as Iraq, and meddling in their affairs.

America must be brought down to size. America must be like every other nation (presumably that means like Syria, Sudan, Iran and North Korea?) and discard the belief in its exceptionalism. That is why Obama tours the world apologizing for what he believes are American transgressions. That is why he bows to foreign leaders and that is why he is intent on furthering on the world stage the same rage that consumed his own father. That is why he is the most radical of all America's presidents and loved by the likes of Venezuela's Hugo Chavez among others.

The president has surrounded himself with American haters over a long period of time. Obama's deep ties to an anti-American fringe has culminated in his White House policy, which has resulted in the passage of bills such as healthcare reform which, hidden away in its two and a half thousand pages, includes an ideological agenda of wealth transfer from the so-called rich to the poor: Healthcare thus being a means to an end. His imperial agenda also allows for the creation of unelected and unsupervised "czars" who are answerable only to the president.

Yet more troubling is the president's relationship with the terrorist Bill Ayers and the anti-American Black Muslim group, the Nation of Islam. Indeed, Obama, while still a Senator, employed Cynthia K. Miller as the treasurer of his Senate campaign. Miller at the time was a member of the anti-Semitic Louis Farrakhan's Nation of Islam, as was Jennifer Mason his Director of Constituent Services.

The Muslim ties and his four formative years in Muslim Indonesia perhaps explain why President Obama is sympathetic to the building of a giant mosque so near to Ground Zero in New York City and why his first overseas trip was to Cairo, Egypt where he addressed the Muslim world.

It is revealing how many anti-Israel individuals Barack Obama was influenced by before he became president. As Gerald Honigman wrote in a June 2010 Op-Ed in Arutz-Sheva's website: "Obama's close associations with well-known anti-Israel politicos, friends, and advisors, such as former Secretary of State Zbigniew Brzezinski, Samantha Powers, Robert Malley, General Tony McPeak ("American Jews are the reason there is no Middle East peace"), etc. are beyond coincidental."

So, while events led then Senator Obama in 2008 to later officially distance himself from some of these folks, the direction that an Obama Administration would be heading in, vis-à-vis, the Middle East was already very clear prior to the November 2008 election.

Honigman continued: "At his best buddy, Professor Rashid Khalidi's private party, it was reported that Obama spoke about 'Israeli genocide' against Arabs. It was caught on tape. During the fight that ensued, Obama's folks managed to see to it that the LA Times would not even release a transcript. The late Edward Said, Ali Abunimah, and other prominent anti-Israel activists were good buddies as well. Abunimah and others have spoken of Obama's frequent attendance at Arab anti-Israel functions and such."

Let us not forget that President Obama was a member of a church for twenty years whose minister, the Rev. Jeremiah Wright, preached black-liberation theology. There is an eerie similarity here with the anti- British and anti-Colonial views his biological, Kenyan father evinced. This has clouded his own views as has his association and friendship with the PLO representative and now professor at Columbia, Rashid Khalidi, one of many Israel-hating people that Obama befriended and allied with.

Honigman then delivered a clincher: "Long before the election, Senator Obama endorsed the Saudi Peace Plan. He said - repeatedly - that Israel would be crazy not to accept it. It's key provisions are a total withdrawal of Israel to the '49 armistice lines – not borders - which made it a mere 9 miles wide at its waist (where most of Israel's population, industry, and so forth are located), and the acceptance of millions of real and alleged Arab refugees into the Jewish sub-rump State. In return, Israel would get some vague recognition and normalization. "Peace" all right…of the grave.

"In other words, then Senator and now President Obama expects Israel to give up the promise of the carefully worded final draft of UNSC Resolution 242, adopted in the wake of the '67 War, that it would finally get real secure and somewhat defensible political borders (instead of armistice lines) as it withdrew (at the conclusion of formal treaties of peace, not cease fires) from some - not all - of the territories it came to occupy in the defensive war it was forced to fight after being blockaded by Arabs, along with other hostile acts, in 1967.

Resolution 242 promised Israel a bit of a buffer in lands where Judeans - Jews - have lived for millennia via territorial compromises with Arabs who are still not reconciled with anyone but themselves having political rights in the region."

And where does this take us? It takes us to the report in the *Debka Intelligence Report* of January 22, 2011 which has as its headline: "Obama to withhold veto from Palestinian UN move to condemn Israeli settlements."

The writer of the article adds that: "A Non-veto would spark a US-Israel crisis." Israel and the US are thus set for a collision if President Barack Obama stands by his refusal to veto a Palestinian-Arab motion due to be tabled at the UN Security Council condemning Israel for its settlement policy in the West Bank and Jerusalem.

If he did, he would be the first US president to let an anti-Israel motion go through the Security Council; building on the West Bank (Judea and Samaria) and even in the forty-year old suburbs of East Jerusalem would become illegal, as would also municipal, police and military actions in these places.

"This situation would throw Israel's relations with the US, the UN and the European Union into deep crisis. By failing to block such a motion, Obama would encourage the Palestinians and hostile Arab states to continue to use the UN Security Council to undermine Israel's legitimacy and even recognize a unilateral Palestinian state within the pre-1967 borders without negotiations."

If the *Debka Report* is corroborated and found to be accurate, then this will be the moment many who support the Jewish state's independence and legitimacy have feared. Those of us who warned repeatedly against voting for Barack Hussein Obama were dismissed as right-wingers and extremists.

The Lefties still to this day mock and smear American patriots such as Sarah Palin as they do Israeli conservatives and patriots. But they still defend the indefensible present day incumbent in the White House. The Left then must be considered complicit with the president in enacting a clear anti-Israel bias. Heaven knows, there are enough examples of left-wing hostility towards beleaguered and embattled Israel.

So will Obama veto the proposed anti-Israel Security Council resolution describing Jewish communities (which will be called by the pejorative term, settlements) throughout the Jewish biblical, ancestral, aboriginal, spiritual and physical heartland as illegal, or will he withhold his veto?

If he withholds his veto power and allows the brutal anti-Israel and anti-Jewish resolution to pass, he will commence what many have said he has always planned to do; set in motion an existential threat to Israel's basic security and very survival.

February 5, 2011

Obama Knows What Chaos He Has Unleashed

Not content with creating havoc in the U.S. economy, setting Americans against each other, and forcing through a health reform act which has nothing to do with health but everything to do with the redistribution of wealth and an immense increase in governmental interference, our president has now opened a Pandora's Box in the Middle East. It may well usher in a catastrophe not seen since World War 2.

From his notorious Cairo speech to the present, President Obama speaks, and disaster follows. Some commentators believe that President Obama and Secretary of State Clinton are so utterly naïve as to make them unable to understand what will happen in Egypt as a result of their undermining of the Mubarak regime.

The question is justifiably asked: Do they truly believe that the next regime that comes to power will have the interests of the U.S. and the West at heart?

My fear is that Obama is not naïve at all, but he instead knows only too well what he is doing, for he is eagerly promoting Islamic power in the world while diminishing the West and Israel, however much innocent blood will flow as a result.

Inevitably, sooner or later, the Muslim Brotherhood will take power, usher in a barbaric Islamist power in Egypt that will control the Suez Canal, and show no mercy to its own people or its perceived foes.

So now we see what the present incumbent in the White House has wrought, and so can our few remaining allies. They must now wonder what confidence they can ever have in any future alliance with the United States.

We should be aware of what endemic Islamic violence has wrought in the past. For example, assassinations of Arab leaders are not an infrequent occurrence. After the 1948 Arab-Israel War, the King of Jordan, Abdullah, was murdered by followers of the Muslim fanatic, the Mufti of Jerusalem.

The Egyptian Prime Minister, Nokrashi Pasha, was also struck down. The forces behind the killings were elements of both Arab socialist movements and the

Muslim Brotherhood. Today, in the streets of Cairo, we have an unholy alliance of the current radical left with the same Muslim Brotherhood.

The Suez Canal is a major lifeline for the economies of Europe and the United States. It has been the source of political disruption in the past, as it may well be in the near future. And the Muslim Brotherhood may soon control it. As always, the past is our guidepost to the future.

In 1952, Gamal Abdul Nasser seized control of the Egyptian state and forged an alliance with the Soviet Union, which provided enormous arms shipments to Egypt.

Feeling greatly empowered, Nasser broke both the 1949 Armistice Agreement with Israel and international law by blocking the Suez Canal to Israeli ships and other vessels bringing cargoes to and from the Jewish state. At the same time, Nasser blockaded the narrow Straits of Tiran at the foot of the Sinai Peninsula, thus preventing Israeli maritime trade with the Far East and Africa.

Nasser eventually nationalized the Suez Canal on July 27, 1956. This illegal act threatened the oil supplies to Britain and France from the Middle East. The economic stranglehold on Israel became intolerable, and Arab terrorism against the Jewish state led to many Israeli civilian deaths. (Incidentally, Arab terrorism began long before the so-called Israeli "occupation," which Arab and pro-Arab propagandists now use as the excuse for present Arab aggression against Israel.)

In October 1956, war by Britain, France, and Israel against Egypt broke out. Israeli forces, in what became known as the One Hundred Hours War, defeated the Egyptians in Sinai and Gaza and broke the naval blockade. Britain and France invaded the Canal Zone to end Nasser's blockade of the Suez Canal.

Under U.S. Secretary of State John Foster Dulles, Britain and France were eventually forced out of Egypt. This was, as future events showed, a dreadful blunder on the part of the Eisenhower administration. It was the beginning of Britain's decline as a world power. It also led to Nasser remaining in power.

The Egyptian dictator's political and pan-Arab ambitions again climaxed in 1967. Nasser again blockaded the Suez Canal to Israeli shipping and reinstituted the naval blockade at the mouth of the Tiran Straits. This in turn led, in 1967, to the hasty withdrawal of the U.N. buffer force that had been in place to prevent further Egyptian aggression against Israel. U.N. Secretary General U. Thant folded under

Arab pressure and arbitrarily withdrew the buffer force. Egyptian armed forces then entered the Sinai, heading for the Israeli border.

The Arab and Muslim world called then, just as now, for Israel's extermination, and huge mobs in Arab capitals uttered lurid threats for Israel's defeat and the slaughter of her people.

The world prepared for Israel's destruction, but everyone was astonished when in June 1967, Israel - forced to fight a defensive war of survival - destroyed the combined Egyptian, Syrian, and Jordanian armies and air forces within six days.

The Suez Canal and the Straits of Tiran were again open for the free passage of Israeli ships. Nasser fell from power and was replaced by Anwar Sadat. However, in 1973, the Syrian and Egyptian armies attacked Israel on the holiest day in the Jewish religious calendar, Yom Kippur, which gave its name to the war.

Israel was hard put to survive initially, but she gradually beat back the Arab threat. Sadat eventually decided that war was not an option for the time being and chose to make peace with Israel.

Israel vacated the entire Sinai desert (95% of the territories Israel conquered) and gave up the oil-producing facilities it had developed at Abu Rodeis - all in return for a signed peace agreement with Egypt. Jordan eventually followed Egypt's decision, but both Arab nations maintained a frigid peace with the Jewish state.

Anwar Sadat was subsequently assassinated by members of the Muslim Brotherhood. His successor was Hosni Mubarak, who, for the last thirty years, has kept control over the seething Egyptian masses and the volatile Arab street.

Now his thirty-year rule has been fatally undermined by U.S. President, Barack Hussein Obama, in a betrayal that is as astonishing as it is deplorable.

It is clear to any child that a new Egyptian regime will, if not immediately, be hijacked by the Muslim Brotherhood, which is now calling for Egypt to prepare itself again for war with Israel and for the blockading of the Suez Canal to American, Western, and Israeli shipping. Obama is no fool; he engineered this.

So, thanks to President Obama, we are back to square one with an Islamic Egyptian regime poised to send Egypt's massively armed army back into Sinai and towards the Israeli border with the aim of exterminating the Jewish state: So much for "Land for Peace."

But what economic turmoil would a new Egyptian Islamic closure of the Canal mean to the West? It is estimated that slightly more than two million barrels of crude oil and refined petroleum products flow both north and south through the Suez Canal every day.

In 2009, for example, almost 35,000 ships transited the Suez Canal, and 10 percent were petroleum tankers. Oil shipments from the Persian Gulf travel through the Canal primarily to European ports, but also to the United States.

Additionally, the Sumed Oil pipeline provides an alternative to the Suez Canal, transporting as much as 3 million barrels of crude oil from Saudi Arabia and several Gulf states. It amounts to up to seven percent of Europe's oil needs. Since the violence erupted in Egypt, European oil prices have risen far more than they have in the United States.

If the Muslim Brotherhood, which was founded in 1928, takes over Egypt, it is more than likely that both the Canal and the pipeline would be shut again, causing oil tankers to travel around the Cape of Good Hope, adding six thousand miles to the journey to Europe alone. Not what an economically strapped Europe wants.

At the same time, the Brotherhood, now governing over 80 million Egyptians and possessing a huge military, would join with a radicalized Yemen in blockading the Bab al Mandeb straits at the foot of the Red Sea.

Add to the noxious mix the Islamic Republic of Iran, and we may well see the closure of the Gulf of Oman, with additional disruptions of oil shipments to the West. The economic reality for America will be catastrophic.

Under Obama's watch, the true democratic revolution against the mullahs in Iran was snuffed out because the American president refused to support the demonstrators in the streets of Tehran. In contrast, the same Obama ordered Hosni Mubarak to leave office and let the rioters in Cairo have "free" elections.

Following Condoleezza Rice's naïve call for "free" and democratic elections in Gaza, a branch of the Muslim Brotherhood (Hamas) used the democratic process to come to power and immediately trashed all semblance of democracy by instituting oppressive sharia law and raining thousands of missiles upon Israeli towns and villages.

The grotesque policies of Obama have caused Lebanon to fall under Islamic occupation, with the Iranian puppet, Hezbollah, now controlling the Lebanese government. Jordan's kinglet, Abdullah, sits on a powder keg whereby his throne is under increasing pressure from violent members of the same Muslim Brotherhood.

So there you have it. Islam increasingly holds Europe, America, and what is left of the free world in its clutches...and the left cheers it on.

Let me close with the words of Michael D. Evans, New York Times bestselling author of *Jimmy Carter: The Liberal Left and World Chaos*:

It's no coincidence that Al Baradei showed up in Cairo only two days after the uprising began and was immediately named a negotiator by the Muslim Brotherhood. In fact, he had been waiting in the wings for quite a while.

He's on the board of an organization headed by George Soros and Zbigniew Brzezinski called International Crisis Group. Brzezinski is the same man who supervised the fall of the Shah of Iran in 1979.

Another board member of the ICC is one Javier Solana. Solana is one of the most powerful figures in the European Union. Because of Solana's Marxist sympathies, and his support for the regime of Cuba's Fidel Castro, Solana was on the USA's subversive list.

Former U.S. National Security Advisor, Sandy Berger, who once smuggled incriminating documents out of the Clinton White House [editor's note: the documents were smuggled out of the National Archives] by hiding them in his clothing, is another Board Member, as is General Wesley Clark, once fired from his NATO command.

Mohamed El Baradei also sits on the ICC's Board and thus, seeing the hand of George Soros along with the other players, who for so long have plotted against the West and Israel, the Islamists are joined together." Mr. ElBaradei suspended his membership from the Board of Crisis Group concurrent with his January 2011 return to Egypt. What, one wonders, will history say of the foreign policies of Barack Hussein Obama?

Take back the Philadelphi Corridor

February 15, 2011

Egyptian President, Hosni Mubarak has been forced to resign and a new and temporary military regime installed. Mubarak was a dictator, which in the Arab and Muslim world is par for the course. Some believe the 83 year old has billions stashed away. That, too, is not uncommon. Arafat stole vast sums from the Arabs who call themselves Palestinians, which his widow now enjoys.

Whatever a new Egyptian government may call itself, it will not be a free and democratic government as we know in the West; even behind an El Baradei or a Suleiman, a Tantawi or whatever fig leaf.

Despite the naivety and idiocy spewed by the international mainstream media, still attempting to liken the demonstrations in Cairo to the anti-Soviet democratic uprisings in Eastern Europe, this will become a Muslim Brotherhood regime with all the anti-Jewish venom and Islamic triumphalism that one expects from such a beast.

Look at the Middle East. Once secular Turkey is no more but is rapidly becoming an Islamic state and thus predictably hostile to Israel. Egypt, despite Mubarak's severe control of the Muslim Brotherhood, is fundamentally an Islamic state in all but name. Its people are overwhelmingly in support of strict Islamic practices.

Look at the demonstrators in the Cairo square; they were all men. The only time women were seen was when they were trotted out for the ever gullible and manipulated Western press. Egyptian women no longer project the free, secular image they once did in the 1950s. I remember seeing old movies of that era and the women looked and dressed like their European and American counterparts. Now they are covered in the Islamic shrouds that so demean their sex.

Mark Steyn, on Fox News, recently pointed out that nine out of ten Egyptian women have undergone genital mutilation according to Islamic practice; a fact that should outrage the Western world but which elicits nothing but deafening silence.

And despite, or even because of, Mubarak's control, the Egyptian state officially spews the vilest anti-Semitic filth seen since Adolf Hitler's Nazi regime. All of this bodes ill for a western style new Egyptian government that will truly honor the peace agreement made with Israel in 1979. And don't forget the security of the West's lifeline – the Suez Canal.

Islam (there is no radical and no moderate Islam) will guide the regime, and the more hateful later writings in the Koran and Hadith will be its roadmap. That being the case, Israel must repossess the Philadelphi Corridor as a most basic but vital military act for its own security and survival. It can still do so while only Hamas rules in the Gaza Strip.

There may soon be no more need for smuggling tunnels beneath the Egyptian – Gaza border. Instead, endless fleets of trucks will bring into the Strip from Egypt – the big Muslim Brotherhood – the most sophisticated weapons and missiles needed for Hamas – the little Muslim Brotherhood. Only by possessing the Philadelphi Corridor again can Israel hope to stem the lethal tide.

The question is, will Israeli leaders, including Defense Minister, Ehud Barak, continue the same fearful and timid policies that too many have shown when dealing with the Quartet, the U.N., the Obama Administration, the EU, ad nauseum. Ehud Barak has a particularly poor record with respect to Israel's security since being a member of subsequent Israeli governments.

He betrayed the Christian Lebanese force in southern Lebanon fighting alongside Israel by ordering the Israeli forces to quit the southern Lebanon Security Zone, thus abandoning Israel's loyal ally, the Southern Lebanese Army (SLA). As a result Israel now has Iran's surrogate, Hezbollah, on the same Lebanese border. Barak's misplaced energies have largely been at the expense of the Jewish farmers and villagers in Judea and Samaria who are routinely harassed and forced to see their homes demolished by his orders in those same ancestral and biblical Jewish territories.

I fear Israel will find that the Gaza Strip becomes an appendage of a new Islamic Republic of Egypt. Gaza has always been a perilous finger pointing into the very heart of the Jewish state. Now it will become even more so, backed by an Egyptian hand armed with enormous and highly lethal amounts of weaponry supplied by the U.S. over many years.

We can only hope that an Israeli leader with foresight and intestinal fortitude will put Israel's needs above all else. Hopefully that leader may yet be Prime Minister Binyamin Netanyahu. But I prefer not to hold my breath just yet. Indeed, Netanyahu's reported "sigh of relief" that Egypt will honor the peace may be tragically premature.

Repossessing the Philadelphi Corridor will no doubt evoke screams of rage from the morally compromised world, but they will always condemn Israel however peaceful the Jewish state acts. So with that truism, it is surely better to be hung in the media and the international corridors of power as a lion than a sheep. Besides, a case can be made that joint Israeli-Egyptian forces working together along the Gaza –Egypt border (the Philadelphi Corridor) will prevent an infestation in Sinai, and along Israel's long southern border, of Hamas banditry and terror.

It is just as much in Egypt's best interests as well as Israel's to frustrate Hamas aggression unless, of course, Egypt's government slides into the Muslim Brotherhood's orbit. Then it is definitely Israel's only hope of security to arbitrarily re-possess the narrow Corridor.

When the peace treaty between Egypt and Israel was signed in 1979, the 14 km long security and buffer zone known as the Philadelphi Corridor was under Israel's control. Its purpose was to prevent the illegal importation into the Gaza Strip from Egypt of weapons and terrorists to be used against Israel.

The Oslo Accords, signed in 1995, allowed Israel to retain the security corridor along the border but it soon became apparent that Sinai Bedouin and the Palestinian Arabs were digging ever more sophisticated smuggling tunnels under the border.

Condoleezza Rice, when Secretary of State, urged Israel to vacate the vital security strip separating Egyptian Sinai from the Gaza Strip as a peaceful gesture to the Palestinian Arabs: Another land for peace disaster in which the Arabs always receive land but in which the Israelis never receive peace.

Following the infamous and tragic disengagement from Gaza in 2005, forced upon the Jewish villagers in Gush Katif by Ariel Sharon, Israel gave up control of the Philadelphi Corridor to the Palestinian Authority in September of that year. Meanwhile, massive smuggling continued.

It was only a matter of time before Hamas, the little Muslim Brotherhood, evicted their Fatah rivals in a bloody coup in 2007. Hamas, with its charter calling for Israel's extermination, has now ruled the Gaza Strip since then, including occupying the Philadelphi Corridor.

According to a recent poll in Yediot Achronot, some 65% of Israelis admitted that the fall of Hosni Mubarak would pose a direct danger to Israel and a majority believed that a Muslim Brotherhood regime would take power. Even earlier, the Palestinian Authority, according to David Poort in Al Jazeera, "had pleaded with the Israeli government to re-occupy the Philadelphi corridor on the Gaza-Egypt border, in order to tighten the siege on Hamas-run Gaza, the Palestinian papers show.

"On January 23, 2008, masked gunmen demolished the steel wall alongside the Philadelphi route in Rafah and hundreds of thousands of Gazans entered Egypt to buy food and supplies.

"Less than two weeks later, in a meeting in West Jerusalem, Ahmed Qurei, the former Palestinian Authority prime minister, asked Tzipi Livni, the former Israeli foreign minister, if Israel could re-occupy the Philadelphi corridor to seal the border and cut off supplies to Hamas." Apparently Livni did nothing and Hamas, as we know, has been greatly strengthened militarily ever since.

Whether one accepts as sincere the deep concerns expressed by the Palestinian Authority leadership regarding Hamas and its urging of Israel, specifically Tzipi Livni at the time, to re-possess the Philadelphi Corridor, it nevertheless is crystal clear that not to do so now, or very soon, will bring dire security problems for the increasingly beleaguered Jewish state.

So take it, Israel, and take it soon, for the Muslim Brotherhood neither sleeps nor rests, and time in this instance is most assuredly not on Israel's side. Despite the present "assurances" from the Egyptian military that they will continue to honor the peace treaty, it is imperative for the Jewish state not to be lulled yet again into a sense of false security.

March 29, 2011

Hillary's War

Let us first look back to the bombing of Serbia by President Clinton and who was most instrumental in encouraging him.

According to Dean Murphy in the New York Times of October 2000,

"Hillary Clinton called for the US to reject isolationism and aggressively engage itself in world affairs in the tradition of President Truman at the end of WWII.

"She cited American involvement in Bosnia and Kosovo as examples of foreign engagements she favored on *moral* and strategic grounds, but also suggested that Americans needed to consider becoming involved in solving crises that are not only military in nature."

In other words Hillary urged Bill to launch the first "human rights war" in Bosnia and Kosovo. But in doing so she laid the foundation for an Islamic beachhead in territory previously fought over for centuries by Christian Serbs who were resisting Muslim invasion and conquest.

Again, according to Gail Sheehy writing on December 9, 1999 in *Hillary's Choice*, page 345: On March 21, 1999, Hillary expressed her views by phone to the President:

"I urged him to bomb. The Clintons argued the issue over the next few days. The President expressed what-ifs: What if bombing promoted more executions? What if it took apart the NATO alliance?

"Hillary responded, "You cannot let this go on at the end of a century that has seen the major holocaust of our time. What do we have NATO for if not to defend our way of life?"

The next day the President declared that force was necessary. Thus it was Hillary Clinton who urged her husband to bomb Serbia. And it was done, predominately, with the use of U.S. aircraft wearing NATO insignia and bombing from thousands of feet. Inevitably such indiscriminate force led to the destruction of bridges in Belgrade with untold numbers of Serbian civilians killed. Some humanitarian war!

The same thread appeared in June 1999 when Hillary spoke at the Sorbonne in Paris. She again defended the bombing of Serbia by claiming that:

"We will not turn away when human beings are cruelly expelled or when they are denied basic rights and dignities because of how they look or how they worship. When crimes against humanity rear their ugly heads, we have to send such a message as an international community."

She was referring to the Muslim victims of the war but she lost sight both of the Serbian victims who had died at the hands of Muslims she was defending or who themselves had been expelled from their lands by Muslim aggressors.

Hillary Clinton misread the strategic and humanitarian disaster to the Serbian people that increasingly jihadist Muslim states in the Balkans were bound to create. It was not America's finest hour.

Now Secretary of State, Hillary Clinton, is doing the very same in Libya that she set in motion in Bosnia and Kosovo. Like the pressure she brought to bear on President Clinton, Hillary has repeated it with President Obama.

So we have Obama signing on to United States bombing in Libya in order to protect the so-called Libyan rebels against the deplorable President Gaddafi. But, like the Muslims in the Balkans that Hillary wept over, we have no true idea who these rebels really are. There are commentators who believe that, as Gaddafi himself suggested, the rebels are members of Al Qaida or the Muslim Brotherhood.

It is instructive to read Tom Dickinson writing in the far from conservative website, *Rolling Stone*, on March 21, 2011. Though Dickinson is critical of Obama, remember it was Hillary Clinton who pressured the present president, as did Samantha Power, one of his most influential foreign policy advisors, and Susan Rice, his ambassador to the United Nations. Dickinson wrote:

"In recent years, at mosques throughout eastern Libya, radical imams have been "urging worshippers to support jihad in Iraq and elsewhere, according to Wiki-Leaked cables. More troubling: The city of Derna, east of Benghazi, was a "wellspring" of suicide bombers that targeted U.S. troops in Iraq.

"By imposing a no-fly zone over Eastern Libya, the U.S. and its coalition partners have effectively embraced the breakaway republic of Cyrenaica.

A West Point analysis of a cache of al Qaeda records discovered that nearly 20 percent of foreign fighters in Iraq were Libyans, and that on a per-capita basis Libya nearly doubled Saudi Arabia as the top source of foreign fighters.

"The epicenter of Libyan jihadism is the city of Derna - the hometown of more than half of Libya's foreign fighters. The city of 80,000 has a history of violent resistance to occupying powers - including Americans, who captured the city in the First Barbary War.

"A surprisingly readable cable titled "*Die Hard in Derna*" makes clear that the city "takes great pride" in having sent so many of its sons to kill American soldiers in Iraq, quoting one resident as saying: 'It's jihad - it's our duty.'"

So here we see Hillary at it again. Having brutally harmed Serbia and forced it to lose its heartland of Kosovo - what Serbs call their Jerusalem - she aided and abetted Muslim jihadist ambitions and is now doing the same in Libya.

Let us also not forget that in Frankfurt, Germany, two U.S. servicemen were recently murdered by a Kosovo Muslim terrorist screaming, *"Allahu Akbar"* (Allah is greater) as the unarmed soldiers sat in a bus at the airport.

Is Hillary so naïve as not to realize that these are not Libyan rebels in the true sense of the word? No, I believe she fully understands what she is doing and that makes for one truly frightening scenario.

The rebels are jihadists, murderers of Americans in Iraq and Afghanistan. They are enemies of the West; enemies of Jews and Christians and of all other non-Muslim faiths. What is shameful is that Americans are being put yet again in harm's way in another Muslim country and at the urgings of the Arab League: that ever corrupt body that is using American and European forces as cannon fodder.

The jihadists are now the creatures that Barack Hussein Obama, with the connivance and urgings of Hillary, Samantha Powers, Susan Rice and so many other "progressive" denizens of the White House and State, are supporting. If this were a novel it would be considered too far-fetched.

It will be interesting to see how the far left views Obama's and Hillary's War? Unhappy, to say the least, with the protracted conflict in Iraq, Afghanistan and now the Libyan imbroglio, one thing is certain: they cannot this time blame Bush.

Oh, what noxious weeds has Hillary Clinton sown!

Cartoon by A.E. Branco

April 6, 2011

Passover's Gift: Promised and Undivided Land

Millions, perhaps billions, of the world's population do not know the meaning of the towering festival of freedom and liberty known as Passover; a festival recognizing an event that has blessed the world for some 3,300 years. The festival begins on April 18th of this year and always on the 15th day of the Jewish month of Nissan. Jews and Christians know from the Bible the story of the Exodus and of the salvation of the Jewish people from centuries of slavery under the Egyptian pharaohs: This creation and deliverance of an entire nation.

Such a seminal event in humanity's history became the foundation for freedom and liberty – created many centuries before democracy was first enunciated by Greek philosophers who nevertheless lived primarily within a polytheistic society. Many people know in varying degrees the Passover story and the birth of the Jewish people and of their undying faith in the One and Only God; invisible and indivisible. Judaism has given the world monotheism in its purest and most undiluted nature. The Unity of God is what Jews have defended against all who attempted to suggest a plurality: Even to enduring martyrdom.

The long suffering Jews under Egyptian bondage were led to freedom by the Jewish prophet, Moses, who brought them to their own very special and promised Land of Israel. Moses spoke with God in Sinai and brought a wondrous divine gift to the Jewish people and through them to all humanity – the Decalogue; the Ten Commandments, and the basis of today's laws of Western and Judeo-Christian civilization and jurisprudence. These ten brief commandments – a mere 120 Hebrew words – are written on the walls of synagogues and churches.

But, as in all Jewish practice, Moses was never deified. He was shown in the Torah, the first five books of the Bible, as a man; nothing else. Indeed in order not to deify him or exalt him over others he is shown in the Holy Bible with human failings and his burial place remains unknown. He sought the mountain top and beheld the Promised Land of Israel, yet was never to enter. In fact, in the Torah Moses is described merely as "the humblest and meekest of all human beings." For in Judaism, only God is divine and besides Him there is none other.

Passover (Pesach in Hebrew) is the first of the Jewish holidays and festivals, coinciding with the coming of the Spring in the Jewish people's ancestral, biblical and native land: the land given by God in an everlasting Covenant to the Jewish people; a land extending from the Jordan River to the Mediterranean Sea and including Gilead (the possession of the tribes of Manasseh, Gad and Reuben) east of the river, in the present day Arab state of Jordan.

The Passover festival precedes two other harvest festivals based upon the agricultural cycles of ancient and modern Israel. Next comes Shavuot, Pentecost, which records and commemorates the giving to Moses of the Ten Commandments followed by Succot, which is known as Tabernacles. Mankind was, and is, blessed through the Passover for it is a veritable gift to those who accept its divine message and perform the ritual meal, the Seder, recording the Exodus story.

But there is an evil in men's hearts, and it is a profound evil, for those who hate and envy this Jewish gift to humanity and its message of freedom, liberty and foundational democracy. They have chosen since time immemorial to rise up to destroy all that it stands for and persecute those – the Jews – who received it from God and who have shared it with all humanity.

Let me recount what Mary Antin wrote in 1911 about the horrors inflicted upon the Jews in Russia as they celebrated the festival of liberty in the Exodus story during the festive Seder meal. Ms. Antin wrote of what routinely took place at Passover and of how Russian neighbors reminded the Jews that for them it was another Egypt:

"... in Russian cities and even more in country districts, where Jewish families lived scattered, the stupid peasants would hear lies about the Jews and fill themselves with vodka. Then they would set out to kill their Jewish neighbors. They attacked them with knives and clubs and scythes and axes, killed them or tortured them and burned their houses. This was called a pogrom.

"Jews who escaped the pogroms came with wounds on them and horrible, horrible, stories of babies torn limb from limb before their mother's eyes.

"Only to hear these things made one sob and sob and choke with pain. People who saw such things never smiled any more, no matter how long they lived and sometimes their hair turned white in a day and others went insane."

In the Passover story, which is enshrined in the Haggadah, the book retelling the events of the Exodus and of the order of the Seder meal, there is a profound and millennial old passage: "Not one man alone has risen up against us to destroy us, but in every generation there have risen up against us those who sought to destroy us; but the Holy One, blessed be He, delivers us from their hands." And so it was and still is.

Just recently, a family in the Jewish Israeli village of Itamar, in biblical and ancestral Samaria, was slaughtered by Arab Muslims whose tracks led back to a nearby Arab settlement. The members of the Fogel family were sleeping in their tiny home on the Sabbath when a Palestinian murderer entered and knifed to death the father, mother, and three children, including a little baby girl only three months old.

Mary Antin spoke about unspeakable horrors inflicted on Jewish families in Russia; atrocities which had been repeated time after time throughout Europe and the Islamic world for 2,000 years or so.

Those relentless persecutions, pogroms and the shattering genocide perpetrated against the Jews in the Holocaust by Nazi Germany, in which a third of the world's Jewish population was exterminated, were done when the Jews were still living in the long night of statelessness after Rome had destroyed Jewish Judea in 135 AD.

Yet today, since the modern miracle in 1948 of Israel's rebirth and reconstitution as a sovereign, independent nation, restored again to its aboriginal, ancestral and biblical homeland, successive Israeli governments since that of Yitzhak Rabin – despite all the overwhelming and empirical evidence of implacable Arab and Muslim refusal to ever accept it as a Jewish state – plead for peace.

It is offered again and again to the Arabs, those who call themselves Palestinians, and again and again rejected by them. Yet still Israeli leaders make unheard of and suicidal offers of "land for peace."

This may seem to many observers as an aberration, an illogical and deeply naïve act in the face of so much evidence of antipathy and loathsome hatred exhibited towards the Jewish state by the Arabs who call themselves Palestinians. What nation would accept such Arab and Muslim barbarity and withstand so many Palestinian crimes against its civilian Jewish population – and still hope for peace?

What nation would continue, despite the rain of thousands of missiles launched from Hamas occupied Gaza upon Israeli women and children, to hold out the hand of peace to a people who display such cruelty and human rights abuses?

What nation, after seeing the horror in the Fogel home, would still harbor hopes of a peaceful Palestinian state living side by side with Israel? What people would still entertain the insanity of dividing up the tiny land under the fatal rubric of a "two-state-solution?"

Well, only a state whose people embraced the Passover message for millennia and of the biblical passage in Deuteronomy 19;18, "Thou shalt love thy neighbor as thyself," would remain convinced of the benefits to all, even to an Arab people who have poisoned and morally crippled themselves for over 60 years with the most abhorrent and loathsome anti-Jewish hatred.

But to give away one inch of the land is a profound rejection of the Covenant made between His people and Almighty God. It is also a strategy of national suicide.

As Passover approaches, again there are insistent reports that Hamas, the branch of the Muslim Brotherhood that occupies the Gaza Strip and ceaselessly calls for the extermination of the Jewish state, plans new atrocities against the embattled people of Israel during the Passover. Remember the words: In every generation.

An Arab terrorist who once planted a bomb in Jerusalem has now become a passionate supporter of the Jewish state. Walid Shoebat stated recently to a Jewish audience in America the following:

"Americans need to start looking at what really happens in Israel. They don't see what happens in their media. They don't see what happens to the religious places in Judea or what the world calls the West Bank. They have never seen what has happened to Joseph's tomb. They have never seen every single holy place, Jewish and Christian, in Judea desecrated by the Palestinian Muslims.

Americans need to see the reality on the ground and what happened to two Jews who got lost in the streets of Ramallah in the Palestinian Authority. If they did they would see the frenzy, the demonic frenzy of the Palestinian Arab population of Ramallah. How they tore out the human hearts, lungs and kidneys of the hapless Israeli victims. "The media in America and around the world must show the reality of how the Jews suffer and of how the Jew cannot go from his home to worship in Joseph's tomb or worship on the Temple Mount."

He also stated that the worst possible mistake Israel ever made was inviting Arafat and his terrorist cronies to end their exile in Tunisia and set up their new headquarters in Judea – Israel's biblical heartland.

This decision by the left-wing Israeli government of Yitzhak Rabin led to Arafat and his terrorist gang gaining international acceptance, the so-called Oslo Peace Accords, which in time became the Oslo War in which thousands of Israeli civilians were murdered and maimed by Palestinian terrorists and suicide bombers.

Walid Shoebat concluded that he sees the Jewish people are afraid of the Arab Goliath. But he, Shoebat, born a Muslim and now a Christian who knows full well the death sentence imposed upon him under Islamic Sharia law, is not afraid of Goliath.

Neither should Israel be afraid, for in truth it is the David, the tiny Jewish state of only 6,000,000 Jews within a tiny land no larger than New Jersey, confronting Goliath, the combined Arab and Muslim world of one and a half billion straddling an enormous land mass dwarfing America plus most of Europe.

And Israel should no longer seek to placate those Europeans and the present U.S. Administration that remorselessly calls for a "two-state- solution, which would reduce the Jewish state at its most populous region to a width of only nine miles: yes, only nine miles wide: A sure and certain recipe for self-destruction within the Middle East, arguably the most evil neighborhood on planet Earth.

So we approach the Passover festival, which brings light and blessings to all humanity but which also brings the maniacal threats of genocide against the Jewish people by those who would unleash unutterable terror and who, like the evil Mahmoud Ahmadinejad, spew hideous ravings and shameless libels against the ever suffering Jews.

A brave and highly principled British journalist, Melanie Phillips, has suggested that Israeli leaders should finally tell the European and American leadership how they are guilty of double standards, moral equivalence and a bias against Israel which is shameful in the extreme. Here are some of her words:

"Israel should be making the case against the western media, and especially the British media, that it is an accessory to mass murder. Israel is always on the back foot. Israel is always on the defensive. It is always saying, '… it is not our fault, we didn't do these terrible things. Can't you see that they are doing it?'

"What Israel should be saying is quite different. Israel should be saying, '… world, this terrible conflict is your fault because you are persisting in supporting Arab aggression and punishing its Israeli victims. While you do that the aggression will simply continue. That's not rocket science, that's human nature. If you reward the aggressor he will have every incentive to continue his aggression.

"What you should be doing, world, is saying to the Palestinian Authority, let alone Hamas, '… what is this? After six decades you still say that you will never accept Israel as a Jewish state? What is this you are saying? If there was a state of Palestine, not one single Jew could be in a state of Palestine? How do you expect us to support such a racist doctrine?

"While you are racists, while you are so anti-Jew, and while you will not accept that Israel has a right to exist as a Jewish state, I am sorry but we, as the civilized world, will have nothing to do with you nor will we continue to fund your incitement and your prejudice. When you decide to join the civilized world we will welcome you. That's what Israel should be saying to the world, but Israel doesn't."

As Caroline Glick reminded Leah Zinder in a recent IBA broadcast, Israel is not alone. There are millions of Americans – the vast majority – who support Israel and want to fight for her in the media and in the political realm against grievous pressure from the Obama Administration but are waiting for Israel to give them the reason to do so.

So these timely thoughts and questions must be urgently considered before, during and after the time of Passover for it surely is humanity's moral barometer. As the great Rabbi J.H. Hertz wrote in 1935:

"Though man cannot always even half control his destiny, God has given him the reins of his conduct altogether into his hands."

May Prime Minister Netanyahu and his government take to heart the pleas of Melanie Phillips, Walid Shoebat, and the millions of Jews who yearn for a principled and resoundingly firm response from him to the ever humiliating demands upon the Jewish state to surrender from the Obama Administration, the State Department, and all the flawed Chanceries of Europe and beyond.

And it would not go amiss to remind the increasingly Godless European Union of Passover's gift to the Jewish people: The promised and undivided land.

Oh, and by the way, for centuries Jews have uttered a prayer at the conclusion of the Passover meal. In Hebrew it is *L'Shanah HaBa'ah B'Yerushalayim*.

In English it means, "Next year may we be in Jerusalem," the 3,000 year old eternal capital of the Jewish people.

But in the beginning of the second decade of the 21st century the world, through the hateful two-state-solution, is forcing Jerusalem to again be divided by a wall of concrete and Arab hate. Those who call themselves Palestinians demand the eastern half of the city and the ancient Jewish prayer at Passover may become a bitter and tragic joke.

Worshipers will be forced into saying, "Next year in West Jerusalem."

A Bit of History Never Goes Amiss

April 12, 2011

President Obama's lugubrious policy of denigrating America whenever he visits developing Third World countries includes craven, mournful apologies for perceived past American sins to some of the world's worst thugocracies. British Prime Minister, David Cameron, alas, appears to be sinking to the same level in apologizing for alleged British sins.

The Prime Minister was recently in Pakistan - that Muslim nation that has just seen U.N. officials beheaded and scores of people murdered by frenzied Muslim mobs upset at the burning of a Koran by an American Christian pastor.

Of course, burning the Jewish Torah (first five books of the Bible), Bhagavad-Gita, (Hindu Gospels), Tripitaka (Buddhist holy book) and the Bible itself would never engender beheadings or murders: such horrors are left to the followers of Islam. But David Cameron has some problems with history, it seems.

His words imply that Britain is responsible for all the ills between India and Pakistan - stating that Britain's, "imperial legacy was to blame for the current conflicts in many parts of the world's trouble spots."

He continued, "As with so many of the world's problems, we are responsible for the issue in the first place."

According to Nile Gardiner, Mr. Cameron, while on a trip to Washington last July, 2010, also described Britain as the "junior partner" to America in fighting the Germans in 1940. Are we to understand that Prime Minister Cameron does not know that Britain fought alone once war was declared on September 3, 1939 and that the US did not enter the war until December 7, 1941, and then only because the Japanese attacked Pearl Harbor?

Again, according to Nile Gardiner, writing in the London Daily Telegraph on April 5, 2011, Cameron's predecessor, Gordon Brown, had responded to an earlier attack on Britain by Thabo Mbeki, then South Africa's president, by declaring that, "… the days of Britain having to apologize for its colonial history are over," and that, "we should celebrate much of our past, rather than apologize for it".

Sir Charles James Napier (1782-1853)

With thanks to Mark Steyn, I am reminded of the words spoken by British General Napier who, in a much earlier time, was faced with a problem confronting British control in India. The problem was the Hindu practice of "suttee" - the grisly tradition of burning widows on the funeral pyres of their husbands.

Gen. Sir Charles Napier was impeccably multicultural, but in a far more positive manner than multiculturalism is practiced today. The general told his Indian interlocutors: "You say that it is your custom to burn widows. Very well! We also have a custom. When men burn a woman alive, we tie a rope around their necks,

and we hang them. Build your funeral pyre. Beside it, my carpenters will build a gallows. You may follow your custom. And then we will follow ours."
India doesn't have suttee any more.

Britain undoubtedly brought enlightenment to much of the world, stamping out endemic horrors such as suttee and creating stable governance and a civil service admired and emulated by native peoples throughout the Empire. But not everything turned out the way it was originally meant to be.

Sometimes, the British civil service operating around the world fell short of its mission because of the prejudices of individual officers and civil servants. Yes, there were abuses of power by minor and senior officials and sometimes they were confronted by brave individuals who succeeded or failed in correcting those abuses.

At the height of Great Britain's Empire, when almost three quarters of the world was governed by Britain, an Austrian Jew by the name of Theodor Herzl was deeply affected by the anti-Semitism he found in otherwise enlightened France.

Albert Dreyfus.

As a journalist for an Austrian paper, Herzl had attended the infamous Dreyfus Trial, which put a Jewish captain in the French Army in the dock charged with high treason. This was a nakedly anti-Semitic falsehood perpetrated by the Army High Command looking for a scapegoat for French military disasters. It initially resulted in Dreyfus being sent to the horrendous penal colony on Devil's Island.

Dreyfus was eventually found not guilty after a campaign by the great French writer, Emile Zola, who in 1898 wrote a letter titled "*J'Accuse*," published in the French newspaper *L'Aurore*.

In his letter Zola listed military personnel and eight politicians (including the President of the Republic) whom he held responsible for the scapegoating, anti-Semitic conviction of Captain Dreyfus three years earlier.

Herzl witnessed the ugly outbursts of anti-Jewish bigotry among the French citizenry, which led him to realize that Jews would forever be victimized and persecuted unless and until they redeemed their ancient Jewish homeland – then under a nearly 400 year old occupation by the Turkish Ottoman Empire.

Seeing there was no escaping the hatred that never dies, he determined to work for the restoration of the ancient and ancestral biblical Jewish homeland in the neglected and impoverished Turkish backwater, which stretched eastwards from the Mediterranean Sea.

He spoke with the world's leaders often with words that thundered with terrible conviction and shattering truths. He did so with the earnestness and fatal speed of those who are to die young. And, indeed, he wore himself out for his heart gave way at an early age. But his message gave hope to a long suffering and stateless people who had lived for nearly 2,000 years dreaming of their final return and redemption in the native land of their biblical and post- biblical ancestors.

Theodor Herzl loved Britain, and in 1900 wrote these words: "England, great England, whose gaze sweeps over all the seas - free England - will understand and sympathize with the aims and aspirations of Zionism."

And so it was that on November 2, 1917, Jewish hopes for a restored and independent homeland were raised by the British Foreign Minister, Lord Balfour, in what became known as the Balfour Declaration.

Great Britain conquered all of Ottoman occupied territory including the geographical territory known as Palestine. After the First World War, the League of Nations gave Britain control of the Holy Land with a mandate to effect Jewish self-government and a national homeland within it. But shortly after Britain obtained the Mandate, she tore away all of the land east of the River Jordan in 1921/22 and gave it to the Arab Hashemite tribe; thus denying Jewish rights in four fifths of the territory.

This was a first White Paper issued by the British Government and dealt a grievous blow to Jewish aspirations and hopes within the Mandatory territory. It also could be characterized as the first "Two State Solution."

Under Colonial Secretary, Winston Churchill, Mandatory Palestine was partitioned and all the territory east of the River Jordan was given away to Emir Abdullah Ibn al-Husseini, who had earlier been driven out of Mecca by the rival Saud family. Abdullah had no historical ties to Mandatory Palestine but nevertheless received nearly 80% of the Mandate. In 1925, Britain further increased the size of his territory.

That country, which sits on nearly 80% of original Mandated Palestine, is the present Kingdom of Jordan and from its artificial inception, Jews were barred from living in it; an early version of Apartheid, Arab style. Jordan consists of an Arab population made up of 25% Hashemite and 75% Palestinian.

In reality, Jordan is Palestine. And interestingly today, the Palestinian leadership in the so-called Palestinian Authority allows no Jew to reside in that territory and will permit no Jewish villages or populations to exist in any future Palestinian state: Again racism and apartheid Arab style.

Meanwhile Hamas in Gaza calls for the extermination of all Jews in Israel. The world, especially the European Union, remains deafeningly silent at such blatant racism and genocidal threats.

Most Arab leaders in the early years of the 20th century acknowledged that they had no historical claims upon the Land of Israel. The area had never been home to an independent Arab state called "Palestine," and even when it had come under the control of the invading Muslim Arab hordes sweeping out of Arabia in the seventh century, it had always remained an unimportant backwater. Since 1517 the land had been occupied by the non-Arab Ottoman Muslim Turks.

In 1936, the British Peel Commission stated clearly that "if the Arabs were given independence in the enormous territories of the Middle East, they would willingly give, "little Palestine," to the Jews."

But "Little Palestine" was now very little, reduced to just one fifth of the original Mandate - the tiny territory remaining between the Mediterranean Sea and the River Jordan - a mere 40 miles at its widest; smaller in size than New Jersey.

It would be instructive for readers to purchase or obtain from their local libraries the remarkably clear and graphic books published by Sir Martin Gilbert, the official biographer of Sir Winston Churchill and Fellow at Merton College, Oxford. The two books are "The Arab-Israel Conflict, Its History in Maps," and the "Jewish History Atlas."

From 1917 to 1922, different suggestions had been offered for the boundaries of the geographical entity known as Palestine and, after 1922, what was left of it west of the Jordan River.

During the 1920s and 1930s, the Arabs rioted against the British Mandatory Authorities and, in the ensuing violence, many Jews were murdered. In 1929, scores of Jews were murdered in Hebron by their Muslim neighbors.

Hebron is Judaism's second most holy city, the other three being Tiberias, Safed, and the jewel in the crown, Jerusalem. Remember, there were no so-called occupied territories then - Israel was not re-born until 1948 - yet Muslim Arabs were busy slaughtering Jews; just as they are today.

In 1936, an organized Arab campaign broke out and armed Arabs inflicted heavy casualties on British forces. In addition, eighty Jews, mostly civilians, had been killed by the time the Arabs called off their "intifada" on October 12, 1936.
Britain, as always, tried to appease the Arabs by appointing a Royal Commission to look into the Mandate.

The Peel Commission recommended a Jewish state and an Arab state with a British controlled corridor from Jaffa to Jerusalem. The Jews reluctantly accepted; the Arabs totally rejected.

In 1937 more Arab rioting took place with yet more Jewish and British casualties. Many of the Arabs who sought peace and coexistence were murdered by their fellow Arabs because they were considered "collaborators." This same murderous activity continues in today's Palestinian Authority and in Hamas occupied Gaza.

The Second World War broke out on September 3, 1939 and Britain, more than ever, needed the oil from the Arab Middle East to survive. Again, it chose to appease the Arabs and in 1940 began restricting Jewish land purchases even though the barren land was often worthless and been neglected for centuries.

Before that, the infamous 1939 British Government's White Paper drastically limited Jewish immigration into Palestine for the next five years, just as the Jews in Europe were falling into the genocidal clutches of Nazi Germany. That was not Britain's finest hour.

Dr. Chaim Weizmann (1874 – 1952).

Chaim Weizmann, who had received from Lord Balfour the earlier declaration in 1917 of a Jewish homeland in geographical Palestine, was distressed beyond measure. He wrote the following about the 1939 White Paper:

"On the basis of a pledge, a pledge confirmed by fifty nations, we have been building our National Home. An international obligation undertaken before the whole civilized world cannot be unilaterally destroyed, least of all by a nation like Great Britain which has always striven, and still strives to maintain respect for law, for treaties and for moral principles in international relations."

Perhaps Weizmann, who became Israel's first president, was too trusting and naïve.

The excellent writer and blogger of RuthfullyYours.com, Ruth King, wrote recently about British worthies during the early 1940's:

"Unlike present day Great Britain, where legislators from both parties vie for the title of most hostile to Israel, there were noble dissenters in Great Britain."

She continued: "On 10 March, 1942, in the House of Lords, Welsh peer (and former Liberal MP) Baron Davies, made a stirring speech criticizing Britain's systematic appeasement of the Arabs of Palestine. In summing up his distaste at what British policy had been and was towards the beleaguered Jews he pointed out how counterproductive British actions had been to the war effort against Nazi Germany. Now, of course, all these Jews who could have been mobilized at that time in what is now enemy-occupied Europe have become, in effect, slaves of Hitler, and they are entirely lost to us."

Perhaps the good Baron dimly knew that, in fact, the Jews were lost for Germans were at the time systematically exterminating one Jewish community after another. He concluded his speech by excoriating the deliberate censorship of the many contributions of Palestinian Jewish fighters to the Allied cause by adding:

"The whole thing has a Nazi smell about it, and I cannot help feeling that it does show the extraordinary way in which our Administration carries on affairs in Palestine."

Britain's relentless appeasement of the Arabs led to a veritable death sentence for millions of Jews. The White Paper, as Ruth King reminds us, "limited immigration to only 75,000 Jews over a period of five years." Ironically and tragically, this was approximately the period that the Holocaust raged until Germany was finally defeated.

Haj Amin el-Husseini collaborated with the Nazis and assisted Eichmann.

Another irony was that appeasing the Arabs failed miserably in gaining their support against Hitler. Indeed, in the Balkans, Muslim SS Units rounded up Jews and Serbs and dispatched them to their deaths in German and Croatian death camps. Many of these Muslim SS squads were formed by the Mufti of Jerusalem, Haj Amin el-Husseini, who lived in Hitler's bunker and plotted the planned extermination of the Jewish community in Mandatory Palestine.

Meanwhile, Palestinian Jews and general Jewish enlistment in the British armed forces provided enormous contributions to the war effort. In particular the Jewish Palestine Brigade fought bravely in Italy against German front line forces and saved many Jewish refugees. (See *The Brigade*, by Howard Blum).

In 1947, after one third of world Jewry had been wiped out, most unable to flee to safety in Palestine because the doors had been shut against them by the British Mandatory government, the United Nations voted to divide the land. This was a further division of the already truncated territory after the original first partition in 1922. The UN voted for a Jewish state and an Arab state. Again, the Jews reluctantly accepted; the Arabs rejected.

The immediate response to the U.N. Partition Plan was the outbreak of yet more Arab aggression throughout Mandatory Palestine. The British still were responsible for law and order but behaved in ambivalent ways. Some police and soldiers even sided with the Arabs against the Jews by handing over to them British forts.

Fast forward to the present and we now live in a time when enemies are embraced and friends and allies are abandoned. President Obama spends his term in office doing exactly that. David Cameron has, in part, followed. Here again are his distressing words to Pakistan: "As with so many of the world's problems, we are responsible for the issue in the first place."

But David Cameron will never say to Israel what he said to Muslim Pakistan. The Muslim world is too important to the Arabist grandees of the Foreign Office with their inherent brand of genteel anti-Jewish and anti-Israel prejudice. Economics, alas, trumps morality and members of the Royal Family frequently are sent on state visits to various Arab emirates and sheikhdoms but never to Israel. After all, the Arabs would get upset and lucrative trade might suffer.

Meanwhile Israel is under intense pressure by a murky constellation of Arab, Muslim and primarily leftwing pro-Arab organizations. The object is to de-legitimize the Jewish state by boycotts and through patently false charges of apartheid.

The UN remains an immoral sinkhole and spends its time courting rogue regimes around the world while heaping one calumny after another upon the besieged Jewish state.

Unbearable international pressure is mounting to force Israel into giving to the ever hostile and genocidal Arabs, those who call themselves Palestinians, the entire "West Bank," which is biblical and ancestral Jewish Judea and Samaria, and again reduce the width of Israel at its most heavily populated region to a mere nine miles.

Yes, only nine miles wide!

President Bush, when Governor of Texas, remarked to Ariel Sharon as they flew over the narrow territory in a helicopter, "… why, in Texas we have driveways longer than that."

It is clear that Israel must retain as much of her ancestral land as possible, whether it be in Judea, Samaria, or the Golan Heights otherwise Israel will have insufficient strategic depth to absorb future Arab aggression. Gaza was already given away to the Palestinians in 2005 in return for hoped for peace. Now Israel instead endures thousands of Hamas missiles aimed at its civilian cities, towns and villages.

The suicidal Two-State-Solution, which repeatedly rises from the grave like some Hammer Films vampire movie, is for Israel another Final Solution (the evil euphemism for the Holocaust). Its implementation drives a stake into the heart of Judaism's very spiritual and historical link to the re-constituted Jewish state, to Jewish history, and to its undeniable biblical patrimony in Judea and Samaria.

With the Islamic Republic of Iran and its Islamist allies, Hamas and Hezbollah, encircling Israel; with Egypt fast becoming the Islamic Republic of Egypt, soon to scrap its peace treaty with Israel; the Jewish state most certainly cannot survive in the pre-1967 boundaries that Israel's earlier Foreign Minister, Abba Eban, once described as the "Auschwitz borders."

But it remains inconceivable that Britain today will ever make a profound and moral statement of support for Israel. The principled speeches and unambiguous support given in the past by the likes of Baron Davies, Lord Wedgewood and others are sadly a thing of the past. They would be howled down in a Parliament whose members, with few exceptions, now bend the knee to the unholy trinity of multiculturalism, political correctness and diversity.

And yet Britain itself is a land under siege by millions of Muslims who have come to its shores not to be proud and productive British citizens but to be the advance guard of Islamic Sharia law and Islamic triumphalism. David Cameron, please note.

May 7, 2011

Mahmoud Abbas: A Wolf in Sheep's Clothing

Current PA Chairman Mahmoud Abbas was a trusted member of Yassir Arafat's inner circle responsible for developing Fatah's networks and raising funds for PLO operations at the time, including the Munich Massacre in 1972.

So Osama bin Laden has been killed by the American military. His friend and second in command, Al-Zawahiri, will most probably now assume the mantle of bin-Laden. Al Qaeda has been hurt but the war will go on and innocents will continue to suffer and die. No doubt, millions of Muslims will consider Osama bin Laden as a "holy" martyr and believe he is now enjoying the first of the 72 virgins in paradise.

But there are other terrorists whose body counts even surpass bin-Laden's. Israel endures the criminal hatred of the two wings of the Palestinian Arab terror organization. These terror bosses include first Mahmoud Abbas of the Fatah wing of the so-called Palestinian Authority.

Fatah occupies parts of Jewish biblical Judea and Samaria, aka the West Bank, given to the Arabs who call themselves Palestinians under the fatally misnamed Oslo *Peace* Accords. They mourn bin-Laden's death and vow revenge.

Ismail Haniyeh's Hamas occupies the Gaza Strip, given idiotically to the Arabs by the ex-Israeli premier, Ariel Sharon, who thought that by being nice to the Arabs it would end their aggression.

A case, if ever there was one, of nonsense piled upon foolishness. Hamas also mourns bin-Laden's death and they too predictably vow revenge.

Both wings of the Palestinian Arab terror organization are in the process of reaching a rapport between them. Both have joined together, no doubt to present in September 2011 to that oh so immoral organization, the U.N, a joint request for world acceptance of a Muslim Arab rogue state to be called Palestine.

What is overlooked is that this state would be carved out of Judea and Samaria, the so-called West Bank, thus forcing Israel back into a nine mile wide border (the earlier described Auschwitz border) at its most populous region.

This armistice line existed from 1948 until June 5, 1967 when, faced with looming genocide, Israel was forced to fight against Syrian, Jordanian and Egyptian criminal aggression during the Six Day War.

What is also overlooked is that Hamas and Fatah demand that all Jews be ethnically cleansed from, and driven out of, their Jewish towns and villages within Judea and Samaria. In other words, Apartheid: Arab style.

Israel has targeted lesser Arab terrorists for their crimes in the past and it remains to be seen if she follows America's example and eventually is forced to eliminate Haniyeh and Abbas. But I don't think so. Ever worried about what the hostile world will think of them, especially the American president, Israeli leaders are fearful and paralyzed.

So it is more than likely that Abbas, for instance, will continue to be sanitized by the world and Israel will refrain from eliminating this Arab Muslim terrorist. Meanwhile Haniyeh will be courted by the groveling Europeans and others as merely a politician.

But let us in particular look at what this Mahmoud Abbas is all about; the same terrorist the world considers a moderate, whatever that word means. For a start, how many of you would ever shake hands with a Holocaust denier or give your money to one? If you answered no to both question then why would you support Mahmoud Abbas whose terror *nom de guerre* is Abu Mazen?

In 1983, Abbas wrote a dissertation for his doctorate degree at a university in the Soviet Union. Remember, the Soviet Union supported the PLO and provided it with lavish funds and diplomatic support.

His hate filled topic was: *"The secret relations between Nazism and the leadership of the Zionist movement."* A translation was provided by the Simon Wiesenthal Center and some of the main claims are as follows:

Abbas claimed that Jews artificially raised the number of Holocaust victims in order to gain world sympathy. He even parroted the denial loonies who suggested that the number of Jews murdered by the Germans was less than 100,000. He ridiculed the fact that six million Jews were murdered or that a war of extermination was aimed primarily at the Jews, claiming that no one can either confirm or deny this figure.

Despite the overwhelming documentary evidence that six million Jews were indeed systematically targeted and murdered by the German Nazi regime, Mahmoud Abbas chose to echo the mendacious words of the malevolent denial industry, thus consigning six million Jewish ghosts to suffer yet again and the remaining survivors to unbearable agony.

Yet Abbas is the darling of the U.S. State Department, as well as not a few in the administration of President Obama and the president himself. Israeli Prime Ministers, at least in the recent past, were seemingly quite prepared to shake the hand of Abbas and trust him as a viable "peace partner." They had even made the same colossal error with Yasser Arafat.

That Mahmoud Abbas still demonizes the Zionist movement, refuses to accept Israel as a Jewish state, is a Holocaust denier and is quite happy to accept that the figure of Jewish victims of the Holocaust could be below one million, did not even seem to outrage past Israeli Prime Ministers.

It is, perhaps, a sad indication of how low the level of moral outrage had sunk. Hopefully, Binyamin Netanyahu, Israel's current Prime Minister has now had his eyes opened wide. But that remains to be seen and his upcoming address to Congress will be the proverbial acid test. But let's also look at the immense con-trick Abbas continues to play on the European Union, the United Nations, the Quartet, the U.S. Administration and successive Israeli leaders.

According to Yoram Ettinger, the highly respected Israeli commentator with the Second Thoughts Educational Foundation, who was talking recently with Frank Gaffney on Secure Freedom Radio, Mahmoud Abbas, aka Abu Mazen, is a serial terrorist whose roots are in the Muslim Brotherhood and who was part of the inner circle of Yasser Arafat.

Ettinger reminds us that Abbas was expelled from Egypt in the 1950s for subversion. He was expelled from Syria in 1966 for subversion. He was expelled from Jordan in 1970 for subversion. He was part of the Arafat leadership which caused havoc in Lebanon and he and Arafat were expelled in 1980 from Lebanon. Sadly, the U.S. provided him and his terror cronies with safe passage to Tunis: Another error, which led to thousands more deaths and misery.

Abbas was part and parcel of the betrayal by the PLO of Kuwait in 1990 when the Palestinian terror machine spearheaded the Iraqi invasion of Kuwait. Most recently, he is the one who instituted hate education inside the Palestinian Authority schools and mosques and state controlled media: This inevitably led to such atrocities as that committed by Palestinian youths who recently slit the throats of an Israeli family including a toddler and a three month baby girl.

In answer to Frank Gaffney, who referred to suggestions by certain media talking heads that Haniyeh joining with Abbas would moderate Hamas, Ettinger replied that it would be similar to the equally absurd assumption that the Boston Strangler's association with Jack the Ripper would moderate the Ripper.

Let us again remember that while under his control as President of the Palestinian Authority, the Gaza territory was handed over to Mahmoud Abbas by Prime Minister Ariel Sharon in the "disengagement" plan.

In addition, James Wolfensohn urged wealthy liberal Jewish Americans to purchase at great cost the existing Israeli green houses and gift them to the Palestinian Arabs to help them create an independent economy. Instead, Abbas allowed mobs of Arabs to destroy the once highly productive greenhouses and permitted the police to simply stand by and watch. None of the Arabs were punished. This took place while under the watch of Mahmoud Abbas.

While Abbas controlled all aspects of the PA, millions of charity dollars were siphoned off into Swiss bank accounts or to Palestinian suicide bombers. None, or very little, of the cash ever reached the ordinary civilian population in order to improve their lives. The U.S. and EU donors simply turned a blind eye to Abbas's connivance with this corruption on a grand scale.

Hamas, now occupying the Gaza Strip (aka Hamastan), strikes at Israel from the south, in the same way that Hezbollah strikes the Jewish state from the north.

Like Hezbollah, Hamas has amassed huge numbers of missiles from the Iranian mullahs and since the "disengagement" and the relinquishment by Israel of the Philadelphi corridor (urged upon Israel by Condoleezza Rice) vast quantities of Iranian lethal weapons have been smuggled into Gaza from Egypt.

In February, 2011, I urged the Israeli government in an article titled - *Take Back the Philadelphi Corridor* - to restore the vital and strategic Philadelphi Corridor to Israeli control as it was clear that the Mubarak regime was about to topple and that inevitably a Muslim Brotherhood regime would take over Egypt. But the Israelis did nothing, presumably out of fear of upsetting the U.S. president.

It was also obvious to all who had eyes to see and ears to hear that Egypt would eventually tear up the peace treaty with Israel and that sooner or later the border between Egypt and the Gaza Strip at Rafah, (where the Philadelphi Corridor exists) would be opened wide and an even vaster flow of lethal weapons would freely enter Gaza from an Islamist Egypt. This flow has now begun.

Much of Judea and Samaria (the West Bank) is now Fatahland and presided over by Mahmoud Abbas. Meanwhile CIA training of Palestinians continues under U.S. General Dayton and yet more "aid packages" are being sent to Abbas and his Fatah party. A Palestinian policeman recently murdered a Jewish worshipper at the biblical Joseph's tomb in Nablus. This was one of General Dayton's trainees: A scandal that continues to exist.

The American taxpayer is being forced to hand over millions of dollars to Abbas and his "security apparatus." According to Patrick Deveny, *"Training our enemies,"* in a report as far back as October 18, 2005, many of the Palestinians trained in various U.S. military installations simply joined the terrorist organizations, such as Hamas, Islamic Jihad, and Fatah itself, and committed atrocities against Israeli civilians. Abbas has simply shrugged.

It would seem that the farcical policy of endlessly throwing money at Mahmoud Abbas and holding him up as the great hope for a true and lasting peace by the Palestinian Arabs with Israel is going to continue, notwithstanding his history of corruption, ineffectiveness, mendacity, Holocaust denial, introducing hate education in schools, and now his sickening embrace of Hamas.

Will Israel, the US and the world ever learn, and will the sanitized Abbas and Haniyeh ever meet the same just fate as Osama bin Laden?

Though Abbas, Haniyeh and Maashal are Arab terrorists, like bin-Laden, they are called Palestinians and the immoral and hypocritical world treats them differently.

With fact and fiction swirling around the life and death of OBL, it is perhaps useful to keep the spotlight on these other terrorists whose ultimate goal is genocide against a member state of the United Nations.

Their followers murder Jews but most of the world has little or no interest in Jewish victims, especially no interest at all in the survival of the besieged and embattled Jewish state.

May 22, 2011

Obama's Call for Israel to Self-Destruct

President Obama demands that Israel withdraw to armistice lines that existed after the Arab-Israel War of 1948 ended. These lines did not constitute a border but merely the military positions that existed after the Arab attempt to annihilate Israel failed.

In six days in June, 1967, Israel was forced to fight another war for its survival against a new aggression by Egypt, Syria and Jordan. All three Arab countries lost territory as a direct result of their new genocidal war against the Jewish state failed again.

As a consequence, Israel threw back the Syrian army from its positions on the Golan Heights; the strategic high ground from which Syria had bombarded and shelled Israeli farmers in the Hula Valley below and Israeli fishermen on the Sea of Galilee.

Egypt lost the Sinai Peninsula and Israeli forces dug in on the eastern bank of the Suez Canal and developed the Abu Rodeis oil field. All the territory and the oil fields were given away to Egypt in return for a piece of paper; a peace treaty which now is at the point of being torn up by a likely new Egyptian government under the influence of the Muslim Brotherhood.

Jordan, which had nineteen years earlier invaded and occupied the territory they subsequently called the West Bank and divided the city of Jerusalem in half, were also thrown back after launching an all-out attack upon Israel.

As a result, the ancestral and biblical Jewish heartland of Judea and Samaria was liberated from Jordanian Arab occupation. At the same time, Jews were able to pray again at their ancient holy places and synagogues in Jerusalem, which had been desecrated by the Muslim Arabs. Jerusalem, under Israel's governance was now for the first time open freely to members of all religions to worship; something the Jordanians had forbidden.

It was immediately after the June 1967 Six Day War that a secret memorandum was issued by the United States Joint Chiefs of Staff (JCS).

Their conclusions were that any peace settlement between Israel and the Arab belligerents would only succeed if Israel retained certain territories vital for its continued existence and survival. These facts have now been deliberately abandoned by the Obama regime after Barack Hussein Obama's outrageous speech demanding that Israel be forced back to the pre-1967 indefensible lines that always constituted an invitation for Arab military invasion.

The areas the Joint Chiefs declared as the minimum defensible borders for the Jewish state included the Golan Heights, the western half of Samaria (the northwestern part of the West Bank), all of Judea (the southern part of the West Bank), the Gaza Strip and several portions of the eastern Sinai Peninsula.

This, of course, occurred before the world became obsessed with the creation of an Arab terror state to be carved out of the narrow territory between the Mediterranean and the River Jordan - a territory some 40 miles wide.

Since that report in 1967, the Begin government gave away all of the Sinai to Egypt. Under Prime Minister Ariel Sharon and his deputy, Ehud Olmert, Israel gave away the entire Gaza Strip in 2005, with catastrophic consequences for the Jewish state. Hamas, the Palestinian branch of the Muslim Brotherhood, now occupies Gaza and has launched to date some 12,000 Iranian supplied missiles at Israeli villages and towns.

Ehud Barak, Israel's present Defense Minister, had years earlier forced the Israeli Defense Forces (IDF) to withdraw from the southern Lebanon security strip, thus allowing the Islamist Hezbollah to fill the vacuum with dire consequences for northern Israel.

A conflict broke out - the Second Lebanon War - disastrously mismanaged by Prime Minister Ehud Olmert. It was launched too late and ended too soon. Now Hezbollah sits in the Lebanese government and its militia is armed with over 40,000 Iranian supplied lethal missiles aimed at every part of the Jewish state.

After Israel endured over 10,000 incoming missiles from Hamas-occupied Gaza, a war was finally launched by Israel. It too began too late and ended too soon. Now the Islamist Hamas has just joined the so-called Palestinian Authority and both terror groups pursue their ultimate ambition to weaken Israel by making its borders ever more indefensible, and by finally destroying what is left of the embattled Jewish state.

Israel is now under the greatest pressure ever from a problematic American administration and pro-Muslim and pro-Marxist murky president to give away the ancestral Jewish heartland of Judea and Samaria. President Barack Obama is perceived by many to be a clear and present danger to the very survival of the reconstituted Jewish state.

But in the aftermath of the Six Day War, the US Joint Chiefs were not interested in Jewish patrimony or Biblical history. They were solely concerned with the strategic necessities for Israel's survival in a very bad neighborhood: A neighborhood now vastly more bloodthirsty and violent than ever before. That is why the Joint Chiefs set out what the bare minimum retention of territory for Israel should be.

Col. Irving Kett (USA, ret.) prepared an Army War College study on Israel's security needs in 1974. His study was called, *"A Proposed Solution to the Arab-Israel Conflict"*. In it, he strongly suggested that, from a military point of view, Israel's borders should be constituted to make it a compact state with natural boundaries on all sides - the Jordan River to the east, Golan Heights to the northeast, the Litani River in the north, the Mediterranean Sea to the west and the historic boundary with the Sinai Peninsula to the south.

As a direct result and consequence of Arab aggression, most of those borders had been attained by Israel at one time or another but then were given away under pressure from respective U.S. Administrations who urged Israel to "take risks for peace." Note that it was always Israel that took the risks; never the surrounding Arab states.

Another memorandum had been produced earlier, on June 29, 1967, for Secretary of Defense Robert McNamara by General Earle Wheeler, chairman of the JCS, at the direction of President Lyndon Johnson.

That study was declassified in 1983 and, as mentioned earlier, it recommended that Israel keep all of Judea, the western half of Samaria, the Golan Heights, the Gaza Strip and two significant parts of east and south Sinai. The similarity between the memoranda was striking.

Colonel Kett pointed out what the IDF has always known, but what too many Israeli politicians preferred to ignore; namely, that there is a vital strategic value in the mountain range which forms the spine running through Judea and Samaria.

The highlands run some 54 miles from Jenin in the north to Hebron in the south and dominate Israel's coastline. The spine is 12 miles wide and Israel simply cannot afford to vacate it, but Obama has decided it must.

It was assumed for years by both the Israeli military and politicians that if a Palestinian Arab state came into existence it would have to permit an Israeli defense line on the Jordan River (the Allon Plan), and that such a state would have to be demilitarized.

The answer, of course, would be to have made permanent at the time the suggested boundaries proposed in both Kett's memorandum and the earlier JCS report of some 40 years ago. But events have moved on since then. The Palestinian Authority in the West Bank would never agree to this and Hamas in Gaza would scornfully dismiss it out of hand. So would Obama.

The Muslim Arabs have become even more vicious in their anti-Jewish and anti-Christian rhetoric and behavior, and a jihadist Iran has all but encircled the Jewish state through its Islamist proxies in Gaza and Lebanon. There is now no chance that a Palestinian Arab state would ever be de-militarized.

The Arab-Israel conflict is not, and never has been, merely a war over territory. It is, and always has been, a religious war. Islam will never accept a non-Muslim state, whatever size or shape it may be, within lands previously conquered by Muslims in the name of Allah. This is a paramount and fundamental fact, which strangely is never understood.

Look at what the Muslims have done to once primarily Christian Lebanon and what fate awaits the Christian Copts in an increasingly Muslim Brotherhood Egypt. That is why "land for peace" is nonsense. Tiny Israel can give precious land away but it will never receive peace from the Muslim Arab world.

Thus the "two-state solution," so beloved of President Obama and President George Bush before him, requires the biblical Jewish heartland of Judea and Samaria (so-called West Bank) to be given away to the Arabs who call themselves Palestinians.

But these Arabs have no intention of making peace, which should be enough for any Israeli government and Prime Minister with intestinal fortitude to defy the world's pressure for the Jewish state to slowly and surely disappear.

After all, Prime Ministers David Ben-Gurion, Menachem Begin and Yitzchak

Shamir, in part, all said "no" to such international pressure in the past and prevailed.

Interestingly, Colonel Kett had also suggested that the Palestinian Arabs be resettled in a state in the Sinai. The other famous suggestion is that Jordan is Palestine, which is based upon the historical fact of the first "two-state solution" enacted in infamy by Great Britain in 1922.

I wrote an article over two years ago, which dealt with this British betrayal that had taken place some 90 years ago. At that time it was 87 years ago but, of course it is now some 90 years ago.

Even President George W. Bush, when visiting Israel as Governor of Texas, was moved to utter: "The whole of Israel is only about six times the size of the King Ranch near Corpus Christie."

He also was shown where the hideously narrow nine mile wide Israeli armistice lines had existed before the Six Day War and quipped, "... why in Texas we have driveways longer than that: "Yet even he, after becoming president, called, in his second term, for a "two-state solution" west of the Jordan River.

Pushing Israel back to the "Auschwitz lines", as Abba Eban, Israel's early UN delegate and former Foreign Minister had called them, where the Jewish state is only nine miles wide at its most populous region, is what the "Two-State Solution" is all about.

This is what Barack Hussein Obama now demands of Israel. That other dread euphemism employed by the Nazis, "The Final Solution," was code for the Holocaust, and now comes chillingly to mind.

Hopefully Benjamin Netanyahu, in stressing the territorial insanity and existential danger to Israel's survival from Obama's demands, will not falter but remain steadfast in his refusal to be brow beaten into becoming an Israeli Prime Minister forced to preside over Israel's national suicide.

Hopefully he will also remind President Obama that such imperious demands from the White House and the State Department are not the way for the United States to act towards its most loyal ally.

May 27, 2011

Trust in the Lord but keep your Powder Dry

America from sea to shining sea is some 3,000 miles wide. Israel, if President Barack Hussein Obama has his way, will be a mere 9 miles wide. Obama has uttered ill-advised words and added to the confusion that many in the West suffer from when considering the Arab-Israel conflict in general, and the Israel-Palestinian conflict in particular.

In this, they make a justified error because millions of words have been written about the conflict, untold numbers of articles and books published, and a mainstream media that gives any and all incidents front page news. It's no wonder that the uninformed masses consider the topic inexplicable and are reduced to utter confusion. But the reality is that it is quite simple to explain.

This is not a conflict over territory, despite all that you read and hear. It is a conflict between civilizations. It is rooted in the Muslim call for jihad against all infidels and for triumphant Islam to rule over the entire world.

Remember when the Muslim shrieks the Arab and Muslim war cry, *Allahu Akbar*, it is not "God is Great; it is 'Allah is Greater." That is Islamic triumphalism in a nutshell.

Whatever so-called peace agreements are made between a Muslim and non-Muslim state, the fundamental reality for both Christians, Jews, Hindus, Buddhists, and all other beliefs, is that Islam will never accept a non-Muslim state in territory conquered by Muslims in the name of Allah.

Thus, for instance, there will never be a true and lasting peace with Israel agreed to by any Muslim state or entity – especially by those Arabs who call themselves Palestinians.

At best, and according to Islamic passages in the Koran and the Hadith, which all Muslims must obey, there can only ever be a truce, a *Hudna*, agreed to by Muslims with those whom they disparagingly call, infidels.

In the case of the Muslim Arab neighbors of Israel, especially Palestinian Arabs, they will wait until they perceive that the Jewish state is weak and vulnerable. At that time, peace treaty document notwithstanding, and according to the precedent set by Muhammad himself, they will tear up the worthless piece of paper and attack with the intention of an all-out war of genocide.

The Arabs have done this repeatedly against Israel since their war to destroy the re-born State of Israel in 1948. This Arab aggression caused all the misery that has enveloped that part of the world for decades and created both the Arab and Jewish refugee problems.

The stark and moral difference in what became an exchange of populations was that all 850,000 Jews who were driven out of their homes throughout the Arab world primarily found refuge in Israel where they were absorbed and cared for.
The Arabs, a smaller number, needlessly fled their homes at the urgings of the corrupt Arab League. They were unable to return because their leaders, who had promised them a "massacre of Jews like the Crusades," failed to defeat the 650,000 Jewish men, women and children living in Israel at the time.

The Arab League then forced these Arabs to live in squalid camps to be used until today as a propaganda tool against Israel. They have virtually imprisoned these people for over sixty years and indoctrinated them with vile anti-Jewish hatred.

All this has been perpetrated with the connivance of a singular United Nations organization called the United Nations Works and Relief Agency (UNWRA). This Arab outrage, aided and abetted by the immoral snake pit that is the United Nations, should be seen as primarily an Arab crime against humanity.

Arab aggression (long before there was any so-called Israeli occupation) led to the 1956 war forced upon Israel by relentless terror attacks from Gaza and from Jordan. It inevitably led to the June, 1967 Six Day War; the 1973 Yom Kippur War; the War of Attrition; the First and Second Lebanon Wars and the two wars against Hamas after relentless Muslim terror attacks upon Israel from Gaza.

And all the while, in between these Arab wars of attempted genocide against the Israeli people, came daily terror against Israeli civilians by the Arabs who call themselves Palestinians.

Despite what liberal and leftwing commenters in the mainstream media endlessly spew, Islam does not mean peace. It means submission; submission to the will of Allah and not, as in our democracy, submission to the will of the people.

Thus, all talk by misguided Israeli, U.S. and western politicians about promoting the "peace process" or, if you like, *"peace in our time"* is as illusory as a mirage in the desert. I wish it were not so.

We live in an era where euphemisms beguile uninformed people. We saw in World War 2 that the German Nazi leadership cloaked the Holocaust under that charnel house euphemism, the "Final Solution," which brought the horrors of Auschwitz.

Today we have two other euphemisms, which are heard repeatedly in relation to the Arab and Muslim world's ambition to annihilate Israel. They are repeated like some diabolical mantra. You have all heard them; they are "land for peace" in which Israel is pressured to give away its biblical and ancestral lands but never receives peace.

The other one is "The Two State Solution." This is so beloved of the Left and literally spells for Israel and its 6,000,000 Jewish citizens a new Final Solution. Presumably, the first six million exterminated Jews are not enough?

We all heard from the lips of Barack Hussein Obama the call for Israel to return to the armistice lines of pre June, 4, 1967 and carve out from Judea and Samaria (the Jewish heartland) the so-called West Bank, a terror state to be called Palestine.
But these lines from June 4, 1967 were merely the armistice lines where the armies halted during the 1948 Arab-Israel War.

Before that Arab imposed war, Israel had reluctantly accepted the 1947 Partition Plan, which then would have created a Jewish and Arab state side by side. But the Arabs, then as now, rejected it outright. They wanted no Jewish state.

When the ceasefire took place, the Jordanian Arab Legion had invaded and illegally occupied Judea and Samaria – known by its Jordanian name, the West Bank. Jerusalem was cut in half and Israel's width at its most populous region was a mere nine miles wide from the Mediterranean to the foothills of the Judean mountain range.

Those lines were described by Abba Eban, Israel's UN ambassador and later, foreign secretary, as the Auschwitz lines.

President Obama demands that Israel be forced back into those outrageous and indefensible lines. He wants Jerusalem, Israel's 3,000 year old Jewish capital, to again be divided as it was during those terrible 19 years from 1948 to 1967. The world cheered when the Berlin wall came crashing down reuniting the city.

President Reagan had called upon Soviet President Gorbachev to "tear down this wall." Now President Obama calls upon Israeli Prime Minister Netanyahu to "build up a wall."

What this president has effectively done is to set an ever present sword of Damocles over Israel's future, which he well knows will become for the Left, for the Muslim world, and for all the haters of the Jewish people and state, an endless and relentless weapon to be used against Israel's survival.

For those who know history, there already exists a Palestinian state in all but name. It is Jordan, which consists of four fifths of the original Palestine Mandate and exists east of the River Jordan.

Britain created it in 1922 from the ruins of the defeated Ottoman Turkish Empire. It was wrenched away from the original Mandate territory and given to the Arab Hashemite Bedouin tribe: An historic and infamous betrayal by a British government of its promise to the Jewish people for the creation within the Mandatory territory of a Jewish National Home.

Immediately Jews were forbidden to live in it, even though it contains the ancient biblical lands that were a possession of the Israelite tribe of Manasseh. That land on the east bank of the Jordan River is Gilead.

Jordan's population is also four fifths Arabs who call themselves Palestinians. The other fifth consists of the Hashemite Bedouin, whose king Abdullah controls the state. But uneasy is his crown.

The tiny remaining one fifth of the geographical territory, which was part of Mandatory Palestine, is all that is left for the Jewish people west of the River Jordan; A distance of barely 40 miles from the Mediterranean Sea to the Jordan River (including Judea and Samaria).

In this ever so small sliver of land, Obama and a hostile world would carve out another Arab state from Judea and Samaria (the West Bank) that will *never* live in peace with Israel.

Palestine is a geographical entity, like Siberia or Patagonia. It has never been a sovereign and independent nation in all of recorded history; certainly not an Arab state.

Let me quote from Professor Bernard Lewis of Princeton University and expert on Islam and the Middle East: "From the end of the Jewish state in antiquity to the beginning of British rule in 1920, the area now designated by the name Palestine was not a country and had no frontiers, only administrative boundaries."

And from Professor Philip Hatti, an Arab historian, writing in 1946: "There is no such thing as Palestine in history; absolutely not."

In 1956, the Saudi Arabian delegate to the UN Security Council said: "It is common knowledge that Palestine is nothing but southern Syria."

So that we see how illusory peace, true peace, can be, the Jewish prophet, Jeremiah lamented in the Bible: "Peace, peace but there is no peace." Jeremiah 6:14.

Those words were uttered after Jeremiah began his prophecies around 627 BC in Judah and before the great catastrophe befell the ancient Jews and the First Jewish Commonwealth was destroyed. Nebuchadnezzar, the Babylonian king came down from the north and destroyed the First Temple in Jerusalem. Jeremiah's words echo across the ages and warn again of the frailty of peace.

The conclusion to all this is that there can never be peace with an Arab people who remain Muslim. Israel must not voluntarily give away one more inch of the God given covenanted land in return for pieces of paper that can be torn up or international guarantees that can evaporate like clouds on a hot summer's day.

Israel must put its trust not only in temporal powers whose leaders - as we see with President Obama - can become a clear and present danger to both Israel and to America.

No, the people of Israel and America – two great democracies and civilizations facing Islam's threats - must always put their trust in Almighty God.

Certainly today there should be no appeasement of a Muslim enemy that hates both Jews and Christians. Instead Israel and America might be wise to follow the words of the brilliant English military leader and devoted Christian, Oliver Cromwell:

"Trust in the Lord; but keep your powder dry."

May 29, 2011

Jews face Jerusalem but Muslims face Mecca

Jerusalem Unification Day has again been celebrated in Israel and throughout the world with the exception of that 7th century alternate universe: the Muslim world.

It marks 44 years since the amazing and miraculous event took place when the Jewish people's 3,000 year old capital city was restored to the Jewish state in the 1967 Six-Day War.

For 19 long years from 1948 to 1967, Jordan had occupied Judea and Samaria (the West Bank) and the eastern half of Jerusalem. Only Pakistan and Britain had ever recognized Jordan's illegal occupation.

The British officered Jordanian Arab legion had forced out at gunpoint the Jewish residents of the Old City and the neighboring Jewish villages: It was Apartheid and ethnic cleansing, Arab style.

The Legion went on to desecrate the Jewish graves on the ancient Mount of Olives and use the headstones as latrines. They desecrated over 50 synagogues and forbade Jewish pilgrims to worship at their holy places. They had turned the Via Delarosa, the Way of the Cross, into a filthy, sewerage strewn alley through which Christian pilgrims were forced to walk.

Jordan cut the Holy City in half with barbed wire and erected walls, complete with snipers along the dividing line who killed many Jews in the western half of the city.

There is another city today divided by Muslims. It is called Nicosia in Cyprus, a country whose northern half is still occupied by Turkey. Strangely, no international calls are heard calling for Turkey to leave or for the city to be reunited.

Another city that was divided was Berlin and President Reagan called upon Soviet President Gorbachev to, "tear down this wall."

The world applauded when the wall came down. Now President Obama and most of the same world in effect is calling upon Israel to re-divide Jerusalem. Obama is essentially calling upon Israeli Prime Minister to "build up a wall."

Only when Israel was able to restore dignity and cleanliness in 1967 to all the holy places was the earlier Muslim discrimination against Jews and Christians finally brought to a long and overdue end.

But this persecution of non-Muslims is par for the Islamic world and it continues today throughout the territory foolishly given to the Palestinian Arabs as a result of the grotesquely misnamed Oslo Peace Accords.

Throughout the Middle East, Christians are fleeing from Iraq, Lebanon, Egypt and the Palestinian Authority itself. The only nation in the Middle East where the Christian population is growing is Israel.

The Palestinian Arabs are now living under the Palestinian Authority - a territory carved out of Judea and Samaria - the Jewish people's ancestral and biblical heartland, incorrectly called by its Jordanian name, the West Bank.

The Obama regime is today backing the Palestinian Authority's spurious claim that the liberated areas from Arab Jordan must be forced back under the occupation and sovereignty of a future PA state.

The PA is demanding that the eastern half of Jerusalem must be given to them in order to declare it the capital of a new Arab state called Palestine.

Such an independent Arab state called Palestine has never existed in all of recorded history. Palestine has always been a geographical area just as Siberia or Patagonia is: never an independent state. Jerusalem has never been the capital city of any Arab or Muslim people.

Jerusalem has been the eternal capital of only one people in all of that same recorded history: the Jewish people. A Kingdom of Jerusalem existed under the Christian Crusaders but this was created by a motley group of European knights who had no historical roots in the land.

The Jewish Bible along with the Talmud and the Midrash tell us that the Torah, (the first five books of the Holy Bible) its light and its message, is to be broadcast to the entire world from one specific place: Jerusalem.

Each time the Torah scroll is taken from the Ark to be read during synagogue services the following prayer is always sung. "For out of Zion shall go forth the Torah (Law) and the word of God from Jerusalem." (Isaiah 2:1 and Micah 4:2)

In the complete Jewish Bible (the Tanach) the words Jerusalem and Zion appear 821 times with Jerusalem appearing 667 times and Zion appearing 154 times. Both Zion and Jerusalem are usually considered synonymous.

In the Christian Bible, itself an account of Jewish personalities whose lives were formed within the then Roman province of Jewish Judea, as well as the Galilee, the name Jerusalem appears 154 times and Zion seven.

In the Koran, Jerusalem and Zion do not appear at all. Indeed, it was only after the Arabs, under their new banner of Islam, conquered Jerusalem in the year 638 that they invented Islamic history in and around Jerusalem.

We are told that Mohammed flew on his magic horse to a place called *Al Aksa,* which means simply the farthest place. Much later, and for political reasons to do with historic, temporal and spiritual Jewish and Christian ties to Jerusalem, did Muslims name the Holy City as their *Al Aqsa.*

After the Holy Temple was destroyed in the year 70 AD by Titus, Jerusalem lay stricken. But Jews still maintained a presence there and continued to suffer under Roman occupation.

The heroic Bar-Kochba Revolt broke out in 135 AD but was crushed three years later by the Roman emperor, Hadrian, who razed Jewish Jerusalem, plowed the city under, and renamed it Aelia Capitolina in part after his own name, Hadrian Publius Aelius. He built a shrine to the Roman god, Jupiter, on the site where the Holy Jewish Temple's Holy of Holies had once stood.

From the 10th century, the Muslim Arabs still called the city various names that echoed its original Jewish origins. For instance they called it Beit al-Makdis, the Arabic version of the Hebrew name, Beit HaMikdash - House of the Sanctuary.

The Arabic name, beloved of Palestinian terrorists, is Al-Kuds, which is derived from the Hebrew, Ir Hakodesh - City of Holiness.

The Christian king, Frederick II obtained Jerusalem, along with Bethlehem and Nazareth, in a treaty with the Egyptian Sultan al-Kamil.

This was a lease agreement given by the Muslim ruler and meant to last some ten years. Frederick subsequently crowned himself King of Jerusalem.

But in 1244 the Muslims retook Jerusalem and the city lapsed into a long, dilapidated slumber and the Muslim shrines on the Temple Mount, which today are a focal point of anti-Jewish and anti-Israel activity, fell into disrepair and abandonment.

Only when Israeli forces in June, 1967 liberated the Temple Mount and east Jerusalem, during their defensive war against Arab aggression, did the Arab and Muslim world suddenly wake up and demand control of the city, or at least the Temple Mount and Jerusalem's eastern half.

It is instructive to note that when the Jordanian Arab Legion occupied east Jerusalem and the Old City in 1948, after driving out its Jewish population, the Arab world again lost interest in the city.

Indeed, King Hussein, Jordan's ruler had little interest in Jerusalem compared to his desire to build up his capital, Amman, which he considered far more important.

Between 1948 and 1967, during the illegal Jordanian Arab occupation of east Jerusalem and the West Bank, no Arab leader ever thought it important enough to visit Jerusalem except King Hussein, but he visited it rarely.

Today, Mahmoud Abbas, the successor to arch terrorist Yasser Arafat and now head of the Palestinian Authority, demands that Jerusalem be divided again as it was from 1948 to 1967 and a new Arab capital - for the first time in history - established in Jerusalem.

Not only the Muslim world, with its 57 member states, but the Europeans and President Obama pressure Israel into conceding parts of its holy capital to further placate the voracious Arab appetite and "further the peace process."

Giving away even one inch of Jerusalem would be to spit in the face of the endless generations of Jews who have held Jerusalem as the central spiritual and physical place in Jewish history.

It would be a cataclysmic and symbolic act of betrayal of Jewish history and faith if any part of Jerusalem is lost to the Jewish people by this generation of Israelis. For Jews, Jerusalem is the spiritual and temporal heart.

It would also be a reverse for the Christian world. Only under Israeli administration has Jerusalem been open for free and unfettered worship to members of all faiths.

The prayer uttered at Passover and Yom Kippur - "Next year in Jerusalem" - must not become an empty phrase made bitter in its very utterance by abandoning much of eternal Jerusalem to placate a fraudulent Arab people called Palestinians and appease a hostile world by succumbing to an equally fraudulent peace.

It is instructive to note that in prayer, Jews in synagogues face Jerusalem while Muslims in mosques face Mecca. This Islamic practice, even on the Temple Mount, speaks volumes.

Tuesday, June 7, 2011

Israel's Missed Opportunities

In my last published article: *In prayer Jews face Jerusalem but Muslims face Mecca*, I received this simple but profound question from a reader.

"You wrote that for 19 long years from 1948 to 1967, Jordan had occupied Judea and Samaria (the West Bank) and the eastern half of Jerusalem. Then why didn't Israel annex the West Bank after 1967 and why doesn't it annex it now?

Indeed, why have the last 44 years since June 1967 been wasted and Judea and Samaria, the Jewish people's biblical and ancestral heartland, not been annexed to the reborn Jewish state?

Unfortunately many Israeli leaders at the time were socialists, leftists and some even atheists. They were not well grounded in the religious history of the Jewish people and its attachments to its holy places.

Despite pleas from religious and conservative Jews, these leftists refused to fully appreciate the precious nature of those lands to the Jewish state: A tragic, missed opportunity.

The leftwing leaders also undertook a repeated policy of appeasement towards the hostile Arabs, and didn't seize the opportunity for annexation that arose in 1967 after the Six Day War.

Israel's left leaning government at the time thought that by not annexing the territory it would lead to goodwill negotiations where everything would be on the table. This, and the failed policy of appeasement, was a historic mistake.

The most extreme example of this appeasement was the immediate turnover of the Temple Mount in Jerusalem (the site of the two Jewish Temples) to the Arab Waqf by Moshe Dayan, Israel's Defense Minister in the then leftwing Israeli government. Now the Waqf is deliberately destroying ancient Jewish and Christian antiquities, which Israeli authorities are unable to monitor.

More appeasement of the Arab Muslim world leading to Muslim desecration and a crime against history and civilization.

Later - and still continuing the failed appeasement policy - subsequent prime ministers under the rubric of "land for peace" caused the woeful surrender of Jericho, of Hebron, (King David's first capital city) of Shechem (Nablus), and so much of Judea and Samaria to illegal Arab development.

Even conservative Prime Ministers like Menachem Begin and Binyamin Netanyahu fell into the trap of believing that the Muslim world would finally accept a Jewish state in return for endless concessions. Begin gave away all of the Sinai peninsula and Netanyahu in his first term as Prime Minister gave away Hebron - one of Judaism's four holy cities.

Again, this was a fatal mistake for the empirical fact is that Islam will never accept a non-Muslim state in lands once conquered in the name of Allah. This simple and enduring truth is nigh impossible for secular westerners - be they Israelis or Americans - to understand and yet without this realization, all talk of true and enduring peace is a grand delusion.

As time went by, fatal euphemisms began to be employed such as "the peace process, land for peace, and the two- state-solution." All these baseless phrases led not to peace but to more Muslim Arab demands, war and terrorism against Israel. Yet still the Left remained deaf and blind.

The "Two State Solution," has now been embraced by politicians and journalists alike, repeated endlessly, and touted as the panacea for a just, equitable solution to the Israel-Palestinian conflict.

It has assumed the repetitious role of a muezzin's call to Islamic prayer. But it is based on erroneous geography and history; on a mixture of wishful thinking, naiveté and a brilliant Arab propaganda campaign of disinformation and falsehood.

The Holocaust denying leader of the Palestinian Authority, Mahmoud Abbas, and Israel's supposed peace partner - a man who is a wolf in sheep's clothing -has publicly rejected any willingness to accept Israel as a Jewish state; a sure indication of the falsity of any Arab claim to live in full and lasting peace with Israel, especially now Abbas has embraced within his government the malignancy known as Hamas.

The creation of yet another Arab state - this will be number 23 - based upon the two-state-solution and carved out of Judea and Samaria within the mere 40 miles separating the Mediterranean and the Jordan River, is a recipe for war and for the piecemeal destruction of the Jewish state.

Israel is being pressured to shrink to a mere 9 miles wide as it was prior to the defensive war Israel was forced to fight in June, 1967. These lines were called the Auschwitz lines because of the impossibility of defending them against Arab genocidal hostility.

Any new Arab state will more than likely fall under the control of the Islamist Hamas movement, itself a branch of the Muslim Brotherhood, which seeks the annihilation of Israel and a worldwide Islamic Caliphate. Gaza, and what it has become, is living proof of Palestinian Arab genocidal intentions towards Israel

The Iranian mullahs, perhaps soon armed with nuclear weapons, will have a command and control base within the territory already given away to the Arabs. They will be ensconced in Gaza on the eastern shore of the Mediterranean Sea, interested in launching ever more lethal terror against what is left of Israel and threatening Europe.

If Israel foolishly gives away parts of Judea and Samaria, there will be no part of Israel or Jerusalem safe from Palestinian Arab missile attacks. When President Bush was still Governor of Texas he flew over Israel's tiny width and remarked, "Why, in my state we have driveways longer than that."

That nightmare for Israel is the most likely outcome of the current proposed Two State Solution west of the Jordan River, which the Obama Administration is pushing with the flawed zeal of a misguided zealot.

Indeed, Barack Hussein Obama is practically demanding Israel be pressured to return to the pre-June 1967 armistice lines; essentially calling for Israel's national suicide. This may well reach a crescendo in September.

But to truly create a just and equitable solution to the Israeli-Palestinian conflict there must be a Two-State Solution, not within the territory west of the River Jordan, but on both sides of the river.

The present day Kingdom of Jordan occupies four-fifths of geographical Palestine and, as the population is three fourths Palestinian Arab, it follows that the solution to the creation of a Palestinian Arab state should be within the present day Kingdom of Jordan and east of the River Jordan.

Let us also be reminded that the Jewish birthrate in Judea and Samaria (the so-called West Bank) is increasing and the Arab birthrate decreasing. The fear of an Arab demographic bomb is receding according to statistics regularly provided by Yoram Ettinger.

If there is a desire within the international community to truly arrive at a "just and equitable" solution, then this would be it. Of course, if this was a perfect world, it would satisfy historical, geographical, religious and ethnic considerations. But, alas, it is anything but a perfect world and the fanatical desire by so many Arab and Muslim nations to wipe out all vestiges of a Jewish state is a depressing reality.

In the 44 long years since Israel liberated the territories from Arab occupation it has missed opportunities to annex Judea and Samaria. History might have been so different if the leaders of the Jewish state had not been ignorant of their biblical and post-biblical history or of their essential Jewish faith; so inextricably intertwined with the Land of Israel and its 3,000 year old Jewish capital: Jerusalem.

So many of the early Israeli politicians were from the Left and were not moved by faith to redeem the hills and valleys of biblical Judea and Samaria - the very heartland of the Jewish people and their history. And still today, the Israeli Left is blinded by a veritable veil of deception.

Peace Now, for example, despite every manifestation of Jew hatred by the Muslim and Arab world, does all it can to drive fellow Jews out of their ancestral lands. And a dominating Leftwing bias among Israeli tenured professors and a left-leaning Israeli Supreme Court often jeopardizes Israeli security.

The corollary to this is that the Jewish state must not succumb to the enemy within - the Left - and the enemy without - the Arab and Muslim world - or give away any more of its native, ancestral, biblical, spiritual and physical homeland to a people whose Islamic religion demands of them no *true* peace with Israel, no *true* negotiations with Israel, and no *true* recognition of Israel as a Jewish state.

There is no time for anymore missed opportunities.

June 13, 2011

The Choice Is Ours: What will it be?

A timeless paean for peace, written millennia ago by the biblical Jewish prophet Isaiah, appears ironically on the entrance wall of the building in New York City housing that most unholy, immoral and unjust organization: the United Nations. The delegates from every part of the world walk by it but see and understand it not.

The words include: And they shall beat their swords into plowshares, and their spears into pruning hooks; nation shall not lift up sword against nation, neither shall they learn war anymore. Isaiah 2:4.

On the other hand, Thomas Jefferson wrote: "Those who hammer their guns into plows will plow for those who do not."

In a perfect world, Isaiah's words should be paramount. But this is not a perfect world; it never has been. Jefferson knew it, and it may be millennia before it becomes such a world as envisioned by Isaiah.

All we can do is strive mightily to bring the world to a better place than it is now. But the first years of the 21st century do not augur well for the human race. It is, therefore, only wise and prudent to maintain personal and national defense against all whom harbor ill will and genocidal ambitions against us.

There is suffocating hypocrisy in the United Nations where up is down, day is night and a veritable Kafkaesque worldview exists. There is towering deceit and mendacity in the international corridors of power. Few nations can be trusted. Most act in their own best interests, despite agreements between them.

Atrocities in Syria, Libya, the Congo, the Sudan, Iraq, Egypt, Nigeria, Iran, Pakistan and Somalia, to name a very few of the world's benighted lands, make the very angels in heaven weep.

Liberals and the all-pervasive and pernicious Left would ban guns for personal and legitimate self-defense if they could; and they try mightily to do so. Similarly, the Left eviscerates national defense whenever it comes into power.

In the 1930s, Britain let down its guard by slashing its military, despite all the clear and present warnings of German rearmament and the strident war cry spewing from the mouth of Adolf Hitler and his adoring German Nazi sycophants.

Winston Churchill, forced into the political wilderness, saw clearly what was coming and he, almost alone, pleaded in the House of Commons for the British nation to wake up before it was too late. For his efforts he was demonized as a war monger for far too long. And we all know how things turned out: That is those of us who still think.

So do we all have to go forward into the past? Do we all have to decry and vilify those who today warn us against the coming new war; a war that will transcend in human depravity even the horrors unleashed by fascism, Nazism and Communism.

It is coming, and it is the same ultimate horrific combination of a religion wrapped in an ideology that the same Winston Churchill warned about many years before the rise of the National Socialists (Nazism) and Communism.

Churchill called it, Mohammedanism, and he wrote the following in his book, The River War:

"How dreadful are the curses which Mohammedanism lays on its votaries! Besides the fanatical frenzy, which is as dangerous in a man as hydrophobia in a dog, there is this fearful fatalistic apathy. The effects are apparent in many countries. Improvident habits, slovenly systems of agriculture, sluggish methods of commerce, and insecurity of property exist wherever the followers of the Prophet rule or live.

"A degraded sensuality deprives this life of its grace and refinement; the next of its dignity and sanctity. The fact that in Mohammedan law every woman must belong to some man as his absolute property, either as a child, a wife, or a concubine, must delay the final extinction of slavery until the faith of Islam has ceased to be a great power among men.

"Individual Moslems may show splendid qualities, but the influence of the religion paralyzes the social development of those who follow it.

"No stronger retrograde force exists in the world. Far from being moribund, Mohammedanism is a militant and proselytizing faith. It has already spread throughout Central Africa, raising fearless warriors at every step; and were it not that Christianity is sheltered in the strong arms of science, the science against which it had vainly struggled, the civilization of modern Europe might fall, as fell the civilization of ancient Rome."
- *Sir Winston Spencer Churchill (The River War, first edition, Vol. II, pages 248-50 (London: Longmans, Green & Co., 1899).*

Not only Winston Churchill saw this fundamental danger to Judeo-Christian civilization but so did other luminaries. Here is what John Quincy Adams wrote about the same 7th century force, and its relentless war against non-Muslims:

"In the seventh century of the Christian era, a wandering Arab of the lineage of Hagar [i.e., Muhammad], the Egyptian, [.....] Adopting from the new Revelation of Jesus, the faith and hope of immortal life, and of future retribution, he humbled it to the dust by adapting all the rewards and sanctions of his religion to the gratification of the sexual passion. He poisoned the sources of human felicity at the fountain, by degrading the condition of the female sex and the allowance of polygamy; and he declared undistinguishing and exterminating war, as a part of his religion, against all the rest of mankind. THE ESSENCE OF HIS DOCTRINE WAS VIOLENCE AND LUST - TO EXALT THE BRUTAL OVER THE SPIRITUAL PART OF HUMAN NATURE.....

"Between these two religions, thus contrasted in their characters, a war of twelve hundred years has already raged. The war is yet flagrant ... While the merciless and dissolute dogmas of the false prophet shall furnish motives to human action, there can never be peace upon earth, and good will towards men."

The twelve hundred year war that Adams wrote of continues today with greater ferocity, fuelled as it is by vast inflows of capital derived from oil.

Atrocities committed in the name of Islam go hand in hand with a stealthy infiltration of Sharia law into every facet of life in the West.

Vast sums of money befoul European and American universities, enslaving their ability to attain and maintain the moral high ground. Instead, insidious examples of moral equivalence abound in what Michael Savage describes as the "colleges of lower learning."

Anti-Semitism corrodes the very fabric of the halls of academia as one beguiled and besmirched student body after another falls victim to the malignant lies and poison of the immensely well-funded Arab and Muslim student organizations whose limitless coffers are enriched by each of us every time we fill our cars at the gas pump.

The students are the leaders of tomorrow. With few exceptions they are now infected, perhaps terminally, with an aberrant hatred of Jews and of Israel.

Remember, the Jews are the canaries in the coal mine and whatever befalls them, eventually befalls all. Everything points to a new dark age with the stench of Arab and Muslim oil suffocating all clarity of thought and, perhaps, finally ushering in the victory that the followers of Islam have sought over those they have impudently called "infidels" since the 7th century.

Remember also, even for those who yet mock the Bible, Genesis 12:3 remains an everlasting reproach to those who would curse embattled Israel and its people.

Churchill, Adams, Jefferson all understood the ever present and mortal Islamic threat. They spoke with conviction and knowledge in an age where the debilitating and impoverishing insanity of political correctness had not yet arrived to stifle free speech. There are those today who also warn us.

But must we be fated yet again to ignore them and walk blindly into the darkest night of all?

Bodies in the Well: Jewish Martyrs of Norwich

June 28, 2011

The news of the discovery in Norwich, England of a presumed mass murder of Jewish men, women and children that took place in medieval times has left hardly a ripple, especially among the present day Anglo-Jewish community.

This is passing strange as it now appears that the bodies – all 17 of them – were found as long ago as 2004 and have been kept in storage all that time without decent or respectful burial.

The remains were discovered during the construction of a new shopping center and researchers from the Center for Anatomy and Human Identification at Dundee University have deduced that all 17 bodies were thrown head first down a well in either the 12th or 13th centuries.

The conclusion from DNA research is that they were Jews and that at least five were from the same family.

Eleven of the bodies were of children from the ages of 2 to 15 with five of them below the age of five.

England was no different from most of Christendom during the medieval period and beyond. Europe then was as much a charnel house for the stateless and hapless Jews as it was during the Holocaust. The same relentless hatred of the Jews lay like a psychosis among the vast majority of Europeans and England was no exception.

Today that same aberrant behavior manifests itself in unfounded hatred towards the Jewish state and in a perverse ultra-support for the Arabs who call themselves Palestinians.

In England, a catastrophe broke upon the Jews during the Third Crusade (1189-1192) when the coronation of Richard Coeur de Lion took place. Anti-Jewish mobs attacked and murdered Jews from Norwich to Dunstable and throughout many English towns because of a false rumor that King Richard had ordered the Jews, who had come to honor him at the palace, to be turned away.

During the king's absence while on the crusade, the Jewish community of York tried to find refuge in the lord's castle from ravening mobs bent on the Jews' destruction. Rather than fall into the hands of the fanatical mob, the Jews, at least 150 in number, took their own lives on March 17th, 1190.

Rabbi Yom Tov ben Isaac uttered these final words: "It is plainly the will of G-d of our Fathers that we die for his holy Law. And lo, death is at our door ... for if we fall into their hands, we shall die in mockery at their arbitrary choice." A rabbinic ban (*cherem*) prohibited Jewish residence in York after that pogrom.

Peter Abelard, the French Christian scholar, himself a victim of persecution by the Church, was a lone voice in sympathizing with the harried and tormented Jews throughout so much of Europe. He wrote in 1135: "No nation has undergone such sufferings for God. Scattered among all the nations, having neither king nor secular prince, the Jews are oppressed with heavy taxes as if they must buy their lives anew every day ... The Jews are not permitted to own fields and vineyards ... Thus the only livelihood that remains to them is usury, and this in turn excites the hatred of the Christians."

One of the earliest cases of blood libel, the rumors of ritual murder falsely spread against the Jews, was recorded in the same Norwich, England. In 1146, the local Jews were accused of having kidnapped, tortured and killed a Christian boy before the Passover. Thus began the blood libel that spread throughout Christendom and resulted for centuries in the massacres of countless Jewish victims. In Poland and Russia at Easter time, which so often corresponds with the Passover festival, Jews were routinely slaughtered in pogroms.

In short, the discovery of the 17 presumably Jewish bodies in the Norwich well attests to the anti-Jewish hatred that permeated every facet of medieval life throughout Christendom from the Popes to the secular kings and princes on down to the superstitious peasants.

That these bodies have been in storage since 2004 with, as far as I am aware, apparently no outrage expressed by the Anglo-Jewish community or its representative Board of Deputies is deplorable. If this story is true, then the bodies of the murdered Jews should immediately be flown to Israel – the Jewish biblical and ancestral homeland – where they will be given the appropriate and dignified burial according to the laws of Moses.

If it has not already taken place, I hope Britain's Chief Rabbi, Jonathan Sachs, will be addressing this appalling situation.

One can only imagine the Muslim riots in British streets if these skeletons had been identified as belonging to Muslims and were being treated in this manner.

Inflamed Christians leaving their respective churches during medieval times, and bent on murdering Jews after hearing vitriolic and hateful anti-Jewish sermons from their priests, were no different from today's Muslims who leave their mosques with a blood lust after hearing their imams preach anti-Christian, anti-Jewish, anti-Hindu and anti-Buddhist diatribes.

In contrast, most Christians in America have historically eschewed the hate that their European coreligionists spewed for centuries. Indeed, millions of American Christians have embraced the Jewish roots of their faith and have been stalwart friends of the re-born Jewish state. Their support has been an immense encouragement to embattled Israel whose enemies encompass it with growing strength and enmity.

Sadly, however, too many liberal churches and denominations in the United States have fallen victim to the lies and modern day anti-Israel blood libels spewed by the likes of the Rev. Naim Ateek and his Sabeel organization – an appendage of the Saudi and oil rich Arab funded anti-Jewish and anti-Israel Palestinian propaganda campaign; a repetitious catalogue of calumnies against the Jewish state that surely gives the ghost of Josef Goebbels great delight.

So if indeed the bodies in the well turn out to be Jewish victims and martyrs, Israel should immediately demand that they be transferred to the Jewish state as the only decent site for their Jewish burial.

Obama and Israel: What if he is re-elected?

July 21, 2011

If by a disaster, Barack Hussein Obama is re-elected for a second term as President of the United States, all gloves will most likely be off when it comes to his plans for Israel. The spotlight thus turns upon how America's Jewish population will vote.

A recent poll conducted by John McLaughlin and Pat Caddell showed that 43% of all American Jews will support and/or vote for Obama in the 2012 general election. Yet 43% is a considerable and significant drop from the 78% who voted for Obama in 2008.

It is received wisdom that Jewish voters are tied by some familial umbilical cord to the Democrat party based upon how their parents, grandparents and great grandparents voted. But the Jewish vote in Florida has now shrunk, according to this poll, to a mere 34% for Obama. And yet more significant, many younger Jewish voters are heading for the Republicans and becoming conservative.

Times are a changing and the GOP contains far more pro-Israel Representatives and Senators than the Democrat party. The Dems have lurched perilously to the Left and it is within the Left and Far-Left that the most egregious anti-Israel sentiments are now to be found. President Obama is the glaring example.

The man-child is the poster boy for the progressives, socialists and all who deride the Constitution. As Commander-in-Chief he can wreak much havoc.

But in a second term all constraints would be gone, he would be free to unleash his scorn upon America as it exists today, and be sorely tempted to withhold America's veto from an Arab-Muslim engineered UN resolution against the Jewish state. So maybe that mystical umbilical cord, which tied Jewish voters to the Democrats and which the leaders of the Dems always relied upon, will at long last wither away.

But there is the black vote, which is practically a given for Obama, whatever financial and social mess he creates. Two superb black politicians, Allan West and Herman Cain, would make outstanding Republican presidential challengers to Obama. Herman Cain has already thrown his hat into the ring. But it remains a conundrum as to how much support either of these patriotic and conservative men would receive from their fellow blacks.

And there is no doubt going to be a major attempt by Obama to win over the Hispanic vote, perhaps by giving amnesty to the 20 million or more Hispanic illegal aliens in the country. Then, of course, there is the Democrat base and the so-called "progressives" who will vote lockstep for Obama. So we can expect a close election.

With so many vested interests involved it will be up to the independents and, perhaps, the Jewish vote this time that will hold the key to the occupant of the White House in 2012.

If Obama wins a second term, the express train taking us to an overwhelming central government on the European model will clatter ever faster even as its couplings leave the tracks.

With so many failed European states providing ample warning to the United States, nevertheless the leftwing ideologues within an old/new Obama Administration will take the train at full speed into financial ruin and oblivion.

If this is not tragic enough for a once great America, the Obama regime's foreign policy will be an even worse catastrophe than it is now. And our allies, what is left of them, will be ill served: None more so than the Jewish state.

In a second term, President Obama will cast his baleful glare upon the reunited city of Jerusalem and will do all in his considerable power to divide it against itself once again.

This was its fate during those heartbreaking 19 years from 1948 until 1967 when Jordan illegally occupied the eastern half of the city, along with the Jewish biblical and ancestral heartland of Judea and Samaria - erroneously called by its Jordanian Arab name; the West Bank.

So would the same world that cheered on the tearing down of the Berlin Wall; an ugly wall that had divided a city, now equally cheer on the building of an equally ugly wall to divide Jerusalem? If so, it will be a very sick world indeed.

Just read the book Obama allegedly wrote, "Dreams from My Father." In it he spelled out his personal commitment for all of his dealings with Israel and her Muslim-Arab enemies: "I will stand with them (Muslims) should the political winds shift in an ugly direction."

Obama has already stated that he wants to push Israel back to the 1949 Armistice lines (which he calls the 1967 border) that existed before the June, 1967 Six Day War Israel was forced to fight against genocidal Arab-Muslim aggression. That line was never a border; it was merely where the opposing armies halted.

Imagine a nation whose neighbors are so endemically hostile that they call ceaselessly for genocide against it. Then imagine that at its most populous region that nation is only nine miles wide. Yes, nine miles wide.

That nation was Israel prior to June 5, 1967. That is where the 1949 armistice lines were, and that is the suicidal border Obama plans to push Israel back into: Lines that Israeli statesman, Abba Eban, once described as the "Auschwitz lines," and with good reason.

I fear that far too many Jewish voters will be suckered yet again by President Obama who, during the next 18 months before the election, will keep his anti-Israel powder dry and pretend that he is the best friend Israel ever had in the White House. And if they believe that, they will, alas, believe anything this man says.

It is that mystical umbilical cord to the Democrat party that still deceives so many Jewish voters. Up until now, they seem to shrug off Obama's close, very close, friendships with the likes of Rashid Khalidi, the "Rev" Jeremiah Wright, and

"Minister" Farrakhan who have spewed, and continue to spew, anti-American, anti-Jewish, and anti-Israel toxic filth.

Do they not remember the despicable manner in which Barack Hussein Obama treated Prime Minister Netanyahu in his first visit to the Obama White House? And have they forgotten how he once labeled the Jewish state as "occupiers?" Here was the same Obama describing the Jewish people living in their biblical and ancestral homeland as "occupiers."

I am reminded of Israeli Knesset member, Yaakov Katz, who wrote the following advice to American Jewish voters: "Even if the Republicans put up a soda-pop can to run against Obama, it would be the better and wiser choice to give your votes to the "soda-pop can."

July 31, 2011

The ship that changed the Middle East

During World War 1, Winston Churchill was widely blamed for the Gallipoli debacle; the attempt by the British to end the war by striking at Germany's ally, the Ottoman Turkish Empire.

But Churchill's decision to invade the Dardanelles, penetrate Europe's soft underbelly, and force an early end to the war was in large part born out of frustration at the exploits of two German battle cruisers, the Goeben and the Breslau.

These two ships had been sailing in the Mediterranean since 1912 and were to embark on an amazing voyage and desperate chase across the Mediterranean once war began in August, 1914.

Indeed, it can perhaps be said that the main reason the Middle East was to change forever was because of the fate of these ships and one in particular, the battle cruiser, Goeben.

On December 7, 1909, the keel of a powerful new addition to the Imperial German Navy was laid. Named after the German general, August von Goeben (1816-1880), a hero of the Franco-Prussian war of 1870, the Moltke class capital ship, Goeben, was eventually commissioned in July, 1912.

Boasting an armament of ten 11inch main guns, mounted two per turret with guns that could fire to both sides as well as forward, the Goeben was to become a thorn in the side of the French and British navies in the Mediterranean.

It also became a source of shame for Great Britain, whose fleet failed to intercept it or bring it to battle, instead allowing the Goeben and the Breslau to escape through the Dardanelles and reach Constantinople, now Istanbul.

On June 28, 1914, while the Goeben was anchored off the coast of Haifa, her Admiral, Wilhelm Souchon, along with the ship's officers were enjoying a reception given to them by the German colony.

Word came that Archduke Ferdinand had been assassinated. Admiral Souchon, sensing that war would soon follow, decided to head for the Austro-Hungarian port of Pola in the Adriatic for needed repairs. He telegraphed for the light cruiser Breslau to join him there.

It is interesting to note that on board the Breslau, a Sub-Lieutenant, Karl Doenitz, was serving; the same Doenitz who was to command the German World War 2 U-Boat fleets and who took over command of Germany in 1945 after Hitler committed suicide.

On July 31, 1914, Winston Churchill instructed the commander of the British fleet, Admiral Sir Berkeley Milne, that his first task was to protect the French transports and be ready to bring to action individual German ships, particularly the Goeben. On August 2, 1914, Churchill issued another order saying, "Goeben must be shadowed by two battle cruisers."

Some 12 hours before war was officially declared, Goeben and Breslau thus found themselves flanked by two British cruisers, Indomitable and Indefatigable, which for political reasons were constrained from taking military action.

Britain, fearing that an alliance would be formed between Germany and the Ottoman Empire, known as the "sick man of Europe" had earlier sent the battle cruisers, along with the Inflexible, into the Mediterranean to intercept the two German battle cruisers and eventually sink them. But the German ships were able to give them the slip.

Immediately after war had officially been declared on August 3, 1914, Admiral Souchon in the Goeben took matters into his own hands, even though he had earlier been ordered by Admiral Turpitz to head for Constantinople.

The powerful German ships headed west along the North African coast, bombarding the port of Philippeville in French Algeria. The Goeben tricked the French by running in under Russian flags.

Goeben then briefly dueled with the British light cruiser, Gloucester, which was unable to close because of the Goeben's greater firing range.

For a brief period, the Goeben and Breslau threatened French troopships bringing French-Algerian forces across the Mediterranean to reinforce the French armies fighting on the fast evolving Western Front.

On August 4, 1914, Berlin again ordered both ships to head for the Dardanelles. In the message received by Admiral Souchon, the German Admiralty baldly stated "... alliance with Turkey concluded August 3. Proceed at once to Constantinople."

The German ships changed course but were again pursued by the Indomitable and Indefatigable. They succeeded in out-running the two British battle cruisers but both Goeben and Breslau were eventually tracked to Messina in Sicily where they were taking on coal.

The British cruisers stood off shore waiting for the German ships to come out of port. Incredibly, the Goeben and Breslau slipped through the waiting British net and made for Constantinople. This was not the British Navy's finest hour.

On December 10, the German battle cruisers approached the straits separating European and Asian Turkey. Instead of being fired upon by Turkish shore batteries, as Admiral Souchon had feared, the German Mission advising the Turkish army had convinced the Turks to permit the Goeben and Breslau safe passage through the Dardanelles.

Everything that had happened up to then led to the eventual diplomatic decision by Germany to hand over the Goeben and Breslau to the Ottoman Empire as a gift to Turkey for allying itself with the Central Powers.

Henceforth the Goeben became the Yavuz Sultan Selim, though the German crew by agreement remained to work the ship and control the future military sorties it carried out in both the Black Sea and the Mediterranean.

Sultan Selim was known in history as Selim the Grim (1470-1520). He was the father of Suleiman the Magnificent who built the walls surrounding Jerusalem and was the greatest of all the Ottoman rulers.

The transfer of both German battle cruisers was both a defining moment and deciding factor in bringing Turkey into the war on the side of Germany and Austria (the Central Powers).

On November 4, 1914, the Russians, smarting after the German-Turkish ships had shelled Odessa and Sebastopol, declared war on the Ottoman Empire. The following day, the British and French Governments also declared war on Turkey.

During 1915, initial plans were drawn up by the Entente powers for the eventual dismemberment of the Ottoman Turkish Empire.

In May, 1916, the Sykes-Picot Agreement was discussed by Britain and France with respect to the geographical areas known as Palestine and Syria. The plan was abandoned at the time of the Paris Peace Conference in 1919.

Ultimately, the Turkish Ottoman Empire collapsed as British forces, including those drawn from the British Empire, rolled back the Turks throughout the Middle East.

In December 1917, Britain's General Allenby entered Jerusalem at the head of his army. Ottoman possessions throughout the Middle East were subsequently captured and initially set up as British Mandates.

Iraq became independent in 1932 and Trans-Jordan in 1946. Former Turkish areas that came under French control in 1920 also subsequently became independent: Syria in 1943 and Lebanon in 1944.

As a result of Britain's victories over Turkish forces in 1917 and 1918, some ten million Arabs in the Middle East were freed from 400 years of Turkish rule.

It is interesting to note that the area set aside for Arab rule in the region was 1,184,000 square miles while geographical Palestine, the only portion set aside for a Jewish National Home by Great Britain under the Balfour Declaration of November 2, 1917, covered less than 11,000 square miles. That area was further reduced through subsequent political decisions by the British Colonial Office.

For instance the Golan Heights, in Anglo-French wrangling, was torn away by Britain from Palestine in 1923 and ceded to France, which made it a part of Syria. And in 1921, Britain arbitrarily gave away all the territory east of the River Jordan, comprising four fifths of geographical Palestine, to the Emir Abdullah and re-named it Trans-Jordan. Jews were immediately forbidden to live within its territory. But that's another story.

The remarkable fact is that all the subsequent internecine conflicts between the artificially created Arab states in the Middle East, as well as the continuing Arab war of aggression against the existence of a Jewish state in the region, can be traced back to the voyage of the German battle cruiser, Goeben.

Its transfer to Turkey, along with the Breslau, led that nation into war and to a crushing defeat, changing the region's map and transforming the Middle East into what it is today.

The Goeben was thus fated to become the ship that changed the Middle East.

August 25, 2011

Tiny Israel: The ultimate rape victim

The world and the national and international mainstream media are eerily silent when Israel and her civilian population are attacked by missiles from Gaza or Lebanon and her people slaughtered by Palestinian terrorists as just occurred.

But if she retaliates, oh my, the same immoral world and mass media scream and condemn her for daring to resist and a predictable anti-Israel censure is issued from that ultimate temple of hypocrisy: the United Nations. Israel is like the rape victim who never receives justice from a series of biased judges.

But it is now even worse for the embattled Jewish state. The most hostile anti-Israel President, Barack Hussein Obama, and a State Department, which is perennially anti-Israel to its core, will never give Israel the green light to finally finish the job by destroying once and for all the murderous terrorists of the Arab and Muslim world.

Does the world care about the tormented Israeli town of S'derot, which is battered relentlessly by missiles from the pitiless Hamas occupied and terrorist infested Gaza Strip?

O little town of S'derot, her suffering people live a mere three kilometers from the Gaza Strip. They have only 15 seconds warning from the next incoming barrage of deadly missiles deliberately fired at them by the Arabs who call themselves Palestinians.

Ashkelon, a large city of over 100,000 souls is another nearby target of Palestinian Arab aggression. Rockets slam into her civilian areas routinely and again the world is silent. Ashdod and Beersheba - all major southern Israeli cities came under a heavy rocket offensive from Gaza lasting from Thursday until Sunday night.

Jews have died, babies and toddlers have been wounded, a synagogue was hit by a Grad missile and a school all but destroyed. Towns and villages have been struck and their civilians terrorized.

Did you hear that on the TV news or read it in the New York Times or Washington Post? If you did it was reported in the fashion that afflicts all news about Israeli suffering: The sin of moral equivalence. In other words, it is a perverse editorial mechanism, which presents the Israeli victim as equal to the Arab victimizer.

Under the latest blatant crime against humanity perpetrated by Hamas, Islamic jihad and Al Qaeda, which terrorized southern Israel, some one million Israelis were under threat as more than 150 Grad and Katyusha missiles from Gaza struck Israeli villages and towns.

By the way, according to reports, many of the lethal Grad missiles were captured from Gaddafi's forces by the so-called rebels in Libya and smuggled into Gaza. These are the same rebels who cried Allahu Akbar, the Islamic war cry, as they stormed into Tripoli.

There is the clue to what will be the new Libya: An Islamic state based upon Sharia law and endemically hostile to the non-Muslim world. Thank you, NATO and President Obama.

Where was the mainstream media during the terrifying bombardment of Israeli civilian targets from Gaza? Where was Hillary Clinton, and oh, where was our President? I'll tell you where he was: Laughing it up on a golf course at Martha's Vineyard while our most loyal ally, Israel, suffered grievously and America's economy continued to sink.

The next target will be Tel Aviv, which is a mere 68 kilometers from Gaza. In the north, Hezbollah is even more deadly. They have received from Iran, through Syria, more than 80,000 deadly missiles all aimed at the Jewish state. Some may even be tipped with chemical and biological weapons. The Greater Tel Aviv area contains almost a quarter of Israel's population

When the next war will occur is in doubt but it will occur - perhaps sooner than later. Meanwhile when it does, hordes of Muslim Arabs, who call themselves Palestinians, will be called upon by the muezzin at the Al Aksa mosque to kill Jews and Christians wherever they are found in the Holy City. These Muslim drones merely bide their time before committing horror and genocide.

Let me quote partially from a recent article by Giulio Meotti, a journalist with Il Foglio, and the author of the book, *A New Shoah: The Untold Story of Israel's Victims of Terrorism*.

"S'derot represents the siege on the Jewish people and the resistance of Israel, but it also reveals the rest of the world's indifference to the genocidal hatred that is Jihadism. Some 70% of Israeli children in the Negev show symptoms of trauma, while thousands of children carry physical disabilities from Palestinian bombs.

"There are children who want to constantly stay inside the bunkers, or in the secured rooms of their homes. There are children who don't get out of bed anymore.

"Little is said or written about the incredible courage being shown by the civilian population of Israel, but it is reminiscent of events 70 years ago, Londoners, who had endured the blitz stoically...the people of Israel are equally valiant, going about their daily lives knowing that Arab killers might explode a bomb or rocket in any public place at any time.

"For Israel, more alarming than the rocket escalation is an eventual Islamist takeover of the mere six miles that separate Netanya on the Israeli coast from the Palestinian town of Tulkarem.

"There is an Arab saying about Netanya as the narrowest and most exposed throat of Israel: 'When we hang you, we will hang you from Netanya.'"

If Israel, heaven forbid, should ever succumb to the relentless and genocidal evil that is the Arab and Islamic world, cheered on by the despicable and terminally misguided Amen chorus from much of the morally degraded West, then the world as we know it will forever end and a new and terrible dark age will descend.

When we see how the mainstream media and the international corridors of power are silent in the face of the crimes of the Palestinian terror machine we should hearken to the words from the ancient Jewish Ethics of the Fathers: "He who is kind to the cruel ends by being cruel to the kind."

But if she retaliates, oh my, the same immoral world and mass media scream and condemn her for daring to resist and a predictable anti-Israel censure is issued from that ultimate temple of hypocrisy: the United Nations. Israel is like the rape victim who never receives justice from a series of biased judges.

But it is now even worse for the embattled Jewish state. The most hostile anti-Israel President, Barack Hussein Obama, and a State Department, which is perennially anti-Israel to its core, will never give Israel the green light to finally finish the job by destroying once and for all the murderous terrorists.

September 18, 2011

Erdoğan's Not-So-Sublime Porte

The Muslim and Arab world smells blood. Like sharks circling their prey, many in most of the world's 57 Muslim states are eager and willing to commit genocide against embattled Israel.

With the Palestinian Authority's leadership pressing ahead with their unilateral bid at the United Nations for a declaration of statehood (by willfully abrogating the Oslo Accords, which required them to negotiate a final peace treaty with Israel), war and Arab violence will now subvert any hope of true peace.

The ridiculously touted Arab Spring has fast degenerated into an Arab Hell. Mobs screaming "death to the Jews" broke into Cairo's Israeli embassy while the police just stood by. The Muslim mob would have torn the embassy staff to pieces if they could, just as a Palestinian mob did with two hapless Israelis in Ramallah during the so-called intifada in 2000.

In Turkey, Prime Minister Recip Tayyip Erdoğan is deliberately ratcheting up an anti-Israel policy that may soon spin out of control. Erdoğan is resurrecting the old Ottoman Turkish Sublime Porte -- the old Ottoman government in Constantinople, named after the symbolic "elevated gate" and the Ottoman Empire's position as the gateway between Asia and Europe.

Millions of Christians in the Balkans and Greece endured Islamic domination during that time. But Erdoğan forgets that the same Sublime Porte became known also as the "sick man of Europe."

In response to Erdoğan's growing anti-Israel threats, Israel's foreign minister, Avigdor Lieberman, has decided to come to the aid of the hard-pressed Kurds who are battling Turkish forces. But this should not be done merely as a response to Turkey's aggressive posture towards the Jewish state. It should be done as a moral imperative, regardless of Turkey's aggression against Israel.

Indeed, under the administration of Prime Minister Menachem Begin, such early attempts to support the Kurds in their struggle for liberation and long-overdue statehood did take place. Israel supported Kurdish aspirations diplomatically and militarily until such support was nixed by U.S. pressure in 1975.

From the time the current Kurdish liberation struggle began in 1961, the Jewish state was the only nation to actively support Kurdish aspirations. According to Mordechai Nisan in his book *Minorities in the Middle East*, published by McFarlane in 2002, the Kurdish leader in 1966, Mustafa Barzani, told a visiting Israeli emissary, Arieh Lova Eliav, that "in truth, only the Jews cared about the Kurds."

Mr. Nisan also added that in 1980, Menachem Begin revealed that "from 1965 to 1975 Israel provided weapons and military advisors to the Kurdish resistance fighting against powerful Arab enemies."

One of the Israeli advisors was Rehavim Ze'evi, who was murdered several years ago by a Palestinian Arab in a Jerusalem hotel. During the period when Israel was assisting the Kurds, the United States became involved and, for a while, helped facilitate the support. But in 1975, America abandoned the Kurds, forcing Israel to follow suit.

Israel has supplied Turkey with UAVs, which Turkey used against the Kurds. This was before the increasingly Islamized Turkish government turned on Israel. Under left-leaning Israeli leaders, including Ehud Olmert, Ehud Barak, and Tzipi Livni, the Jewish state had copied the mendacious policies of other nations -- namely, putting political and economic expediency above morality. These leftist leaders should have known of the agony the Kurdish people were enduring, then as now, not only from Turkey, but also from Iran, Iraq, and Syria.

Of all the current stateless people in the Middle East, the 35 million Kurds - whose territory straddles a landmass from Iran to Turkey - deserve more than any others a sovereign, independent homeland.

An article some years ago by James Lewis in American Thinker was titled "Can Israel make it alone?" In it, Mr. Lewis suggested that, "nations have no permanent friends, only permanent interests - like survival."

With an Obama administration which is profoundly unfriendly towards Israel, Lewis suggested that "if the United States abandons the Jewish State, Jerusalem will have to seek new alliances."

President Barack Obama acts in just such an unfriendly way. Moving forward, however, any new Israeli alliances should include the restoration of a profoundly just, moral, and enduring pact with the Kurdish people, further including assistance towards them in creating a future independent State of Kurdistan.

In a previous chapter, I quoted in part a plea I received some two years ago, before Turkey's infamous flotilla campaign. It came from a Kurdish friend who is very supportive of Israel's struggle to survive among its hostile Arab neighbors. But it is so compelling that I feel it is worth repeating once more.

He is very supportive of the Jewish people; he knows of the shared ethnicities that exist between Jews and Kurds dating back millennia. He wrote:

"I wish the Jews in Israel and abroad would know better about the policy of their leaders concerning the Kurds, because it happens in the name of Israel, and that should matter to all Jews. The cooperation by Israel with the Turkish military is no secret, but Turkish oppression of the Kurds is unknown to most Israelis.

"It is hard for me to understand how Israel's cooperation, which benefits Turkey, does not take into account the misery that it imposes upon the Kurdish people who yearn, as the Jews have for centuries, to be free from terror and persecution. We Kurds remember fondly the Jews who lived with us for centuries.

"But the Turks waxed and waned in their attitude towards the Jews; sometimes they were tolerant and sometimes hostile. There are many Turks today who share Islamist ideas and proclaim hostility towards the Jewish state. Within Turkey lies the same pestilence of anti-Semitism that exists throughout the Arab and Persian world.

"Arming Turkey, our people's oppressor, is morally and geographically not to Israel's advantage. Israel's cooperation with Turkey is, in reality, a misguided support for political Islam and its oppression of the Kurds.

"The legitimate arguments and rights Israel has are the same rights and truths it denies in its official policy towards the Kurds. For now and for the future, everything looks black. I fear the worst for us. The whole world is against us, and on the Turkish side there is no change."

Though Israeli Foreign Minister Avigdor Lieberman is correct in now supporting the Kurdish struggle against Turkey, he is coming to the table late. Support by Israel and the West for the Kurds must never be part of a geopolitical maneuver; it must be done in recognition of a matter of paramount moral justice.

Turkey's Erdoğan is planning soon to send Turkish warships in support of a new and aggressive flotilla towards Gaza, thus inflaming already dangerous acts of Turkish brinkmanship.

But the world should be reminded that in 1974, a different flotilla set sail from Turkey. No, it wasn't destined for the Gaza coast, carrying thugs and jihadists masquerading as human rights activists - as ill-armed Israeli commandos discovered to their cost. No, this was a flotilla of naval ships sailing towards Cyprus as a full-fledged invasion force, illegally employing U.S. arms and equipment.

After Greek Cypriot resistance had been crushed in the north of the island, Turkish forces began to ethnically cleanse almost half of the island of its Greek population. The Turkish military employed hundreds of U.S. tanks and airplanes and 35,000 ground troops, with the result being a land-grab by Turkey of 37.3% of Cyprus. Turkey later sent additional flotillas to the island - ships containing 150,000 Turkish settlers, who proceeded to colonize the land after 200,000 Greeks had been driven out and made into refugees.

The capital city of Cyprus, Nicosia, remains today a city divided, with barbed wire marking the border like an ugly scar. Though relatively quiet today, pockmarks still cover the walls where bullets struck civilians and snipers held sway.

This was how Jerusalem and its Jewish population suffered during the illegal Jordanian occupation from 1948 until 1967. This division of the holy city left its eastern half and the biblical and ancestral Jewish homeland of Judea and Samaria, known by the world as the West Bank, under Arab occupation. Jews were driven out, and only Britain and Pakistan recognized Jordan's annexation.

In a truly moral world it would be eloquent justice for flotillas containing true humanitarians to sail towards Turkey and publicly demand restoration of the national integrity of Cyprus and removal of all Turkish military occupation.

It would also be eminently just to demand the rights of the Kurdish people for an independent State of Kurdistan as well as to finally require that Turkey admit the horrors it perpetrated against the Armenian people.

Finally, Turkey, which is fast becoming Erdoğanistan, must come to its senses by accepting Israel's inalienable right to defend itself against Arab and Islamist aggression emanating from Gaza.

September 25, 2011

Netanyahu's Speech and the Deafening Silence

If Israel shrank to just one downtown city block in Tel Aviv, it would still be reason for an all-out war of extermination by the Arab and Muslim world against the Jewish state.

Those of you who saw Netanyahu'speech at the United Nations, that Temple of Hypocrisy and Moral Turpitude, will have noticed the polite but tepid applause from a few along with the deafening silence from oh, so many of the international delegates.

I fear that calling, nay begging, for peace by successive Israeli Prime Ministers is an exercise in futility. The stark fact, which nobody wants to hear, is that Islam will never make peace with a non-Muslim state, especially if the Muslim foot trod triumphal upon that same territory once occupied in the name of Allah.

Even though the Jewish people in the Land of Israel pre-date Islam by millennia, nevertheless for Muslims in general, and for those Arabs who call themselves Palestinians, all the territory is theirs and they will call it by its fraudulent name: Palestine, which is a name that had nothing to do with Arabs living in the area.

As I have written before, if Israel shrank to just one downtown city block in Tel Aviv, it would still be reason for an all-out war of extermination by the Arab and Muslim world.

Until people understand that it is not "radical" Islam which creates the horror and misery that burdens all mankind but simply Islam, there can be no understanding of the existential threat we face in what is left of the Free World.

There is no moderate Islam and no radical Islam; there is only Islam. It is a bitter pill to swallow and no amount of sugar coating can ever make it palatable.

Netanyahu uttered the words: "West Bank" over and over again. This is a fundamental mistake. He must, and all of us must, call the territory by its Jewish biblical and ancestral name, Judea and Samaria, and then call it "aka the West Bank."

The inextricable Jewish connection with this G-d given promised land - attested to in the Torah and Tanach - must be proclaimed again and again and again in the halls of international diplomacy and the international corridors of power.

So it is the same with the counter-productive word, "settlements" – which in the English language is a pejorative term. These Jewish communities are not the outposts of an alien presence in another people's land.

No. These are Jewish villages and towns populated by the Jewish descendants of biblical and post-biblical native Jewish ancestors who for untold generations farmed and tended the hills and valleys of this Jewish heartland: Judea and Samaria.

All of us must call the territory by its Jewish biblical and ancestral name, Judea and Samaria, and then if we must, call it "aka the West Bank."

In conclusion, the endless and repeated begging for peace from a perverse and irretrievably hostile Muslim and Arab world must stop. The reality is desperately hard to acknowledge and accept, but it is an Islamic fact that Islam and its adherents will never make peace with non-Muslims.

The Muslim is enjoined by the later writings in the Koran and Hadith to lie to the non-Muslim if it advances Islam in the world. The Muslim must break all and every agreement entered into with non-Muslims if it advances Islam in the world.

This is the bitter reality non-Muslims must come to understand for if it is dismissed it guarantees war and all the horror of violent and evil terror perpetrated in the name of Allah.

For Israel the course is clear. The Arab and Muslim world has proclaimed everlasting enmity towards the non-Muslim; those which Islam arrogantly dismisses as infidels.

Thus, no Muslim state or its leader will ever recognize Israel as a Jewish state for that is to deny Islam; a word, by the way, which means submission - not to the will of the people as in a democracy - but only to the will of Allah.

That is an empirical fact.

The Muslim Arabs who call themselves Palestinians have made their bed. Now they must lie in it for their words of deceit and venom have consequences. Historical correctness must always trump political correctness.

That being said, Jordan is Palestine. That is also an empirical fact.

And one other fact. A Two-State Solution - that appalling euphemism - describing Israel and a Muslim terror state existing within the narrow strip of land from the Mediterranean Sea to the River Jordan will be for the Jewish people a repeat of that earlier dread euphemism, one the Nazis used to describe their extermination of the Jews: "The Final Solution."

October 31, 2011

Palestinian Arab Aggression Will Never End

Hamas footage of missiles being fired from Gaza towards Israel.

No, the terror will continue so long as Israel and the IDF merely retaliate against each and every separate Muslim Arab crime against the Jewish state's civilian population. As one person, commenting on a blog, stated: "Israel's taking out a few rocket launchers is like giving aspirin for cancer. It's only a band aid - not a cure."

These last few days, Israeli cities and villages have been bombarded with dozens of Grad and other missiles from Gaza; lethal weapons, many brought in from Libya. Last Wednesday, October 26, 2011, a Grad rocket brought into Gaza from one of Gaddafi's looted weapons stockpiles, was fired into an Israeli town. This began a relentless daily barrage.

There was no Israeli response until the following Saturday when a gang of Palestinian Islamic Jihad terrorists were spotted preparing to launch several more Grad missiles at Israeli civilian targets. They were killed and the Grads and their multi-barreled launchers destroyed before they could be fired.

Predictably, the mainstream media attacked the victim, Israel. The BBC, CNN, and the New York Times all blamed Israel during this latest unprovoked Palestinian attack, giving the usual pass to the terrorists. This twisting of the truth must give great joy and comfort to the ghost of Josef Goebbels; Nazi Germany's Minister of Propaganda.

But if the Israeli government does not inflict far, far more intensely painful responses to the terror bosses of Hamas, Islamic Jihad, Al Qaida, the Muslim Brotherhood, and all the human cockroaches who infest the Gaza Strip, then the missiles will continue to strike at southern and central Israel with increasing lethality and horror.

The Israel Defense Force (IDF) produces charts and graphs showing the ever increasing capabilities and destructiveness of the terrorists' weapons caches. The deadly flow of Grad missiles entering Gaza - with Egyptian complicity - from the looted arms stores of Muammar Gaddafi in Libya exposes the real meaning of the Arab Spring. The so-called rebels, who were aided by NATO, are not the democratic loving folks who Hillary Clinton and her boss, Barack Hussein Obama, claimed them to be.

Along with all the European heads of state who gleefully joined in the lust for Libyan oil that masked their hollow claims of bringing democracy to Libya, Clinton and Obama have unleashed a Muslim Pandora's Box, which will create in the Maghreb (North Africa) an Islamist, Jihadist and Sharia compliant wave that will eventually engulf Morocco and Algeria. It will extend west to Mauritania and its loathsome tentacles will then reach south beyond the Sahel and into equatorial Africa.

Like Hillary's and Bill's destruction of the Serbs, which allowed the ancient Serbian heartland of Kosovo to become a Muslim beach-head in the Balkans, so too Hillary's and Obama's misguided policies - under the guise of an Arab Spring - have plunged the world into an endless and perilous cycle of violence in which untold horrors will plague the entire globe.

The Islamic tide is rising. With every foreign policy misstep by the Obama Administration and the grotesque mishandling of her term as Secretary of State at the State Department, Hillary Clinton and Barack Obama are emboldening the Islamists in their aim of a creating a worldwide Caliphate.

Nowhere has their ideological foolishness and political ineptitude been more glaring than in their relentless obsession with what they call Israeli "settlements." They even go as far as to denounce the construction of homes within Jerusalem's city limits as "impediments to the peace process." Again Palestinian Arab terror, the real impediment to peace, is cynically ignored.

Jerusalem, north, south, east and west is Israel's capital. It was her capital city 3,000 years ago - millennia before the United States was created and Clinton and Obama came to power.

Judea and Samaria is the biblical, ancestral and aboriginal heartland of the Jewish patrimony going back to the time of Joshua's entry into the Promised Land. Before that, Abraham, Isaac and Jacob, the Jewish patriarchs, lived in the land some 4,000 years ago and are buried in Hebron, Judea; one of Judaism's four holy cities.

Jews have always lived in this tiny sliver of land in whatever numbers they could maintain and the hills and valleys of Judea and Samaria are dotted with Judaism's shrines, holy places, villages and ancient cities from time immemorial. The very ground embraces its Jewish heritage and patrimony. Ask the archaeologists. Read the Bible.

Yet here come Obama and Clinton, et al, parroting the mendacious and deceitful lies of the Arabs, those who call themselves Palestinians, that Judea and Samaria is Palestinian territory and that Jewish villages are "settlements." Even Judaism's holy shrines, such as the biblical Joseph's tomb in Shechem - the city now known by its Arabic name, Nablus - are Islamized by the Palestinian Authority and attempts by Muslim Arabs to desecrate it and turn it into a mosque are all too frequent.

Clinton and Obama employ today, as so much of the world sadly does, the Jordanian Arab name of "West Bank" for the territory instead of biblical Jewish Judea and Samaria. This is the territory the Arabs want to take as a Palestinian state - a first stage before taking what is left of Israel. But it must be repeated again and again that there has never in all of recorded history existed a sovereign, independent nation called Palestine; and certainly not an Arab one.

This "West Bank" was seized by the British officered Jordanian Arab Legion when it invaded and occupied the territory in the 1948 Arab-Israel War. The Jordanians drove out the Jewish population, including from the Old City in Jerusalem, and the subsequent illegal Jordanian occupation was recognized only by Britain and Pakistan.

Yet the thousands of years that the land was known as Judea and Samaria are forgotten and sublimated to the name, "West Bank," which refers to the term given to the mere 19 years of Arab occupation that lasted from 1948 to June, 1967. How strange!

So many times have such slanders and falsehoods about this Jewish heartland been spewed by Arabs and their supporters that now the world cannot comprehend the immoral, unspiritual and unhistorical fabrication that they have perpetrated.

That the morally bankrupt United Nations vomits such lies endlessly is one thing, but that Hillary Clinton and United States President, Barack Obama, repeat it and hurl it at Israel is shameful. But we know by now that neither of them are true friends of the Jewish state: Anything but.

So, in the face of the villainous campaign to delegitimize and demonize the embattled Jewish state by the Arab League, the Muslim world, the Left and the execrable international and national media - with few honorable exceptions - Israel must realize that it is time to weather the storm by responding both to Hamas and terrorist crimes and aggression with a terminally painful and crushing rejoinder.

It must also decide that, if needs be, it is better to be hung for a wolf than a sheep. After all, whatever restraint Israel shows in the face of Muslim Arab terrorism and barbarism, she will still be vilified, slandered and pilloried by a hostile and unsympathetic world. And whatever concessions she makes, one truism will always remain: Palestinian Arab aggression will never end.

Conclusion:

In the first volume of *Politicide* I ended the conclusion page as follows:

"I for one realize that Islam will never accept a non-Islamic state in lands once conquered in the name of Allah ... Therefore I will no longer end my articles or essays with the phrase, 'Victor Sharpe writes about Jewish history and the Arab-Israel conflict.' Instead, I will state that, 'Victor Sharpe writes about Jewish history and the Islamist-Israel conflict. Alas, that is what it is, what it always has been, and what it always will be.'" I wrote that at the end of 2006.

In Volume Two, which ended in December, 2009, I concluded with these words:

"The appeasement of the Arab and Muslim world will bring the exact opposite of what the appeasers seek. Winston Churchill wrote the following: 'Appeasement is like feeding a crocodile in the hope he will eat you last.'"

I went on to add: "The crocodile has no feelings of sympathy, nor does the Muslim Arab whose culture considers concessions a form of weakness and will offer no reciprocal concessions but cruelly demand more and more. It reminds me of the ancient saying from the Jewish Ethics of the Fathers: 'Whoever is merciful to the cruel, ends by being cruel to the merciful.'"

This third volume of *Politicide: The attempted murder of the Jewish state* includes example after example of just such appeasement by growing numbers of individuals in the West towards the voracious Muslim appetite for world conquest, for a Caliphate and for triumphant Islam. Those individuals include politicians, tenured professors, journalists, entertainers, et al.

Nations seek to gain time before the Islamic tide washes over them through appeasement. They do so by ever growing hostility towards the embattled Jewish state in the hope of assuaging the Islamic appetite. But it is all folly.

Western European nations are now submerged in an ever growing, Sharia compliant, Islamic monster that is within the gates. In a generation or two, France, Belgium, Spain, Germany, the Scandinavian countries and Britain may no longer retain a Judeo-Christian culture or civilization except in small pockets, always besieged by a Muslim majority they so foolishly allowed to grow and strengthen within their borders.

The world is changing, as both Adrian Morgan and Steve Myers so eloquently warn in their forewords to my book. And Israel, the one Jewish state, now finds itself, after years of foolish concessions to an implacable Muslim and Arab foe, left with so little land, and with a Palestinian Authority occupying territory in the very heartland of the Jewish people's patrimony - Judea and Samaria - called by its Jordanian Arab name: the West Bank.

And then there is the Gaza Strip: A finger of land pointing into Israel's heart like some cancerous tumor. This territory is occupied by Hamas, the Muslim Brotherhood branch of the so-called Palestinian Arabs. As Adrian Morgan pointed out, this Islamic organization is motivated by an abiding hatred of Jews and not only wishes to exterminate the Jewish state and all its citizens, but seeks to destroy Jews throughout the world.

And after Israel in 2005 drove out its own citizen from their villages and farms in the Gaza Strip, 10,000 Jewish exiles from Gaza were forced to live as refugees within Israel, their lives embittered by such a breathtakingly stupid Israeli concession.

Since Israel withdrew from Gaza in the hope that the Arabs would live peaceably with them and share in the benefits for all that comes from a true and lasting peace, Israeli villages and towns in southern and central Israel have endured a relentless barrage numbering some 12,000 deadly missiles.

As I write this, lethal Grad missiles, looted from Muamar Gaddafi's Libyan weapons caches, have been brought overland into the Gaza Strip - with Egyptian complicity - and are raining down upon the Israeli cities of Ashkelon and Ashdod Israeli civilians are being killed and maimed.

So many Israeli concessions forced upon past, weak Israeli leaders by friends and foes alike have endangered Israel's existence more than the combined military and terroristic Arab aggression against her since her reconstitution as a Jewish nation in 1948.

As you will have read in the many chapters of this volume, and the two previous volumes, Israeli concessions have never been met by Arab and Muslim concessions: Never. And I make no apologies for repeating it again and again.

The outrageous euphemisms employed to mask Israeli capitulation are well known. "Land for Peace" is the term used to sanitize Israeli national suicide. Land, precious land, with spiritual, historical, and strategic value to Israel, is given away to persuade the Muslim Arab enemy to join in the benefits of peaceful coexistence.

But it is a disastrous charade played upon the Jewish state for, in return for painful Israeli concessions of territory the Arabs, who call themselves Palestinians, never, ever offer peace.

Another suicidal euphemism to mask Israel's gradual destruction is, "The Two-State-Solution." This abomination has permitted a delusional belief that two states can live side by side in peace with each other. One state is Israel, a democratic nation. The other state would be "Palestine," an artificial creation and a terrorist entity that would live and breathe in relentless and genocidal aggression towards its neighbor, Israel.

For such a state to exist that patently and demonstrably has no desire, because of its adherence to its Islamic faith, to ever give up its ambition to destroy the Jewish state, will be the ultimate fatal error of any Israeli government.

It is national suicide and the very euphemism, "Two-State-Solution," echoes in its hideous similarity that other euphemism employed by Nazi Germany as it systematically exterminated 6,000,000 Jews: "The Final Solution."

Let me quote from words I wrote in one of the chapters in this book; words which, I believe, must be stated over and over again.

"Even though the native and indigenous peoples of Israel are the Jews, and even though the Land of Israel was given to the Jewish people in an eternal covenant with God, it does not matter to Islam's adherents, for wherever the Muslim foot has once trod triumphal, that territory is forever regarded as Islamic.

"If such territory is lost to Muslims, then Allah has been diminished and the land must be retaken. Peace, then, is merely a mirage in the desert sands.

"Too many world leaders fail to understand the Muslim mindset. Israeli leaders, who of all people should know better, still fall into the fatal trap of believing that the Western model of lasting peace between nation-states can equally apply in the Middle East between Muslim and non-Muslim nations. It is a fatal fallacy."

Thus we reach the end of 2011 with this third volume of *Politicide*. It is a year in which anti-Semitism is on the rise in quantum leaps and the international guilt that permeated nation states after the Holocaust is fast withering away. The spectacle of the individual Jew as a victim is now increasingly replaced with the Jewish state itself now cast in the role of the persecuted Jew.

The baffling alliance of the Left with Islam is a phenomenon stalking the world. Its target is the Jewish state even though the Left is protected and free to exercise its political will within the Israeli democracy, yet forbidden to challenge all powerful Islam within the fifty seven Muslim nations: Even proscribed brutally by them.

And today, the extreme Left has unleashed an anti-Capitalist, anti-Free Market, anti-American, anti-Israel and anti-Jewish army of radical students and mostly young people, many brainwashed by their tenured leftist professors in colleges and universities, with the usual aging hippies and useful idiots among them. This movement is the so-called, "Occupy Wall Street."

Many cities in the United States and throughout the ever decrepit West are allowing these demonstrators to take over parks and squares, turning public places into unhealthy quagmires. Among the leftist placards are those with pro-Palestinian, anti-Israel and anti-Jewish slogans.

Phyllis Chesler, the feminist writer, saw as far back as 2003, what horrors were emerging in the West. Writing in her book, *"The New Anti-Semitism: The Current Crisis and What We Must Do about It,"* she penned the following:

"When feminists, gay rights groups, and civil rights activists choose to support Islamic countries where women are subject to honor murders, where homosexuals are imprisoned and sometimes executed, and - in the case of Sudan today and Saudi Arabia before 1962 - slavery is practiced, something irrational is at work. Only anti-Semitism can explain this weird Marxist-Islamic alliance."

Indeed the Left and Islam in their unholy alliance target the Jewish state. That Islam will turn upon the leftists is guaranteed, yet it will let the Left work its evil upon Israel before, like Churchill's crocodile, it devours its erstwhile partner.

In the Passover story, which is enshrined in the Haggadah, the book retelling the events of the Exodus and providing the order of the Seder meal, there is a profound and millennial old passage:

"Not one man alone has risen up against us to destroy us, but in every generation there have risen up against us those who sought to destroy us; but the Holy One, blessed be He, delivers us from their hands." And so it was and still is.

So let me end with the words of Steve Myers from his foreword to this third volume of *Politicide*:

"Every word of Victor Sharpe's trilogy is well-chosen; even the titles.

"He points out that, as Israel finds itself in dire straits, it often forgets God's promises to the Jewish people. Even Israel's own leaders seem willing to compromise and allow Israel to fall into the abyss. If Israel's leaders will not defend its right to its land: Who will?"

Hopefully you, dear reader, will become one of those who choose to defend and support Israel's struggle to survive and prosper in an ever darkening world.

VICTOR SHARPE

Far too few people truly understand how tiny is the State of Israel. This map shows the 22 Arab countries stretching from the Atlantic Ocean to the Indian Ocean. The speck of land you see at the eastern end of the Mediterranean Sea is the Jewish state.

Israel, however, is shown including Judea and Samaria (the West Bank) as well as the Gaza Strip. Without them, Israel is reduced even further. If Judea and Samaria, the Jewish ancestral and biblical heartland, is given away to the Arabs who call themselves Palestinians, then the Jewish state will be only nine miles wide at its most populous region. That is what the so-called Two-State-Solution will create. One more Arab state will come in to existence but the Arab League, and the Muslim world, will still not be satisfied until Israel ceases to exist.

If the chapters in this book – all derived from previously published articles – have not yet convinced you, dear reader, of embattled Israel's vulnerability and miniscule size, this map should make it very clear.

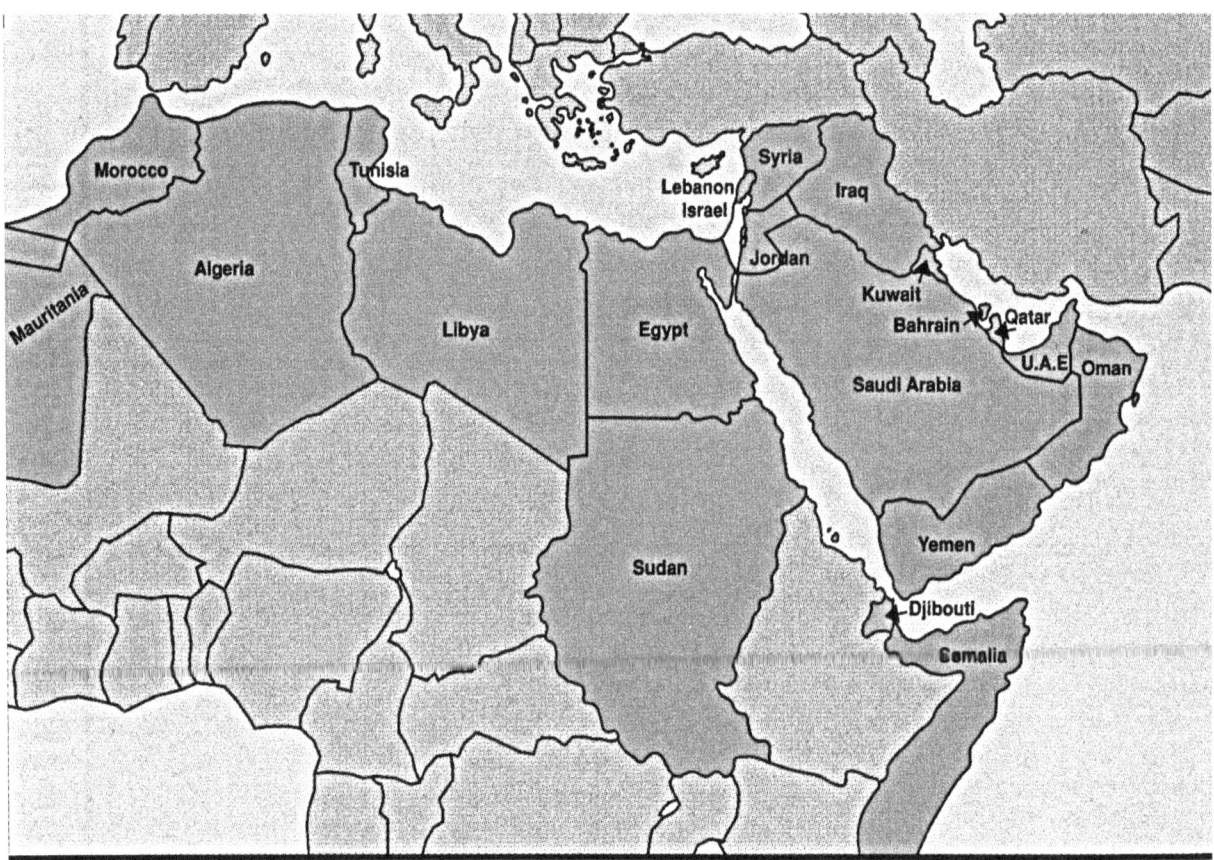

Israel and the Arab States

Politicide

www.ingramcontent.com/pod-product-compliance
Lightning Source LLC
Chambersburg PA
CBHW080539170426
43195CB00016B/2609